T. MACCI PLAUTI

RUDENS

PLAUTUS

RUDENS

EDITED WITH INTRODUCTION, NOTES
AND VOCABULARY

BY

H.C. FAY, M.A. Ph.D.

Formerly Head Master of the Classical Department
Royal Belfast Academical Institution

Bristol Classical Press

First published in 1969 by University Tutorial Press Ltd

This edition published in 1983 (with minor corrections) by
Bristol Classical Press
an imprint of
Gerald Duckworth & Co. Ltd
61 Frith Street
London W1D 3JL
e-mail: inquiries@duckworth-publishers.co.uk
Website: www.ducknet.co.uk

Reprinted 1993, 2001

A catalogue record for this book is available
from the British Library

ISBN 0-86292-063-9

Contents

INTRODUCTION

PART I

PART II

CONTENTS

iv

Acknowledgement

The text follows the Oxford Classical Text, reproduced by permission of the Clarendon Press, Oxford. The following emendations have, however, been made:

Line	Oxford Classical Text	Fay	Authority
9	Iuppiter,	, Iuppiter,	Fay
19	iterum . . . iudicat;	(iterum . . . iudicat)	Fay
79	eius	eiius	Lindsay's footnote
106	unam habui	unam quam habui	Seyffert
113	†praetereat†	haud praetereat	Acidalius
161	qui | Herculei	qui et Herculei	Marx
164			
166			
167			
168			
169			
170	No change of speaker	Changes of speakers	Marx
173			
174			
175			
176			
187	med	me	MSS
189	2nd hancine	hanc	Fay
192	si | erga . . . me inpiavi	si me erga . . . inpiavi	Bothe
194	tum | hoc mi	tum mi hoc	Fleckeisen
197		minus *after* sceleste	
198	me	med	Lindsay's footnote
206a	obviam	ob viam	Fay
210	†diu†	etiamdum	Seyffert
211	saltem | aliquem	aliquem saltem	Schoell
218	quasi	quam si	MSS
273	voluisti	voluistis	Hermann
304	incenati	cenati	Reiz
315	semihomines	secum homines	Mitscherlich
329	, sacerdos Veneriá haec si	hanc—sacerdos Veneriá si	hanc sacerdos MSS
329	quid	quidpiam	quidpiam Schoell
375	facere [ego]	faxere	Sonnenschein
418	munerem	mulierem . . .	Lindsay's footnote says: cod ut vid

v

ACKNOWLEDGEMENT

Line	Oxford Classical Text	Fay	Authority
425	te sic placide bellam	te sic placidule bel-lam	Fleckeisen
430	petere aquam iussit [sibi]	a vobis iussit petere aquam	Ussing
457	suppetit, subita via	suppetit subitaria	Ussing
481	Agasi	exi	Seyffert
485	†sese†	esse sese	Bentley
528	algeo	al-algeo	} Seyffert
529	ullum | instruit	ull-ullum	
533	| uterer	ut-uterer	
534	| ex aqua	ex aq-aq-aqua	
537	†lavisse†	ela-lavisse	
538	quia |	qui-quia	Seyffert
579	quod elavi	quod semel elavi	Müller
599a	ut in omnibus xxx	(omitted)	
639	exoptavi	exopto	Marx
656	fecit hercle ⎫ arrangement of lines	hercle *before* cum magno	Brix
675	par moriri est ⎬	nos par est moriri	Fay after Sonnenschein
677	has ⎭	illas	Sonnenschein
678	opsecro, quis est	opsecro, nam quis est	Sonnenschein
693	moeniá hinc ego	moeniá haec; hinc ego	Lambinus
694	Venús alma	Venus almă	Fay
728	argentum!	argentum?	Sonnenschein
735	tu es	tu's	Sonnenschein
750	nescio,	nescio—	Fay
760	∫ votas, utramque . . . ⎰ semul.	votas utramque . . . ⎱ semul . . .	} Fay
763	messis in ore fiet mergis	mergis in ore fiet messis	Fay after Sonnenschein
765	ignem	lignum	Schoell
765 and 769	DA	TR	Schoell
771	no change of person	DA	(consequent on the above)
829	†ut potest, ignavi†	ut potis est, ignavi	Bothe
843	lapidibus nequissu-mum?	lapidibus? nequis-sumum.	Fay
859	| in ius rapiam | exulem	in ius rapiam, exi-gam exulem	Schoell
884	semel bibo	sat semel bibo	Fay prompted by Lindsay's foot-note

vi

ACKNOWLEDGEMENT

Line	Oxford Classical Text	Fay	Authority
888	nam | in columbari collus	nam collus in columbari	Fleckeisen after Osberu
920	nimisque	nimi'que	Fay
925	hic inest	*omit* hic	Sonnenschein and one MS
927	†... liberes ... praeter te† ⎤	liberet ... praetor te	Fay after Lindsay's footnote
933	circumvectabor. ⎥	circumvectabor,	Fay
933	clara, ⎥ arrangement of lines	clara.	Fay
935	ibi qui ⎥	ibi	Sonnenschein
936	vidulum ⎥	vidlum	Fay
956a	noveram ⎦	noram	Lindsay's footnote
967	*first* quoius (? a slip by Lindsay)	quoiius	
997	GR quo colore est, hoc	quo colore est ? GR hoc	MSS
999	vidulum	vidlum	Fay after Lindsay and Sonnenschein
999	te bis	piscem te	Sonnenschein; MSS te piscem
1014 / 1015	GR	Transfer GR to beginning of next line	Fay
1040	ibo	eo	Sonnenschein
1072	dico.	dico ...	Fay
1082	istic	isti	Lindsay's footnote
1114	tacita bonast	tacitast bona	"alii" in Lindsay's footnote
1131	ut	uti	Lindsay's footnote
1132	ex proclivi planam	ex ardua planam	Fay
1137	sed si erunt	si erunt	Müller
1143	⎰ GR hoc habet, solutust. DA aperi. video cistellam haecinest ⎱	TR hoc habet. GR solutumst. DA aperi. PA video cistellam. DA haecinest	Bothe, Marx, Weise, Sonnenschein
1152	te	ted	Lindsay's footnote
1195	ego | hodie	ego hodie qui	Sonnenschein
1270	censeo	censeo ...	Fay
1290	[est]	indicate lacuna	Seyffert
1314	Philippea	Philippa	Seyffert
1316	bene ego hinc	bene hercle ego hinc	Sonnenschein
1338	GR	no new speaker	Sonnenschein
1342-3	tum ego huic *once*	tum ego huic *twice* and person changes ⎱ Schoell	

vii

ACKNOWLEDGEMENT

Line	Oxford Classical Text	Fay	Authority
1345	†si†	si quid	Seyffert
1359	†infuere†	no obeli	Fay
1382	DA	*omit* DA	Marx
1406	LA *after* Ampeliscam	LA *before* Ampeliscam	Fay
1424	DA	OMNES	Fay

Introduction

I

PLAUTUS: HIS DATE, AND HIS BUSINESS

Tradition gives our author the name T. Maccius Plautus, and says that he came from Sarsina in Umbria, that as a young man he had experience in the theatre (whether as stage-hand or actor is unknown), and that later he took to writing plays after financial disaster in trade; and though none of this is very certain, none of it is in itself improbable.[1] His plays were written and produced around 200 B.C., say ten years on either side (the last known date is 191 B.C. for the *Pseudolus*): he is therefore the earliest Latin writer whose work survives in bulk; he belongs to the generation that fought Hannibal. His work consisted in adapting for performances in Rome Greek comedies written a hundred years earlier for performance in Athens. We have twenty of his plays, and parts of another: there were probably more; but on the other hand one or two of the twenty have been suspected to be by someone else.[2] Terence, who wrote a generation later than Plautus, has left us six plays; and these twenty-six plays, or twenty-six and a half, comprise what

---

[1] For almost all this Introduction, consult, for confirmation, expansion, or contradiction, W. Beare, *The Roman Stage*, hereafter cited merely as "Beare".

[2] See Beare, p. 37.

we possess of Latin comedy; so it is obvious that in this branch of literature Plautus is a major figure.

Since his plays and all the other Latin comedies that we have are derived from Greek plays, we must, in order to see what he was doing, have a look at Greek drama as well as Roman.

ANCIENT DRAMA, (I) AS A LITERARY TYPE

The Greek "Old Comedy"

In origin Greek drama was not primarily an entertainment but a religious exercise. Both tragedy and comedy, though the two were always kept distinct, alike sprang from the singing and dancing which celebrated rustic holidays, especially those of the harvest and vintage, and which were taken over by the state as national festivals. The actors began as chorus leaders, who took solo parts and so in time evolved into independence. Comedy was therefore a stylised version partly of drunken revelry, partly of rites intended to induce fertility in soil and beasts. For both reasons it contained, and was expected to contain, a good deal of obscenity in language, in action, and in costume. With this went personal and political abuse, singing, poetry, and much humour and fun. To give an impression of the "Old Comedy", the best thing is to describe a play by its great practitioner Aristophanes, the *Birds*.

An enterprising Athenian, Pisthetaerus, disgusted with life in Athens, decides to emigrate with a friend to Bird-land. By the good offices of the hoopoe (in mythology once king of Athens), and by his own quick wits and persuasive tongue, he not only weathers a hostile reception, but is elected to a position of responsibility, in which he organises the building and fortification of a capital city, "Cloudcuckoo"; meanwhile he deals unsympathetically

2

with a queue of would-be immigrants, representative of Athenian social pests. Reports soon come in of the successful building operations: particularly valuable service, it seems, has been given by wood-peckers in timber-work and by cranes in hoisting loads. Soon an embassy arrives from the gods in heaven, who have thus been cut off from the offerings of the faithful on earth: Pisthetaerus insists on stiff terms for the lifting of the blockade. The embassy consists of Neptune, Hercules, and a barbarous god, Triballus. Hercules (notorious for his voracious appetite) will concede anything in the hope of a square meal, and Triballus knows no Greek. The gods give in: among the terms of the treaty is the marriage of Jove's daughter, "Empire", to Pisthetaerus; and the play closes with the marriage festivities. The birds form the chorus, and at intervals sing and dance.

The "New Comedy"

The Old Comedy was at its height in the last third of the fifth century B.C., and in the following hundred years gave place to the so-called "New Comedy", with which we are more directly concerned, because it was the Greek New Comedy that the Roman playwrights adapted. There were four reasons for the change:—

First was expense: the training and dressing of a chorus had always been a costly burden, undertaken by wealthy and public-spirited citizens in the days of Athenian empire. When Athens became poorer, and perhaps less public-spirited, this burden could no longer be shouldered. Already, in Aristophanes's lifetime, the chorus began to fade out: in his last play, the *Plutus*, though it exists and takes part in the play, it is shorn of its former fantastic splendour; and at five points no ode is written for it, but only a direction "Chorus-business"—presumably a dance,

3

and perhaps not a new one. In the New Comedy these dances were all that was left to the chorus: they divided the play into five parts, which we know as the five "acts".

Secondly, with the loss of empire, national politics became less absorbing, and as community spirit waned, local personalities meant less; hence, from politics the dramatists turned to social phenomena, and from personalities to types.

Thirdly, with the increase both of urbanisation and of urbanity, the rustic traditions of comedy faded, and its deliberate obscenity, losing its religious motive, was felt to be disgusting.

Fourthly, there were influences from other forms of literature. The philosophers and the speech-writers had argued about morality and had studied psychological types, and had put their views before the public in popular form:[1] the dramatists used these theories in framing situations and in drawing characters, as Ben Jonson and George Chapman did for their "Comedy of Humours"[2] in Shakespearian times. In tragedy Euripides had popularised deserted heroines[3] and had elaborated the technique of recognition scenes:[4] the comedians took advantage of both, as we see in *Rudens*.

The New Comedy, whose greatest writer was Menander, was popular on the stage for the next two hundred years, and for four hundred more was widely read and admired; but till this century we had no considerable remains either

---

[1] The *Characters* of Theophrastus, a contemporary of Menander, was perhaps intended as a guide for comedy-writers: see the introduction to Ussher's edition.

[2] Not the name of a play, but of a type of play; Jonson's *Every Man in his Humour*, is a well-known example.

[3] *E.g.* Helen, Iphigenia.

[4] Especially in his *Ion*; in his *Electra* he severely criticises the technique of his predecessor, Aeschylus.

of Menander's plays or of his contemporaries' and successors'. We now have, from Egyptian papyrus finds, parts of several plays, and within this decade one play, Menander's *Dyscolus*, virtually complete. Till then we had to rely on Roman adaptations; and even now, since the *Dyscolus* happens not to show a number of characteristics which ancient testimony abundantly attributes to Menander's work, I choose for illustration of a typical New Comedy an adaptation by Plautus (the original play and author are unknown), called by him *Curculio*, "the Weevil".

An independent but impecunious young gentleman of Epidaurus is in love with a slave-girl, whom, in the temporary absence of her owner (he, a dyspeptic *leno*, is seeking a cure in Aesculapius's temple) he serenades and interviews: we learn that he hopes to raise the money to buy her. These hopes are dashed by his returning messenger, Curculio, a hungry "parasite" or sponger (the ancient equivalent of the hitch-hiking student); but the same Curculio reports that he has met a soldier who had already paid for the girl, has made him drunk, and has stolen his signet. With the help of the signet and a forged letter, the *leno* is tricked into handing the girl over: the soldier, on arriving, gets no satisfaction from the *leno*, and can only storm. A happy ending is found when the girl recognises the signet as her father's heirloom, and thereby establishes her birthright of freedom, and finds that she is the soldier's sister; the *leno*, convicted of selling a free-born girl, is made to disgorge the purchase-money; Curculio claims permanent dining-rights with the happy couple.

Despite the low ethics of the plot, there is hardly any verbal obscenity; the characters, though exaggerated, are all such as were known in Athens around 300 B.C.; and the incidents, though they involve improbable coincidences, are at least not so wildly fantastic as building a city in mid-air and starving out the gods: coincidence apart, kidnapping by pirates or abandonment at birth (the fate of several New Comedy heroines) were happenings only too familiar. Typical of New Comedy are the characters: the young lover and his girl, who is owned by a *leno*, a cheeky slave, a money-lender, and the rich and boastful soldier (a product of Alexander's oriental conquests); typical above all is the bold schemer, here a parasite, but more often a slave, on whose deceptions the play turns. Absent from the *Curculio*, but common elsewhere, are the old men, either jovial abettors of the young, or stingy fathers who are to be cheated of their money. Typical incidents are the despair of the impecunious lover, the deception practised on the *leno* (it is equally often practised on the young man's father), wrangling and threats of court action, and the discovery of the girl's parentage.

The scope of New Comedy is thus in a sense narrow; a number of characters and situations appear again and again. But Menander (we gather) and Terence (we know) were adepts in portraying individual variations within their stock framework; and even Plautus can make some distinctions: for example, among his soldiers, Pyrgopolinices (of the *Miles Gloriosus*) has the brains and morals of a parish bull, but Therapontigonus (of the *Curculio*), though an ass, is a gentleman, and the unnamed "Miles" of the *Epidicus* is not entirely a fool. Plautus takes little trouble over the girl's recognition in the *Curculio*; but in Terence's *Phormio* the discovery of the lost daughter, instead of occurring abruptly when the plot needs it, is anticipated by many slight hints, so that when it comes, one's reaction is not "Of course! The old stale trick!", but "Of course! *That's* who she was! I ought to have guessed". In the *Rudens* there is preparation for the recognition in lines 106, 215-19, 388-9, 739-44, whether we ascribe these hints to Diphilus or to Plautus; and when the recognition does come, the playwright is quick to forestall any derisive laughter (see note at line 1175).

We have so far considered New Comedy as though there were no distinction between the Greek and Latin examples of it; and what has been said of it applies to both. For in adapting Greek plays the Romans did not change their setting: even though Latin jokes and Roman allusions sometimes intrude, the scene, the names, and the costume are always Greek; and for this reason the plays are sometimes called "fabulae palliatae", "plays in a Greek cloak"—not in a Roman toga (there were "fabulae togatae", but none survive).[1] This allowed the Romans to enjoy themselves laughing at human weakness, and yet feel that they, as a nation, were above such things: similarly in the 1930s, translations of P. G. Wodehouse (whose Bertie Wooster and Jeeves would fit very easily into Greco-Roman comedy) amused fascist Italy, and editors explained that they gave a picture of "England's jeunesse dorée" ("la giovinezza dorata d'Inghilterra"). However, the Romans did make some changes when they took over the plays, and here are three:—

1. They omitted the chorus entirely: to the Greeks it was traditional, to them a useless expense. Its absence sometimes leads to a blurring of the act divisions, though these are distinct in the *Rudens*.

2. They introduced much singing,[2] not as choral odes, but for the single actors: the singing may go on for pages, and be shared by two or three actors in dialogue. If we ask why the Roman dramatists brought song into comedy again—for it had almost died out in Greek comedy—there is no answer, and no need for an answer, except that they and their audiences liked it; Roman tragedians did the

[1] Beare, ch. XV.
[2] But see p. 28 for doubts about the meaning of this word.

7

same.[1] There was certainly a native tradition of singing, dancing, and instrumental music, though not much is known about it[2]. But how the Romans learnt the techniques of the songs which appear in drama is more puzzling; for their metres, though rough, are Greek, both in their several rhythms and in being "quantitative".[3] How did Plautus learn them? In general terms, one must suppose that he was familiar with musical performances of one sort or another, vocal, but not necessarily dramatic, in the Greek cities of Italy.

3. Though it cannot properly be said to apply to the *Rudens*, it is known that Plautus made a poor job of some of his adaptations. We have Horace's criticism,

> gestit enim nummum in loculos demittere, posthac
> securus, cadat an recta stet fabula talo.

"He is in a hurry to shovel the cash into his money-boxes, and after that he doesn't care whether the play falls down or finds its feet." About a rather later writer, Caecilius, there is definite evidence; for Aulus Gellius[4] reinforces some severe criticism by a detailed comparison of a scene of his with its Menandrian original. But as for Plautus, the fact that some of his plays are both short and in parts uncomfortably compressed[5] suggests that he reduced or summarised passages which seemed to him unlikely to amuse his audience; elsewhere he certainly expanded.[6] Till we possess for comparison at least a considerable part of one of the originals which he adapted, we cannot, even if

[1] Beare, p. 19.
[2] Beare, pp. 11-13, 19.
[3] See p. 19 for the term "quantitative", and pp. 24-8 for the lyric metres.
[4] *Noctes Atticae* II. 23; see Beare, p. 78.
[5] E.g. *Curculio*, Act II, scene 3; *Epidicus*, Act III, scene 1.
[6] See note on *Rudens* 1212.

8

a play strikes us as a poor bit of work, say for certain whether Plautus chose a bad or spoilt a good one: however, it seems a safe guess that his contribution to comedy was not careful verisimilitude and psychological probability (where his plays have these, we guess that they have them from the Greek originals), but exuberant high spirits, which show themselves in song, knock-about, word-battles and abuse, alliteration and puns, and jokes of all sorts, clean and unclean, good and bad. His form is (more or less) the form of Menander, but his spirit is like that of Aristophanes.

There is indeed much pleasure to be got from reading Plautus, and much more from acting him; but the student must not spoil his pleasure by expecting what he will not get. Some of the conventions and limitations of New Comedy have already been pointed out: one more must be emphasised in connexion with the *Rudens*. The story deals with a beautiful girl, in the romantic circumstances of shipwreck, rescue from a villain and re-union with her beloved: but do not expect a full and glossy treatment of the love theme. Palaestra's rescue is not effected by her gallant lover, and she is not seen in his arms; she never speaks to him on stage, and has to share with Ampelisca the only line (878) that he speaks to her. Love was indeed a standard theme of the New Comedy (not of the Old), but it did not mean to the ancients what it does in Hollywood or in 'teen-age magazines. The ancients regarded sexual love as a ridiculous weakness, like the parasite's appetite or the slave's roguery: when a loving couple are allowed to embrace, the dramatist stations another character beside them to ridicule them (e.g. *Curculio* I. 3); and if at the end of the play they are happily united, he grants it merely from the same geniality as allows the parasite to get his meal, the slave to escape a whipping, and even a *leno* to be invited to dinner.

INTRODUCTION

ANCIENT DRAMA, (2) ON THE STAGE

Both Greek and Roman plays were produced in the open air, in daylight, and at public expense as part of holiday celebrations.

In the Greek world, where drama was an old and respected institution, most cities had, by Menander's time, a permanent stone-built stage and auditorium. But in Rome the stage was put up temporarily (we may guess that it was stored and re-erected from year to year), and the seats, if there were any (this has been denied, see Beare, pp. 233-9) were of scaffolding. In front of the Greek stage was a circular space for the chorus, called the "orchestra" (this Greek word means "dancing-floor"); the stage itself, of considerable length, was backed by a flat-roofed building with three doors, which were used for entrances and exits in the play; characters supposed to come from a distance presumably came on round the ends of the building. Of the Roman stages and stage-houses we can say very little, except that they must have been cheap copies of the Greek. The *Rudens* only needs two doors, and does not use the flat roof (unless Arcturus does); but the same set had to serve also the other plays that were presented at the same festival: perhaps the unwanted door was concealed by a curtain; perhaps the audience was trusted to assume that if it was not used it did not exist. The Romans needed no *orchestra*, for they had no chorus; and later on, when they built permanent theatres, this space was used to seat dignitaries. There was a limited use of scene-painting in later Greek and in later Roman theatres (Beare, pp. 267-70), but Plautus is unlikely to have had that luxury.

We have presumed that entrances from a distance were made round the ends of the stage building; but unfortunately archaeologists have not yet given a clear statement about this; and it is a question that a producer needs to have answered. For one of the phenomena of ancient comedy is what is called the *servus currens*. This means a low-life character, usually but not always a slave, who enters running vigorously towards the doors or the characters on the stage: his opening speech, sometimes punctuated by remarks from watching characters, lasts perhaps a dozen lines (Curculio has over twenty), during which he must be audible, and (one would think) also visible to the audience. When permanent Roman theatres were built, their stages were flanked by return walls, and entry from a distance can only have been by doorways or arches in those walls; so the *servus currens*, if he was visible, can only have run to and fro along the front of the stage. But when these theatres were built, comedies were no longer the Romans' main interest. Was there in Plautus's time a longer visible approach? Of his theatre there are of course no remains; and the remains of Greek theatres of Menander's time apparently do not answer the question conclusively.

It is sometimes stated that the great length of Greek and Roman stages made such scenes easy. But not even the longest of known stages would be enough for Curculio's speech; and it is not certain that the temporary stages of Plautus's time were on a magnificent scale. We have one bit of evidence in *Bacchides* 832: the distance from one door to another was *tris unos passus*—"only three paces". Assuming three doors set symmetrically, that gives four times *tris passus*, viz from end of stage to first door, from first door to second, from second to third, and from third to the far end of the stage; and a *passus* is about five feet. That gives a total of sixty feet, whether for Plautus's theatre or for his Greek predecessor's—spacious enough, but quite insufficient for Curculio's entrance, or even for the fast-walking Labrax of *Rudens* 485–92. The *servus currens* may not have been realistic, but some sort of distant approach would have eased the problem of producing him.

Greek actors were free men and professionals; festivals, eked out by travel abroad or in the villages, gave them, it seems, full-time occupation and some social status. Roman actors had fewer opportunities and a lower standing: the actor manager might well be a citizen, like Ambivius Turpio, who produced all Terence's plays, and T. Publilius Pellio, who produced Plautus's *Stichus* and *Epidicus*, and quarrelled with him before the *Bacchides* (*Didascalia* prefixed to *Stichus*; *Bacchides* 214–15); but some of the players were certainly slaves, and we hear jocose references to the whipping that awaits those who forget their part (*Cistellaria* 785), and to the risk that actors will steal and sell their costumes (*Curculio* 464; *Trinummus* 858–60).

The word for a company of actors is *grex* or *caterva*: how many there would be in this is disputed. Old Comedy in Athens, though it had a chorus of a dozen—perhaps more—only used three actors proper, one the "protagonist", taking the leading character, and the other two taking a succession of minor parts. But as the chorus dropped out, the importance of the actors grew; and in the tightly knit plays of New Comedy, characters re-appeared in different combinations, and required a bigger cast, even though the dramatists, out of old habit, still wrote each scene for three speakers only, though more might be on stage. If we do not believe in an enlarged cast, we must suppose single parts to have been shared by two or more actors; see *The Dyskolos of Menander*, edited by E. W. Hanley, pp. 26–30. The *Rudens* in any case has six speakers on stage together in Act III—seven if both *lorarii* speak. These speakers do not, it is true, speak together, never more than three in any scene. But the two girls who are silent after 701 do not leave the stage, and so their actors cannot take other parts. This has been denied; *e.g.* Marx asserts in his edition that before sitting by the altar, they disappear into the wings (were there any?), to hand over their masks and costumes to two supers, and to become Labrax and another actor (the two supers being the same who briefly re-appear at 1049 as the *lorarii*); and that this is why Daemones does not at line 707 immediately see them (*sed ubi sunt?*). But Trachalio's repeated *has . . . his . . . has . . . harum* indicates, as clearly as language can, that they are present during lines 702–5; and so no time is left for the change to be effected. It is indeed likely enough that in Diphilus's play the girls' parts were so doubled; but if so, the girls will have been mute throughout the act, and their lyric scene with Trachalio is an addition by Plautus: we have already seen that lyrics are a specially Roman development of New Comedy. But, for Plautus's play, there must be six or seven speaking actors.

And since by doubling of parts, but without splitting them, only eight actors are needed for the *dramatis personae* of thirteen, it would seem to have been a false economy to keep the number down to six or seven, at the cost of splitting the part of, say, Plesidippus, who might play Daemones in Act III, were it not that he meets him in Act I, and Sceparnio, who could be played by Labrax in Act I, were it not that he meets him in Act II. With eight actors, Trachalio can take on Charmides (the change at 859–68 is tight but possible), Sceparnio the leading fisherman and a *lorarius* and Gripus; and anyone but Sceparnio can be Arcturus: the three friends of Plesidippus remain silent, and therefore do not count; the rest of the Fishermen (despite what is said in the note at II. i) might also be silent.

Doubling was made easy, and even the splitting of parts conceivable, by the use of masks. (The view that masks were not used in Plautus's time rests on inconclusive scraps of literary evidence, and is in itself improbable.) Where reference is made to change of facial expression (none, as it happens, in the *Rudens*), it demanded the audience's imaginative co-operation, as a stage blush does to-day. Since all the actors were male, and so far as we know adult, there can have been no great difference between the voices of male and female characters; this again would facilitate doubling. But one wonders how far doubling could go. What attention was paid to stature? Definite and unmistakable references to it are few, though there are undersized boys at *Persa* 231 and *Pseudolus* 783; but can one suppose, as Marx does, that the same actor could play in one act a girl *forma scitula atque aetatula* (*Rudens* 894), and in another a *lorarius* who looked like a statue of Hercules (*Rudens* 822–3)? I do not believe it.

Yet it has to be admitted that the ancients' sense of dramatic propriety was not ours. In staging they certainly accepted what would be quite implausible to us: the *servus currens* has been mentioned, and the action in *Rudens* I. iii–v is another example (see Appendix A). Again, some authorities assert that the flute-player played during all scenes except those written in six-beat iambics; and though I find this incredible, it is generally agreed that he stood on stage; indeed there was no other place for him: he would have been no use behind scenes, shut off from the action by a solid door. And the same consideration shows that the prompter (he is not mentioned, but there was never a play that could do without him!) must have been visible to the audience.

Costumes were in general the normal Greek dress of about 300 B.C.: on the feet low sandals or slippers (*socci*), which were symbolic of comedy, as the calf-length buskins (*cothurni*) were of tragedy; and for clothes a shirt (*tunica*), sleeved or sleeveless, and a cloak (*pallium*), which gave its name to this type of comedy (p. 7). This cloak was just a rectangular blanket; the Roman *toga* differed from it in being semi-circular and more voluminous. Of course there could be variations in the length and quality of the garments to suit the characters, but tunic and cloak of some sort were common to all classes. Soldiers, besides carrying weapons, wore a special short cloak (*chlamys*, line 315) and a sun-hat. A farm labourer's tunic was of goat-skin; Sceparnio probably wore one; and he seems to have had no cloak, but used a rush mat instead (line 576 and note). The players' costumes were paid for by the aediles in charge of the games, out of public money usually supplemented by their own. They were kept and issued by the property manager (*choragus*), who in view of the difficulty of recovering them after the performance might charge a deposit (*Curculio* 464, *Trinummus* 858).

STAGING LATIN COMEDY TO-DAY

In staging, the modern producer has two main problems to face, doors and the *servus currens*. To stand up to the *iniuria* of which Sceparnio complains at line 414, the doors must be solid, and so must their frames, or the whole of the scenery will be convulsed. If you cannot be given solid doors, fix a block of wood just out of sight within the doorway, and bang on that. Best of all is if you can use the real doors of the hall. To give room for the *servus currens*, and indeed for all entry from a distance, come in from the back of the hall and up the steps on to the stage; the stage steps then also provide a convenient place for the unobservant and the unobserved during long asides and eavesdropping scenes.

Costumes are simple to contrive, and are perhaps already in the school wardrobe. Masks, though they are not necessary in a modern production, yet have two advantages. One is speed of changing persons, when parts are to be doubled: this is irrelevant if there are enough actors to match all the parts, but is very important to a skeleton cast on tour, and may be valuable even in a local performance, supposing only a few enthusiasts can be found to take parts. The other advantage is most relevant to a local performance: a mask can do more than grease paint to disguise the actor from his school-fellows in the audience, and encourage them to regard him in his dramatic character rather than in his own. If the producer does decide to use them, he may be able to buy them at fancy-dress shops and adapt them; but if not, or if only brittle plastic is available, he may make them as follows:—

Inflate a balloon to the size of a head, grease it, and plaster it all over with scraps of newspaper soaked in paste; after two layers of paper, a layer of scraps of cloth; then two or three more layers of paper: after each couple of layers, hang the thing up to dry over night. When it is complete and dry, deflate the balloon and extract it (it can be used again), and cut the shell in two lengthwise with strong scissors or a sharp knife. Take one half, and with knife or scissors, scraps of cardboard, paste, and a stapler, shape nose and chin, and cut out the mouth and the eyes. Half of the other half can be attached for the scalp: thus one mask requires three-quarters of a shell, and three shells make four masks; but if scalps are unnecessary (and in younger parts the actor's own hair probably need not be disguised), then each quarter of a shell, if it is made pretty large, will give one mask. Unravelled woollens can be pasted on for hair and eyebrows (Labrax's should be a work of art, see line 318), and strips of nylon stocking can hold the mask on behind the head. Paint it; and finally paste in paper whites to the eyes, leaving the eyeball open to see through. Individual tailoring may be necessary, and practice in wearing certainly is.

In training the cast, of course, the task is harder if you venture a production in Latin. Drill the actors thoroughly in reading their words before they attempt to learn them.

Give prime attention to the rhythm of the lines and the correct stressing of words and phrases, particularly, of course, the operative phrase in each sentence. It will be found again and again that the metre is an aid not only to memorisation, but also to intelligent emphasis. Given the correct stress, the refinements of elision, synizesis, and so on can be left to look after themselves. Correctness of quality in vowels and consonants, though no doubt desirable, matters incomparably less than rhythm, which is a matter of syllable-length and stress. This is treated in the next section of this Introduction. But whatever sounds are current with your cast, insist on clear and emphatic mouthing of them; and when the time for stage-rehearsal comes, or even before, emphasise them heavily with gestures. You must act with the whole body to put the meaning across; and ancient pictures and statues give us every reason to think that this was the Greek and Roman style of acting. Drive the cast to vivacity, whether you play in Latin or in English.

To ease the audience's comprehension, let a commentator (in *Rudens* this will naturally be Arcturus) sit at the side of the stage, and at suitable moments let him interrupt the play with brief and informal explanations of what is happening. Suitable moments in Act I are after lines 88, 159, 186, 219, and 257—not all, it may be observed, at the formal beginning of a scene. For example, in our school production of 1954–5, at line 186, after Palaestra had sung a couple of lines, she stood pathetic and silent, while Arcturus said, "This is one of the girls, Palaestra, separated from her friend, and too blind with exhaustion and grief to see where she is"; then Arcturus sat down, and Palaestra resumed her singing. At line 641, after *mulieres*, Arcturus said, "So at last Trachalio gets it out! Labrax is using force to recapture the girls, even in the temple sanctuary. Daemones leads a rescue party"; then Trachalio went on with *duae innocentes intus hic sunt*.

Whether in Latin or in English, the lyric passages need to be sung, and it is not easy to find music for the Latin, or to get it written. If you can, provide your composer with metrically equivalent English words to work on: this is the main purpose of the versions on pp. 26-7 and in Appendix B; but perhaps even nonsense syllables of the right metrical pattern would serve the purpose. You will be wise to cut the lyric passages drastically; yet it is a great loss to cut them out entirely, or merely to speak them.

If you are content with an English performance, there are translations of several plays available, including *Rudens*; but if you choose a prose version, at least rewrite part of the lyrics into a shape that can be sung—not, of course, necessarily the original Latin rhythms.

On particular problems in the staging of *Rudens*, suggestions are made from time to time in the stage-directions, notes, and appendices of this edition.

II

SPEAKING AND SINGING

Metres

Like all ancient drama, the *Rudens* is in verse, and whether it is read for study or for pleasure (better still for both), both understanding and pleasure will be less if its verse is not understood. The student need not necessarily master the technicalities in the account which follows, but if he is to imagine the lines as spoken or sung (and much more if he is to speak or sing them in a performance!), he ought to listen for their rhythms and recognise them.

Latin Verse in General

The student has presumably learnt to scan the metres of Vergil and Ovid, and so knows that, whereas the patterns of English verse are made by syllable-stress, the patterns of Latin verse are made by "quantity"—"longs and shorts", as they are usually called, though the terms "heavy" and "light" are perhaps better for syllables, leaving "long" and "short" for vowels. But the matter is not so simple, even in classical Latin verse. For quantitative verse was not naturally Latin, but Greek; and its patterns, imposed on Latin out of respect for Greek literature at a time when Latin had no literature, needed considerable adaptation to the new language. Latin had, what Greek had and English has not, a natural distinction between short and long vowels, light and heavy syllables; but Latin also had, what English has, but Greek had not, a strong stress accent; and between these two, quantity and stress, there is often disagreement: the syllable which by quantitative verse takes the beat may be by nature unstressed, and natural stress may fall where the quantitative metre puts no beat. In the two centuries between their earliest attempts at Greek metres and their full achievement under Vergil, Horace, and Ovid, the Romans worked out a balance. Plautus had to work out his; and because he had no significant predecessors, he had to learn by the hard way, and the results are sometimes clumsy. Horace's comment was:—

> At vestri proavi Plautinos et numeros et
> laudavere sales—nimium patienter utrumque.
> (*Ars Poetica*, 270-1)

"Your ancestors approved of Plautus's versification and jokes—their standards were low in both." Doubtless their approval mattered to Plautus more than their standards; but he could also reply, firstly that dramatists' metres were not Horace's, and secondly that a comic writer, seeking to echo in his verse the sound of talk, must positively avoid formality and stateliness—except on special occasions such as a priestess's utterance or a star-god's.

The Position of the Stress-accent

It will be as well at this point to review the rules that governed the position of the stress-accent.

1. Apart from monosyllables, no Latin word is naturally stressed on the last syllable, and the weight of the last syllable is irrelevant to the position of stress. Apparent exceptions are easily explicable, e.g.: *illíc, vidén* (for *illíce, vidésne*); and even these tended to become *íllic, víden*.

2. If the last syllable but one (the "penultimate") is heavy, it takes the stress, e.g. *vidébant, domínúsque*.

3. If the penultimate is light, the stress goes back to the syllable before it (the "antepenultimate") whether this is heavy or light, e.g. *intérdius, exóritur*.

4. But if the syllable before the antepenultimate is also light, giving a run of three lights before the last ($\smile\smile\smile\veebar$), the stress goes back to that syllable, e.g. *máriaque, múlieres*. This fact, less commonly known than the first three rules, is of some importance for reading Plautine verse, *e.g.* 36:

> neque is adeo propter málitiam patria caret.

It was not invariable (lines 26 and 54 imply *facílius* and *Sicíliam*), and it apparently died out later; but it was still in force in Vergil's time, and accounts for such scansions as *arjete, tenvia*, for *áriete, ténuia*; and in Seneca's tragedies the type *scéleribus* is still as common as *scelèribus*.

There follow a couple of riders: (i) In a long word there is a secondary stress before the main, placed by the same principles, e.g. *legèrupiónem, pùgilatórium*. (ii) Pairs of words that belong closely together are sometimes stressed as one word, sometimes as two, e.g. *apúd me*, 1358, but *àpud mé* 183. The same applies even to compound words, e.g. *légĕ-rŭpă* at 652 is stressed as two words (as one it would be *legérupa*), whereas *legèrupiónem* (see above) is stressed as one (as two it would be *lége-rùpiónem*).

PLAUTINE METRES, (1) SPEECH

1. *Six-beat Iambics* (an iambus is $\smile\_$). This is the metre of the great bulk of Greek drama, as the five-beat iambic line is of Shakespearian; and the *Rudens* opens with it. Its pattern at its simplest is:—

$$\smile\_\ |\ \smile\_\ |\ \smile\|\_\ |\ \smile\|\_\ |\ \smile\_\ |\ \smile\veebar$$

and line 556 may be an example of it:—

iam ĭs exµ ĭbeb|ĭt ‖ hīc | mĭhĭ | nēgo|tĭum

But, as in other metres, two light syllables could be put for
one heavy; and moreover already in Greek drama the light
syllable of the odd feet (1st, 3rd, 5th) could be replaced by
a heavy, or even, within limits, by two lights; the Greek
comic writers took more liberties, and Plautus took more
still: he is content to have a heavy syllable or two lights
doing duty for a light in any foot but the last; and perfect
iambic lines are rare. The six feet are divided, by a break
between words in the third or fourth foot (often in both),
into 2½+3½ or 3½+2½: by this arrangement, inherited, as
it happened, from the Greek, the metrical beat and the
Latin stress coincided around the middle of the line.

   2. *Seven-beat Iambics.* The pattern at its simplest is:—

ᴗ _ ᴗ _ ᴗ _ ᴗ _ ‖ ᴗ _ ᴗ _ ᴗ _ ᴗ ᴗ̆

and examples of the metre are 293–4

Nēcess|ĭt at|ĕ quid|quĭd est ‖ dŏmī jd | săt est | hăbend|um.

nōs iam | dē ornat|u prōpe|mŏdum ut ‖ lŏcŭple|tes sim|u'

[scī|tis.

or, imitated in English:—

   "To be content with what he gets is simply necessary.
   And as for us, you may guess at our wealth by the outfit
   which we carry."

As the second of these lines shows, variations were allowed
similar to those in six-beat iambics: one that needs to be
particularly observed in reading is the substitution of ᴗ ᴗ ᴗ̆
for the final _ ᴗ̆, e.g. *hódie* 305, *véniat* 328. There is a
break after (not *in*) the fourth foot; and indeed the line has

a tendency at this point to fall apart and allow what only happens properly at the end of a line, an unelided vowel or a light syllable for a heavy, *e.g.* lines 354, 393. In this metre, as in six-beat iambics, metrical beat and Latin stress coincide very frequently.

3. *Eight-beat Trochaics* (a trochee is ‿ ‿). Their scheme at its simplest is:—

$$ - \cup | - \cup | - \cup | - \cup || - \cup | - \cup | - \cup | \times $$

and examples of it are 706–7:—

Exi͜e | fano, | natum | quantumst | hominum | sacrileg|issum |e͞!

Vos in | aram a|bite | sessum! || sed ubi | sunt? — huc | respi | ce.

or, imitated in English:—

> "Out you come and leave the temple, impious, sacrilegious hound!
> Girls, take refuge at the altar! Why, where are they?—
> Look around!"

Variations were allowed, as in the iambic metres; a line of perfect trochees is rare. The last trochee, like the eighth iambic of the seven-beat iambic line, is incomplete. (The description is conventional; from another point of view the trochaics could be described as iambics, and the iambics as trochaics, each *beginning* with an incomplete foot.) The technical name for such a line is *catalectic*, "stopping short"; the opposite is *acatalectic*, and the terms will occur again. The line is normally, though not always, broken after the fourth trochee, and hiatus is sometimes found there, *e.g.* 643, 646.

In these three metres the main business of the play is carried on. The six-beat iambics are normally the quietest, the other two more lively, but the difference is not rigid, *e.g.* 860–85, in six-beat iambics, contain some vigorous action. Trochaics appealed to the Roman ear: not only

23

are they Plautus's favourite metre, but in tragedy too Ennius chose to use them in adapting part of the *Medea* which Euripides had written in iambics (see Beare, p. 65). The choice of metre seems to have been largely arbitrary; but there is sometimes great dramatic effect in the change from one to another; for example when Sceparnio erupts from the farm-house at 414, when Trachalio rushes out of the temple at 615, and when Labrax is ejected at 706; or, in the reverse mood, when Daemones addresses Labrax with icy calm at 780, and when Labrax sanctimoniously takes his oath at 1338: Beare (p. 218) gives more examples from other plays.

PLAUTINE METRES, (2) SONG

The metres which we have considered are used either to carry on the business of the play, or at least to make jokes; the passages written in them are, we may suppose, intended primarily to be understood. These metres fit the natural rhythm of Latin speech, and are used for long passages without a break. Those that we consider next sometimes change rapidly into one another; they do much violence to the Latin stress-accent; and they are not, for the most part, used to advance the plot, nor to entertain us by verbal humour, but just to express emotion—sorrow, joy, or mere high spirits: such passages are *Rudens* 185–289, 664–81, 906–39. I call them "song", despite the objections to be mentioned on p. 28, because that is how they would be treated in a modern performance; and indeed "lyric metres" is their traditional description. The following are found in the *Rudens*:—

1. *Anapaests* (⏑ ⏑ —). These are found not singly but in multiples of two; the typical line is of eight beats, acatalectic (see p. 23 for this term), or of seven beats, catalectic, thus:—

‿‿ — | ‿‿— | ‿‿ —|‿‿ —‖

{ ‿‿ — | ‿‿ —|‿‿ — | ‿‿ — acatalectic

{ ‿‿—|‿‿—|‿‿—| — catalectic

Since there is normally a break after the fourth foot, the eight-beat line may often just as well be considered as two four-beat lines. In Greek a heavy syllable could be put for any two lights, and vice versa, provided that four lights did not come together—but Plautus throws this proviso to the winds.

Anapaests were a favourite metre in Greek drama, but did not come easy to a Latin writer. For, because the break in the line comes immediately after the metrical beat, this beat can seldom coincide with the natural stress, and the disagreement works back to affect the other stresses; thus in the lines now to be quoted the metrical beats are *meliúst*, *sécludám*, *pectóre*, and *exánimalés*, but the natural stresses are *méliust*, *seclúdam*, *péctore*, *exanimáles*. Partly because of this, and partly because Latin words in which two lights alternate with one heavy are not very common (it exercised Ovid's skill to devise them), Plautus was sometimes driven to desperate shifts to make his anapaests scan (*e.g.* 927, 934), and Terence hardly ever used the metre. Anapaestic lines are:—

Quid mihi | meliust|, quid magis | in remst‖, quam a cor|pore

vi|tam ut se|cludam ?

ita male | vivo, at|que ita mihi | multae in ‖ pectore | sunt

cu|rae exani|males (220-1),

25

or, imitated in English:—

> "Oh, what shall I do, oh, what better thing, than to sunder my
> soul and my body apart?
> For my life is a grief; and my breast, it is full of cares and of
> sorrows that wring my heart."

These are acatalectic lines; 225–6 are catalectic:—

Neque eam us|quam inveni|o, neque | quo eam. ‖ neque qua |

quaeram | consul|tumst;

neque quem | rogitem | respon|sorem ‖ quemquam in|terea |

conveni|o.

or, in an English imitation:—

> "And she cannot be found, and I know not the way, and am all
> at a loss in my seeking;
> And there isn't a human soul to be seen, who would grant a
> reply to me speaking."

Gripus has anapaests at 926–37, and shares some with
Trachalio at 956–62. Tunes can be provided for anapaests
by adapting English tunes for what the hymn-books call
"Long Metre".

2. *Bacchiacs* (‿ _ _) and *Cretics* (_ ‿ _). Two light
syllables are allowed for either heavy or both, and even
further an unstressed heavy or two lights are allowed to
stand for the single light. Examples of bacchiacs are:—

Nam hoc mi sat | laborist | laborem hunc | potiri,

si me erga | parentem aut | deos inp|iavi (191-2),

26

which may be imitated in English:—

"For enoúgh wère my hárdships and sóre tribulátiòns,
For wrong done to gods or my nearest relations. "

Cretics are:—

$$\overline{}\;\overset{\smile}{}\;\overline{}\,\big|\,\overline{}\overset{\smile}{}\;\overline{}\,\big|\,\overline{}\;\overset{\smile}{}\;\overline{}\,\big|\,\overline{}\;\overset{\smile}{}\;\overline{}$$
Hŏc quŏd in|dūta sum, | summae opes | oppĭdŏ;

$$\overline{}\;\overset{\smile}{}\;\overline{}\,\big|\,\overline{}\;\overset{\smile}{}\;\overline{}\,\big|\,\overline{}\;\overset{\smile}{}\;\overline{}\,\big|\,\overline{}\;\overset{\smile}{}\;\overline{}$$
nĕc cĭbo, | nĕc lŏco | tēctă quo | sīm scĭo (207-8),

or in English:—

"All my wealth, all my good, is the dress on my back;
I can find neither food, nor the roof which I lack."

The two metres are in general effect similar, but bacchiacs seem to move more slowly than cretics, and cretics to be more agitated than bacchiacs; cf. the notes in Appendix B on the metre of I. 5 and III. 3. Musically, cretics can be treated either as ♩♪♩. or as ♩.♪♩, and bacchiacs in similar time. I have performed Gripus's, not without applause, to raucous variations of "Loch Lomond".

3. *Iambics* and *Trochaics,* other than those already described under Speech; *e.g.* two-beat iambics (206), four-beat trochaics (923).

4. *Aeolic,* a rhythm built round _ _ _ _ (called a *choriambus*) by additions before and after; one common type, called *glyconic,* is _ ⏑ | _ _ _ _ | ⏑ _. This rhythm is fundamental to much Greek lyric and to most of Horace's Odes, but is not very common in Plautus; see, however, the notes in Appendix B on lines 217-18, 945-8, 952-5, with English imitations.

5. There are various short tags, mostly iambic or trochaic, added from time to time to other metres, mostly bacchiacs and cretics. They are best noted as they occur; but one particularly common, originally aeolic, _ ⏓ _ _ ⏓ _, but with

many variations, is called, after the scholar who observed it, *Colon Reizianum*, or "Reiz's Tag": variant examples are *miserae memorantur* (185), *ornatu ornatam* (186), *honor apud vos* (196).

It should be said at this point that the division of the metres between speech and song is not the one made by late Roman writers and by some old MSS of the plays. Their division is into six-beat iambics on the one hand, which they call *diverbium* (apparently "dialogue"), and *canticum* ("song"), which includes all the rest. The distinction simply does not correspond to dramatic function. In view of this Beare (p. 224) says: "It is probable that in his day (i.e. Plautus's) the very idea of 'song' (in our sense of the word) did not exist." He and other writers on Latin drama accept it as true that all passages except six-beat iambics were declaimed to a musical accompaniment. I simply do not believe it.

PLAUTINE METRES, (3) PATTER

Lines 938–62, the beginning of the altercation between Gripus and Trachalio, occupy an intermediate position between speech and song, and to that extent support Beare's view that there was in Plautus's time no such division in fact. The emotional and poetic level is lower than the girls' lamentations, the Priestess's grandiloquence and Gripus's exultation; and the words achieve some advance in the plot and some verbal joking, which the author would not wish us to miss: so far the lines resemble speech. Yet the metres, mostly short trochaics and anapaests, are what I have listed under "Song"; and whatever they are, there is a clear change at 963, when the dispute begins in earnest, into eight-beat trochaics. For this reason I describe the passage rather as "Patter" than as either "Speech" or "Song". There are plenty of similar scenes elsewhere in Plautus, *e.g.* at the beginning of *Epidicus* and at *Captivi*, 498–532.

PLAUTINE SCANSION

Whatever metre he used, prosody (the rules for deciding whether a syllable was heavy, light, or elided) was for Plautus basically the same as for other Latin poets: a syllable was heavy if it contained a long vowel or diphthong, or if it was followed by two consonants (with the known exceptions); but a vowel-ending or an *-m* ending disappeared in scansion before a following vowel or *h*. But certain special phenomena are important.

1. *Final s.* This, in older Latin, was, it seems, very lightly pronounced, and could be ignored in scansion: the practice is continued even by Lucretius, a contemporary of Cicero, though by his time it was probably out of date. *Rudens* 103 *salvo(s) sis* is an example. But *s* was not so dropped as to cause elision, except with *es* and *est*, e.g. *usust* (100), *essuru's* (183).

2. *Hiatus.* An unprotected vowel or syllable in *-m* is not always elided. The commonest type of hiatus (and in Plautus it is very common) is a heavy *stressed* monosyllable lightened but not elided, e.g. *quĕm ego* (158), *vĭ agis* (733). It is probable that when elision took place the elided vowel was in fact vestigially heard, and lightening without elision is a half-way step. Even Vergil has *quī amant* (*Eclogues VIII.* 108) and *té, amice* (*Aeneid VI*, 507).

Hiatus after an *unstressed* vowel is usually to be defended by a pause, such as may occur between two halves of a

INTRODUCTION

verse (715), or be caused by syntax (61), or be made for
dramatic reasons (7, 637, 646, see notes); if no such
defence can be offered, editors suspect that the text is
corrupt.

3. *Old Vowel-length.* Some inflexional endings that
were later light were, or could be, heavy in Plautus's time:
e.g. *-or* in nouns and verbs, and in verbs *-at, -et, -it* except
in present indicative of 3rd and 5th conjugation and
futures in *-bit*. Also *es(s)* ("thou art") and *-es(s)* (as in
miles, dives) could still count an invisibly doubled *s*. The
old pronoun-forms *mēd* and *tēd* were quite common.

4. *Synizesis.* This means that vowels which are normally
separate were run together, e.g. *eọrum* (15). Whether *eius,
huius, quoius* are monosyllables by this phenomenon, or two
light syllables by §6 is not clear; anyhow, when the longer
pronunciation is required, we print (after the OCT) *eiius,
huiius, quoiius*. There is similar slurring of *illius* and *istius*.

5. *Bıeves Breviantes* ("Shortening Shorts"). This is
the name given to the following very important phenomenon:—Given two syllables, the first light but stressed,
the second naturally heavy, the second tended to be
lightened; especially was this so if another stressed syllable
immediately followed. [It is sometimes claimed that a
following stress could effect the lightening even without a
preceding stress, *e.g.* that at 913 we have *pīsci(um) ūll(um)
ūnci(am)*, with *ull-* lightened by *ūnc-*.] This lightening
took place whether the second syllable was heavy by vowel-
length or by consonants, or even if it was a separate monosyllable, e.g. *mánĕ* (1026), *sénĕx* (35), *cápe hănc* (481).

The effect of *Breves Beviantes* was in some words permanent: *bénĕ, nĭsĭ, sciŏ*, for example, all became regular. But
it did not occur invariably, and Plautus could choose what
suited his metre: nevertheless, it is almost unknown to

30

have two iambic words scanning as such ($\smile \_ | \smile \_$) at the end of a line; they would have sounded like $\smile \smile \smile \_$; so, at 884, where the MSS give *semel bibo*, the OCT editor comments *diiambus in fine versus vix ferendus*.

6. *Familiar Slurring.* Some common short words (*e.g.* demonstratives, conjunctions) were lightened in one way or another in unemphatic use, e.g. *ille, illic, iste, istic, ecce, eccum, nempe, quippe, atque, esse, hercle, inde, unde*. Whether these became, for example, *i'lĕ, nĕ'pĕ, u'dĕ*, or *ill', nemp', und'* (even before a consonant), is not certain; nor need they all have the same explanation. For *nempe* the latter explanation seems right: it scans as one heavy syllable equally before vowels and before consonants; and the classical usage of *atque* (*atque* before vowels, *ac* before consonants) is similar. The particle *quidem* tended to lighten a monosyllable before it, with which it practically formed a single three-syllable word; so we get *sĭquidem, tŭquidem*, and so on: if this lightening does not take place, we print them as two words, *si quidem*, etc., after the OCT.

III

PERSONS AND INSTITUTIONS: THE BACKGROUND OF LIFE

(i) Respectable citizens and their servants (Daemones, Sceparnio, the lorarii; Plesidippus and Trachalio)

Though the scene of the play is Cyrene, two of its characters, Daemones and Plesidippus, are Athenians. Daemones has emigrated because he can live more economically on a Cyrenaican farm. We are told he is poor; but he is not destitute: he has kitchen utensils that are worth borrowing (line 134-5); he has lambs and pigs to sacrifice on a fit occasion (line 1208); and he has a farm and a staff of at least four male slaves. Perhaps, though he is still proud of being an Athenian (lines 741, 1197), he has acquired Cyrenaican citizenship; at least he identifies himself in sentiment with the people among whom he lives: *ita est lex apud nos* (line 724); so might an English exile in Ireland speak! His role in the play makes it clear that he is a decent old fellow; but he is not quite to be trusted with pretty girls—his wife's opinion, which we hear reported at lines 895–6 and 1046–7, receives some support from the tone of lines 893–4. There are no perfect heroes in comedy.

Of his four servants whom we meet, three, Sceparnio, Turbalio, and Sparax, are, we take it, farm-hands: the appellation of *lorarii* under which the last two (and other slaves in other comedies) appear, only applies to them for the nonce; a poor farmer could not afford to keep two specialist constables on his staff. These two are large, muscular, and taciturn. Sceparnio on the other hand is loquacious even to the point of insolence (lines 104-17). He has (as the same lines show) the rustic's dislike of strangers, a trait which is displayed by his counterpart Davus in the *Dyscolus*. He has a weakness for pretty girls, though he does not often meet one (lines 415, 462). Daemones's other slave, Gripus, we shall consider later.

Why Plesidippus was in Cyrene is never explained; only late in the play do we learn that he is an Athenian, nay more, a relative of Daemones. He is a young gentleman of independent means, apparently known and liked in Cyrene; he has friends to support him in his prosecution of Labrax, and he gets justice without any difficulty, despite the prejudice of local courts against foreigners; but the prejudice against the *leno* was still greater.

His man Trachalio has the biggest part in the play. He is portrayed as a decent fellow, industrious and loyal to his master, sympathetic to the girls in their distress. But the reader, and still more the actor, must beware of making him a hero. Against Labrax, a scoundrel but a free man, his valour is never tested: he relies on Daemones and the *lorarii*; against Gripus, a slave like himself, he blusters (lines 1007-9), but declines actual fisticuffs (line 1011). He has (like his counterpart Getas in the *Dyscolus*) a great appetite for a free meal (lines 342-7); and amid the pathos of the girls' distress (lines 663-704) his comments are banal, even lewd. He is a comic slave; and a slave in comedy is simply not allowed by his author to be heroic—unless, like Tyndarus in the *Captivi*, he has the rare destiny to discover a birth-right of freedom.

33

(ii) *A country shrine (Venus and her priestess)*

The worship of Venus and the character ascribed to her varied greatly. Her temple at Corinth was famous (or infamous) for its staff of 1000 prostitutes: but, on the other hand, she was not only the goddess of sex, but also, for example, of good luck; and her worshippers were not all of Labrax's quality; she was the family patroness of the Julian Caesars. On the respectability of her temple near Cyrene the play casts no doubts: Labrax's suggestion at line 727 is coldly received. In appearance, though *lepidus locus* and *decorus dis* (lines 255–6), it is clearly modest, like Daemones's farm-house: it is long before the girls notice it. Its only staff consists of a respectable old lady with an aristocratic name (line 481), who lives in the building, but has no income from it (line 283).

Naturally, its statue indoors and its altar outside conferred sanctuary on suppliants, so that they might not be forcibly dragged away; but other means short of force might be used to dislodge them, such as smoking them out (lines 761–8 and note) or blockading them (line 838). Offences against the goddess would normally be her concern (lines 1345–9) rather than the state's (*deorum iniuriae dis curae*, Tacitus, *Annals* I. 73), but at Cyrene it seems that the right of sanctuary was also supported by state law, which Labrax affects to find surprising (lines 723–4); its violation, with assault on the Priestess, naturally causes local indignation (lines 645–56). But against an unscrupulous man the rule was impotent without enforcement; so that even in the Priestess's presence the statue is of no avail to the girls, and the altar is only more effective because Trachalio and (more important) Daemones and the *lorarii* are there.

Though it is some way from the city, the temple is, like Pan's grotto in the *Dyscolus*, the scene of sacrifices and

subsequent picnics; to such Labrax invites Plesidippus.
But it is not provided with utensils, and these the guests
must either bring themselves or borrow from the neighbours
(lines 133–6); this situation is also amply illustrated in the
Dyscolus.

(iii) *The slave-trade and the status of women (Labrax and Charmides, Palaestra and Ampelisca)*

Labrax is a *leno*, and so perhaps is Charmides—he is
described as Labrax's *hospes*, but we should think rather of
a long-standing business association than of a personal
friendship. In the ancient world the *leno's* business,
though disreputable (as was any slave-dealing, *Captivi*, 98–
100), was quite legal. He was a slave-dealer who specialised
in attractive girls; these he either sold at a profit, or hired
out to amorous young men. If the girls were hired, they,
like other slaves (cf. p. 39), would be allowed to keep
part of their earnings and, if they saved up their money,
could use it, like other slaves, to buy their freedom; thereafter they could set up in business on their own account,
still looking, as *clientae*, to their former owner, now their
patronus, for general assistance in business matters, and
owing him in return occasional services.

So far as buying and selling went, the *leno*, of course,
made his money by buying his wares cheap, improving
them, finding where they were most in demand, and selling
them dear (lines 53–6, 540–2). Thus Palaestra was bought
as a child, and was being trained in social accomplishments
when she caught Plesidippus's eye (lines 40–3); and up to
this point her upbringing may have been entirely respectable: Planesium, her counterpart in the *Curculio*, says,
bene et pudice me domi habuit (*Curc.* 698). Ampelisca, to
judge from her price, was probably grown up before she

was bought, and had perhaps (we are not told) earned her keep since; Labrax would sell her at a 50 per cent. profit (lines 1405–9).

If, as was most likely, the *leno's* customer was a young gentleman whose father was still alive, he was unlikely to have the money ready, and could only take an option on the girl, getting the *leno* to promise not to sell her before a given date, a promise which, *fide lenonia*, might not be kept: equally it was the *leno's* complaint that his customer did not in the end produce the money (*Pseudolus* 282, Terence, *Phormio*, 520–1): neither promise could be enforced at law. But Plesidippus had money, and paid a first instalment of the price (lines 46, 860). Therefore Labrax, when he tried to evade the contract, was legally liable, and when Plesidippus got him into court, the court punished him by forfeiture of the goods in dispute. This was simply a matter of commercial dishonesty; apart from that he had committed no crime, except perhaps sacrilege in Venus's temple: Trachalio's mention of the hangman (line 778) is brag, and Plesidippus's (line 857) is jocular; and the references to prison and collar (lines 715, 876, 888) are to the plaintiff's temporary lock-up, where the defaulter might be held before the trial and till he paid the damages (cf. Terence, *Phormio*, 325, 336). In respect of the sacrilege it seems no charge was brought: the treatment by the *lorarii* had been severe enough.

Apart from liability for breach of contract, the greatest risk for the *leno*, as for any other slave-dealer, was the *mancupium*, the legal ownership, involving the guarantee that the person sold was of slave-status (*recte servire*, line 777) and was the property of the vendor. Ultimately this could only derive from evidence of how he (or she) became a slave—*e.g.* slave parentage (line 218) or (as in *Captivi*) capture in declared warfare; but practically it rested with the vendor to offer this guarantee. If he did not, the buyer's risk lowered the price; but for that very reason the buyer might take a chance, and hope that the birthright of his purchase might never be discovered or proved: this is played out in full in *Persa*, 493–672. If it were proved, he lost the slave without compensation, as Dordalus does in *Persa*. If, on the other hand, the vendor had guaranteed the *mancupium*, the price could be recovered from him, if he did not go bankrupt; this is the fate of Cappadox in *Curculio*. For Palaestra Labrax had no *mancupium*, though he probably told Plesidippus that he had. For receiving this type of stolen goods there was no further penalty than forfeiture, though the original kidnapper was, of course, subject to penalties if they could be enforced: and so Labrax took his chance (line 40). The lack of *mancupium* might have been his downfall in this play, as it is of his confrères in *Persa* and *Curculio*: but by the time Palaestra's birthright is established, he has already lost possession of her.

A girl in slavery to a *leno* had a better chance than most other slaves of a quick release, if a lover could raise the money to buy and free her; and this situation contributes to the plot of many other comedies besides *Rudens*. On being freed she could not legally become her lover's wife (his wife must be a free-born citizen), but only his *concubina* (*Epidicus*, 465–6, *ego illam volo hodie facere libertam meam, mihi concubina quae sit*). So far as their domestic life went, a *concubina*'s relationship might differ little from a wife's; but the *concubina*'s children could not legally be heirs or citizens; and her patron could terminate the connexion at will, leaving her destitute except for what he chose to give her. This danger was real; for the man might well decide (perhaps under family pressure) to take a legal wife and rear a legitimate family; and on this danger are based the plots of Terence's *Andria* and Menander's *Samia*. If the girl was not freed by her purchaser, she became his *paelex*

37

("concubine" in our sense of the word); and if or when he was married, a jealous wife would make her life, and perhaps his, hard indeed (cf. lines 895–6, 1045–7). So, for Palaestra to have a happy end to her troubles, it was necessary not only that Plesidippus should acquire her, but that her birthright should be recognised, and with it her eligibility to become his wife.

For Ampelisca there is no real claim to birthright freedom, despite Trachalio's bluff at line 736. On being set free, she is to settle down happily as the wife of another freed slave, Trachalio. Their position will be that they have no political rights, but enjoy the protection of the laws and the normal freedoms of every-day life: from the Roman point of view they will be "clients" of their "patrons", Daemones and Plesidippus (cf. note on 1266).

The girls' characters are differentiated according to their status (it must be admitted that some, though not all, of the following instances depend on my own assignment of lines to speakers). Palaestra, free-born, maidenly, and educated, feels slavery acutely (lines 217–18), and even contemplates suicide (lines 648–6); she understands the Priestess's exalted language, and answers courteously (lines 265–9, 288–9); she is strongly, though conventionally, pious (lines 187–97), and leads the prayers to Venus with dignity and correctness (lines 257–8, 694–9). Ampelisca is more level-headed and vulgar: convention and her author would not allow it otherwise. She has perhaps already had some experience of her profession and uses it just enough to get Sceparnio to do what she wants (lines 426–7, 436–9); Palaestra would not even have known what Sceparnio meant at lines 429 and 435, let alone have promised co-operation. Again, Ampelisca's familiarities with Trachalio in lines 331–403, though harmless, would not befit the virginal Palaestra; still less would the thought that crosses Ampelisca's mind as they take refuge at the altar (lines 699–701). But

Ampelisca is warm-hearted, and sincerely attached to her friend, whom she not only laments when she is lost (lines 220–8), and pities in her grief (lines 387–403), but also, which is harder, congratulates without envy, when she, but not herself, has found freedom and parents (line 1183).

(iv) *Slavery and freedom, litigation (Gripus, Labrax and the* vidulus)

Gripus, the fourth of Daemones's slaves, apparently lives in the farm-house, and does odd jobs (lines 1299–1302); but he carries on business as a fisherman on his own account, owns his own boat and tackle (line 1020), and sells his fish in the market (line 974); part of the profit goes to his master (this is implicit in lines 918–22), the rest he keeps.   He regards himself as a worthy and industrious man (lines 914–23), and as such it is naturally his intention to save money, buy freedom, and set up in business for himself.   How much money he would need, must be settled with his master by bargaining: the sum would depend partly on the cost of a replacement, partly on what his master thought he could exact.   Hence the need that Gripus should cunningly conceal his wealth till he is free and only then display it (lines 928–30).

He is naturally delighted with his strange catch, even without verifying his guess at its contents.   Legally, as his master tells him (lines 1227–33), it is still the owner's property, if the owner can trace it and prove ownership. Unfortunately for Gripus, Trachalio intervenes, partly in the interests of Palaestra, partly (he is himself inconsistent about this, lines 1119–23) to demand a share for himself as hush-money.   The two slaves wrangle vigorously for several pages, and then agree to arbitration.   Arbitration was the common practice among citizens, in preference, or as a preliminary, to fighting the case in court. The arbitrator might be appointed by a magistrate, or, as here, be chosen by mutual consent (lines 1033–44), a man of substance (lines 712–13); he listened to both sides and gave his verdict. It was not legally binding, and a discontented party could go to court, as the disappointed Cappadox threatens to do in *Curculio* 719–22; but there the very fact of the award would tell against him. Gripus and Trachalio imitate this procedure, as no doubt slaves and other humble folk often did. Menander's *Epitrepontes* ("The Arbitration") takes its name from just such a scene.

Later, when Gripus claims his talent from Labrax, there is a different procedure; for then Daemones interferes not by invitation, but as a party to the dispute: he is Gripus's master and therefore protector. Gripus had no right to withhold the *vidulus* from its owner; but neither was he bound to inform the owner where it was; and so he bargained for a reward, which Labrax promised. But Labrax's promise had only religious sanctions; it was not enforceable at law, and in any case not by Gripus, whose case must be put by his master. Why, then, does Labrax give way? Partly because of the difficulty of proving ownership (though it is not disputed, the *onus probandi* lies on him, lines 1392–3); partly because he finds that Gripus's owner is the formidable figure whom he had met, to his undoing, earlier in the day, and who might well give him further trouble if he again came before a court; we may perhaps add that Plautus (or Diphilus) thought it time for the play to come to an end. Anyway, he gives in, and payment is eased by being made partly in kind: part he must make in cash, but for the other half he may give up Ampelisca, generously valued at 30 *minae*. He gets back his valuables, which he had never expected to see again (lines 545–6), at a not unreasonable cost: we hear that at least 320 *minae* were in the *vidulus*, besides gold and silver vessels (lines 1313-19).

On being handed over, the reward belongs legally not to Gripus, but to Daemones; for a slave's possessions were his master's. Gripus is outraged, and indeed everybody in the audience would sympathise; for if not by law, at least by custom slaves were allowed to keep property; nor in fact does Daemones intend to override this custom. He takes, as it were, a commission on the deal, by accepting Ampelisca as part of the price; she momentarily becomes his property: as things stood at line 1220, it was Plesidippus who would be expected to foot the bill for her; he could, it is true, afford to do so, being spared the expense of buying Palaestra. Gripus gets the rest of the reward, in the form of his freedom. Does he know this by the end of the play? Sonnenschein supposes not, saying "Gripus is left in ignorance of his master's kindly intentions to the end of the play" (note on line 1414). Whatever the ethics of this, it seems a bit unsatisfactory as drama; and I think the offer of freedom is conveyed and acknowledged in the last line by the invitation to dinner (see note on line 1423); the scene can at any rate be played so.

Plesidippus, as a foreigner in Cyrene, has his complaint against Labrax heard by a special court (note on line 1282).

(v) *Money*

The monetary system of Greco-Roman comedy is this:—

6 *oboli* = 1 *drachma*.

2 *drachmae* = 1 *nummus*.

10 *nummi* = 1 *Philippus* (or *nummus aureus*).

5 *Philippi* = 1 *mina*.

60 *minae* = 1 *talentum* (*talentum magnum*).

A talent therefore contained 3,000 *nummi*, a *mina* contained 50. Payment of the larger sums, talents and *minae*, would usually be made in the golden Philip or *nummus aureus*, coined by Philip of Macedon a little before Diphilus's time, and highly esteemed throughout the Greek world (and even imitated in first century Gaul). So, at line 1313, the sum of "a hundred odd *minae* Philip" would be made up of 500 *nummi aurei*, more or less, or the appropriate number of these and other coins—Philip also coined double *nummi aurei*. In his haggling with Gripus, Labrax is forced up from 300 *nummi* (not *aurei*) to a talent, ten times as much. In his final settlement with Daemones he agrees to pay half a talent, 30 *minae* (in consideration of which Daemones will release Gripus), and instead of the other half talent to release Ampelisca, this being half as much again as he had paid for her when he bought her.

In an age of currency reform and inflation it would be vain to quote modern values: we can only observe what prices were. An obol was almost worthless, though it is mentioned in Terence's *Andria* 369 as the price of *holera et pisciculos minutos*; Gripus names a three-obol bit as a most trifling sum (line 1330). If a *drachma* was equivalent to a *denarius*, we may remember the values implied in Matthew xx. 2 and Luke x. 35, the parables of the labourers in the vineyard and of the good Samaritan. A decent town-house, sold for 40 *minae*, was dirt cheap (*Trinummus* 1081–2); even at two talents it would be a good bargain (*Mostellaria* 5, 637–49).

As for attractive girls, the commodity most often priced in comedies, a grown-up one might cost from 20 *minae* upwards (*Pseudolus* 52, *Rudens* 1406); the commonest price quoted is 30 *minae*, as in *Rudens* 45 and 1408–9. Sixty, quoted in *Epidicus* 468 to a wealthy and amorous soldier, was a very stiff price; and in *Persa* 665 the same sum is paid by a *leno* for what he takes to be a foreign princess in captivity; the sum there is the more outrageous because no guarantee of *mancupium* is given, and 10 more *minae* are charged for her dress and ornaments. A little girl fetches 10 *minae* in *Curculio* 528, a little boy 6 in *Captivi* 974. Gripus, a steady and useful man, was, as we have seen, worth 30.

Of course, we may suspect that some of these prices are dramatically exaggerated, and that neither did anybody in his senses part with 70 *minae* for a girl, nor could one buy even a few cabbage leaves and scraps of fish for an *obol*.

LANGUAGE

Plautine Latin is less unlike classical Latin than it seems at first sight. The differences fall into two categories: unfamiliar spellings and inflexions, and unclassical syntax. To the former the reader must accustom himself as quickly as he can: help is given in the notes and vocabulary. The most disconcerting difference is probably the use of *o* for *u*, after *v* or another *u*, giving for example *aequos, servos,* for *aequus, servus*. The verbs *es* and *est* are often attached to terminations which would be elided before them, giving, e.g. *acceptumst, opust, cenaturu's,* for *acceptum est, opus est, cenaturus es*. Plautine syntax is less troublesome; its variations consist chiefly in not observing certain rules which were more strictly kept in classical Latin, *e.g.* certain cases after certain verbs, subjunctive with causal *quom* (*cum*) or in Indirect Question. They, too, are noticed in the notes, but more to warn the reader off from imitation when he composes Latin himself than because of any difficulty in translation. But one characteristic worth mentioning here is *parataxis*, the use of co-ordinate clauses unconnected by a conjunction, where we should expect one clause to be subordinated. Examples are *scibis faxo* (line 365), "I'll let you know", and *vim adferam adigit* (line 681), "makes

43

me use force", where we should expect *faxo* (*faciam*) *ut scias* and *ut vim adferam adigit*. Even in classical Latin parataxis is found, particularly in the colloquial language.

For further information, see W. M. Lindsay, *The Syntax of Plautus*.

MANUSCRIPTS AND THE TEXTS

Like all ancient literature, the plays of Plautus were published and preserved by hand-written copies of hand-written copies; and the copyists, being human, made mistakes, which modern scholars have done their best to recognise and correct. Textual criticism is not the purpose of this edition, but the following summary, gleaned from Lindsay's preface to his Oxford Text, may be interesting.

All the manuscripts of Plautus but one appear, by the similarity and character of the mistakes that they contain, to have been derived from one copy, written about the ninth century A.D.; these MSS are collectively called by Lindsay *P*. The one exception is the "Ambrosian Palimpsest", or *A*. A palimpsest is a parchment which has had the old writing scraped off and another text written on: this was done in the middle ages because parchment was scarce and dear. If the older text is detected, it can be made legible under the newer one by chemical treatment. The Plautine text of *A* dates from the third or fourth century A.D.: it contains its own errors, but they are different from those in the *P* manuscripts. Therefore where *A* and *P* have the same reading, we may assume, not indeed that it is necessarily what Plautus wrote, but that it was to be found in all or most of the copies in existence in the third century. Where *A* and *P* differ, either or both may be wrong. *A*'s text is not complete; parts of *Rudens* and other plays are missing; but it has parts of one play, *Vidularia*, which is not in *P* at all.

44

INTRODUCTION

The *notae personarum* (indication of speakers) are haphazardly given in MSS. In *A* they are missing; in other MSS the change is often indicated by no more than a dash; and we know from papyrus remains of Greek plays that this was normal in the classical period. An editor is therefore within his rights in so assigning words to speakers as to make the best sense he can.

RUDENS

DRAMATIS PERSONAE

(In order of appearance)

ARCTURUS, a star-god.

SCEPARNIO, slave of Daemones.

PLESIDIPPUS, a young gentleman of Athens.

DAEMONES, an old gentleman-farmer.

PALAESTRA
AMPELISCA } slave-girls, owned by Labrax.

PTOLEMOCRATIA, Priestess of Venus.

FISHERMEN.

TRACHALIO, slave of Plesidippus.

LABRAX, a slave-dealer.

CHARMIDES, his business associate.

TURBALIO
SPARAX } *lorarii*, slaves of Daemones.

GRIPUS, a fisherman, slave of Daemones.

FRIENDS OF PLESIDIPPUS.

Scene: the countryside of Cyrenae, close to the sea.

48

PROLOGUE

Of the doors of the stage-building (see p. 10), that to the audience's left is open, and represents the Temple of Venus; that to their right is shut, and represents the farm-house of DAEMONES. *The God* ARCTURUS *enters, perhaps on the roof, perhaps through the central door; his costume is adorned with a star.*

AR Qui gentis omnis mariaque et terras movet,
eiius sum civis civitate caelitum.
ita sum ut videtis, splendens stella candida,
signum quod semper tempore exoritur suo
5 hic atque in caelo: nomen Arcturo est mihi.   5
noctu sum in caelo clarus atque inter deos;
inter mortalis ambulō interdius.
et alia signa de caelo ad terram accidunt:
qui est imperator divom atque hominum, Iuppiter,
10 is nos per gentis alios alia disparat,   10
qui facta hominum moresque, pietatem et fidem
noscamus; ut quemque adiuvēt opulentia.
qui falsas litis falsis testimoniis
petunt, quique in iure abiurant pecuniam,
15 eorum referimus nomina exscripta ad Iovem;   15
cottidie ille scit quis hic quaerat malum:
qui hic litem apisci postulant peiiurio
mali, res falsas qui impetrant apŭd iudicem
(iterum ille eam rem iudicatam iudicat),
20 maiore multa multat quam litem auferunt: 20
bonos in aliis tabulis exscriptos habet.
atque hoc scelestĭ ín animum inducunt suom,
Iovĕm sé placare posse donis, hostiis,
et operam et sumptum perdunt; id éŏ fit quia
25 nihil ēi acceptumst a peiiuris supplici: 25

facilius si qui pius est a dis supplicans
quam qui scelestust inveniet veniam sibi.
idcirco moneo vos ego hoc, qui estis boni,
quique aetatem agitis cum pietate et cum fide:
30 retinete porro, post factum ut laetemini.   30
   nunc huc qua caussa veni argumentum eloquar.
primumdum huic esse nomen urbi Diphilus
                              (*he indicates the district in general*)
Cyrenas voluit.   illic habitat Daemones,
                              (*he points to the farm-house door*)
in agro atque villa proxuma propter mare,
35 senĕx, qui huc Athenis exul venit, hau malus;   35
   neque is adeo propter málitiam patria caret,
   sed dum alios servat se impedivit interim;
   rem bene paratam comitate perdidit.
   huĭc filiola virgo periit parvola.
40 eam de praedone vir mercatur pessumus;   40
   is eam huc Cyrenas leno advexit virginem.
   adulescens quidam, civis huiius Atticus,
   eam vidit ire e ludo fĭdicinio domum;
   amare occepit: ad lenonem devenit;
45 minis triginta sibi puellam destinat,   45
   datque arrabonem et iure iurando adligat.
   is leno, ut se aequom est, flocci non fecit fidem
   neque quod iuratus adulescenti dixerat.
   ĕĭ erat hospes par sui, Siculus senex,
50 scelestus, Agrigentinus, urbis proditor.   50
   is ïllĭus laudare infit formam virginis
   et aliarum itidem quae eius erant mulierculae.
   infit lenoni suadere ut secum simul
   eat in Sicíliam: ibi esse homines volŭptários
55 dicit, potesse ibí ĕŭm fieri divitem,   55
   ibi esse quaestum maxumum meretricibus.
   persuadet.   navis clanculum conducitur;
   quidquid erat, noctu in navem comportat domo

50

    leno; adulescenti qui puellam ab eo emerat
60 ait sese Veneri velle votum solvere   60
    (*he points*) (id hic est Veneris fanŭm), ét eo ad prandium
    vocavit adulescentem huc. ipse hinc ilico
    conscendit navĕm, ávehit meretriculas.
    adulescenti alii narrant ut res gesta sit,
65 lenonem abiissĕ. ád portum adulescens venit: 65
    illorum navis longe in altum apscesserat.
    ego, quoniam video virginem asportarier,
    tetuli ét ei auxilium et lénoni exitium simul:
    increpui hibernum et fluctus movi máritumos.
70 nam Arcturus signum sum omnium unum acerrumum: 70
    vehemens sum exoriens, quom occido vehementior.
    nunc ambo, leno atque hospes, in saxo simul
    sedent eiecti: navis confracta est eis,
    illa autem virgo atque altera itidem ancillula
75 de navi timidae desuluerunt in scapham.   75
    nunc eas ab saxo fluctus ad terram ferunt,
    ad villam illius, exsul ubi habitat senex,
    quoius deturbavit ventus tectum et tegulas;
    et servŏs íllĭc est eiius qui egreditur foras.
80 adulescens huc iam adveniet, quem videbitis,   80
    qui illam mercatust de lenone virginem.
       valete! ut hostes vostri diffidant sibi!—   *Exit.*

ACT I

I i   *Enter* SCEPARNIO *from the farm-house, with a digging tool.*

SC Pro di inmortales, tempestatem quoiusmodi
    Neptunus nobis nocte hac misit proxuma!
    detexit ventus villam—quid verbis opust?   85
    non ventus fuit, verum Alcumena Euripidi:

5 ita ŏmnís de tecto deturbavit tegulas;
inlustriores fecit, fenstrasque indidit.

He turns and surveys the building.

I ii   *Enter from the town (audience's right)* PLESIDIPPUS *and three friends*
         wearing military cloaks and swords. They do not observe
         SCEPARNIO, *nor he them.*

PL   Et vos a vostris abduxi negotiis,
neque id processit qua vos duxi gratia,   90
neque quivi ad portum lenonem prehendere.
sed mea desidia spem deserere nolui:
5 eo vos, amici, detinui diutius.
nunc huc ad Veneris fanum venio visere,
ubi rem divinam se facturum dixerat.   95
SC   *(turning to the front)* si sapiam, hoc quod me mactat
concinnem lutum,
PL   prope me hic nescioquis loquitur. *Enter* DAEMONES *from*
the farm-house.   DA   heus, Sceparnio!
10 SC   qui nominat me? DA   qui pro te argentum dedit.
SC   quasi me tuom esse servom dicas, Daemones.
DA   luto usust multo, multam terram confode: 100
villam integundam intellego totam mihi;
nam nunc perlucet ea quam cribrum crebrius.
                              PLESIDIPPUS *approaches* DAEMONES.
15 PL   pater, salvetō, ámboque adeo. DA   salvo' sis.
SC   sed utrum tu masne an femina es, qui illum patrem
voces? PL   vir sum equidem. SC   quaere, vir, porro
patrem.   105
DA   filiolam ego, unam quam habui, eam unam perdidi:
virile sexus numquam ullum habui. PL   at di dabunt.
20 SC   tibi quidem hercle, quisquis es, magnum malum,
qui oratione hic occupatos occupes.
PL   isticin vos habitatis? SC   quid tu id quaeritas?   110

52

quon mox furatum venias, vestigas loca?
PL peculiosum esse addecet servom et probum,
25 quem ero praesente haud praetereat oratio,
aut qui inclementer dicat homini libero.
SC et impudicum et impudentem hominem addecet   115
molestum ultro advenire ad alienam domum,
quoi debeatur nil. DA tace, Sceparnio.
30 quid opust, adulescens? PL istic infortunium,
qui praefestinet, ubi erus adsit, praeloqui.
sed nisi molestumst, paucis percontarier   120
volo ego ex te. DA dabitur opera, atque in negotio.
SC quin tu in paludem is exsicasque harundinem,
35 qui pertegamus villam, dum sudumst? DA tace.
tu, si quid opus est, dice. PL dic quod te rogo:
ecquem tu hic hominem crispum, incanum videris,   125
malum, peiiurum, palpatorem? DA plurumos:
                                    (*he indicates the audience*)
nam ego propter eiius módǐ viros vivo miser.
40 PL hic dico, in fanum Veneris qui mulierculas
duas secum adduxit, quique adornaret sibi
ut rem divinam faceret, aut hodie aut heri.   130
DA non hercle, adulescens, iam hos dies complusculos
quemquam istic vidi sacruficare; neque potest
45 clam me esse si qui sacruficant: semper petunt
aquam hinc aut ignem aut vascula aut cultrum aut veru
aut aulam extarem, aut aliquid: quid verbis opust?   135
Veneri paravi vasa et puteum, non mihi.
nunc intervallum iam hos dies multos fuit.
50 PL ut verba praehibes, me periisse praedicas.
DA mea quidem hercle caussa salvǒs sis licet.
SC heus tu, qui fana ventris caussa circumis,   140
iubere meliust prandium ornari domi.
DA fortasse tu huc vocatus ēs ad prandium,
55 ĭlle qui vocavit nullus venit? PL admodum.
SC nullumst periclum te hinc ire impransum domum.

Cererem te meliust quam Venerem sectarier: 145
amori haec curat; tritico curat Ceres.
PL   deludificavit me ille homo indignis modis.
60 DA   pro di inmortales!   (*He points to the audience's left*)
                                          quid illuc est, Sceparnio,
hominum secundum litus?   SC   ut mea opiniost,
propter viam illi sunt vocati ad prandium.   150
DA   qui?   SC   quia post cenam, credo, laverunt heri.
DA   confracta navis in mari est illis.   SC   ita est.
65 at hercle nobis villa in terra et tegulae.   DA   hui!
homunculi quanti estis!   eiecti ut natant!   154-5
PL   ubi sunt ei homines, opsecro?   DA   hac ad dexteram.
viden? secundum litus.   PL   video.   séquimini.
utinam is sit quém ego quaero, vir sacerrumus!
70 valete.—SC   si non moneas, nosmet méminimus.
        Exeunt PLESIDIPPUS *and friends.* SCEPARNIO *suddenly becomes excited.*
sed, o Palaemo, sancte Neptuni comes,   160
qui et Herculéi socius esse diceris,
quod facinus video!   DA   quid vides?   SC   mulierculas
video sedentis in scapha solas duas.
                Both DAEMONES *and* SCEPARNIO *gaze intently.*
75 DA   ut adflictantur miserae!   SC   eugae eugae, perbene!
ab saxo avortit fluctus ad litus scapham.   165
DA   nequé gubernator umquam potuit tam bene.
SC   non vidisse undas me maiores censeo
DA   salvae sunt, si illos fluctus devitaverint.
80 SC   nunc, nunc periclumst.   unda eiecit alteram.
DA   at in vadost; iam facile enabit.   SC   eugepae!   170
vidĕn alteram illam ut fluctus eiecit foras?
surrexit; horsum se capessit.   salva res.
DA   desiluit haec autem altera in terram e scapha.
85 SC   ut prae timore in genua in undas concidit!
DA   salvast: evasit ex aqua. iam in litore est.   *He relaxes.* 175
SC   sed dextrovorsum avorsa it in malam crucem.
hem!   errabit illaec hodie.   DA   quíd íd refert tua?

SC si ad saxum quo capessit se ea deorsum cadet,
90 errationis fecerit compendium.   179-80
DA si tu de illarum cenaturus vesperi es,
illis curandum censeo, Sceparnio:
si apŭd méd essuru's, mihi darí operam volo.
SC bonum aequomque oras.   DA sequere me hac ergo.—
                                    SC sequor.—
                              Exeunt to farm-house.

I iii *Enter* PALAESTRA *from the shore (audience's left), wet. She sees
       neither the temple nor the farm-house. She sings:*

       Nimio hóminum fortunaé minus
                miseraé memoràntur   185
           quăm in úsu experiúndo is
                    dátur acèrbum.
       Satin hóc dẹo complacitúmst, mĕ hoc
                ornatu ornàtam
           in ĭncértas regiónes
                    tímidam eièctam?
    5 hancíne ego àd rem nátam miserám me memorábo?
       hanc égo partem cápio ob pietátem praecípuam?   190
       nămhŏc mí sat labórist labórem hunc potíri,
       si me érga paréntem aut deós inpiávi:
       sed íd si paráte curávi ut cavérem,
   10 tum mi hóc indecórē, iníque, inmodéste
           dati', dí; nam quid habebúnt sibi
                signi ínpiĭ pòsthac,   195
           si ad húnc modum est innóxiis
                    honōr apùd vos?
       nam mé si fecísse aut paréntes sceléste
       sciám, minu' me míserer.
   15   sed eríle scèlu' me sóllicitat,
                eiiús med ìnpietás male habet:

                         55

is návem atque òmnia pérdidit
ín mari.
haéc bonorum eíius sunt
réliquiae:
étiam quae simul 200
vécta mecum ín scaphast,
éxcidit;
égo nunc sola sum.
quaé mihi sí foret sálva saltém, labor
20 léniōr ésset hic
mi éiius opera.
nunc quám spem aut opem, aút consilí quid capéssam?
ita híc sola sólis locís compotíta. 205
hic sáxa sunt, hic máre sonat,
neque quísquam homō mi ob viăm venit.

   ★ ★ ★ ★ ★

25 hóc quod induta sum, summae opes óppido;
néc cibo néc loco técta quó sim scio.
quáe mihist spés qua me
vívere velim?
néc loci gnára sum, néc etiamdum híc fui: 210
áliquem saltém velim quí mihi ex hís locis
30 aút viam aut sémitam
mónstret: ita nunc
hác an illác eam, incérta sum cónsili;
néc prope usquam híc quidem cúltum agrum cónspicor:
álgor, errór, pavor,
me ómnia tenent. 215
haéc, parentés mei, haud
scíti' miseri,
35 mé nunc mise-
ram ésse ita utĭ sum.
56

leíbera egō prognáta fui
máxume; nequiquám fui:
nunc quí minu' servió quam si
servā forĕm nata?

neque quícquam umquam illis prófuit qui mé sibi eduxérunt.

She swoons, back stage.

I iv

Enter AMPELISCA *from the shore, wet.   She sees neither the temple,
nor the farm-house, nor* PALAESTRA.   *She sings:*

AM Quid míhi meliust, quid mágis in remst, quam a
    córpore vitam ut sécludam?   220
ita mále vivo atque ita míhi multae in pectóre sunt curae
    exánimales.
ita rés sĕ habent: vitae haú parco; perdídï spem qua me
    obléctabam.
omnía iam circumcúrsavi atque omníbu' latebris perréptavi,
quaerére conservam, vóce, oculis, auríbus, ut pervestígarem.
neque eam úsquam invenio, néque quŏ eam neque quá
    quaeram consúltumst;   225
neque quém rogitem respónsorem quemquam ínterea
    convénio;
neque mági' solae terraé solae sunt quam haéc loca átque hae
    regiónes;
neque, sí vivit, eam víva umquam quin ínveniam desístam.

PALAESTRA revives and listens.

10   PA quoianam vóx mihi
          prope híc sonat?
      AM pertimuí: quis hic
          loquitúr prope?   230
      PA Spes bona, ópsecro,
      subventá mihi.
      AM eximés ex hoc
          miserám metu?

PA cérto vox múliebris aúris tetigít meas.
AM múlier est, múliebris vóx mi ad aurís venit.
PA num Ampelisca ópsecrost? AM tén, Palaestra, aúdio?
PA quín voco, ut me aúdiat, nómine illám suo?   236
20 Ámpelisca! AM hém, quis est?
                  PA égo Palaestra.
AM díc, ubi es? PA pól ego nunc ín malis plúrumis.
AM sócia sum, néc minor párs meast quám tua.
séd videre éxpeto té. PA mihi ēs aémula.   240

They seek each other.

AM cónsequamúr gradu vócem. ubi ēs? PA écce me.
25 áccede ad me átque adi cóntra. AM fit sédulo.

They meet, stage left.

PA cédo manùm. AM áccipé.   *They embrace.*
                  PA dic, vivisne? ópsecro.
AM tú facis mé quidem vívere ut núnc velim,
quóm mihi té licet tángere. ut víx mihi   245
crédo ego hoc, té tenere! ópsecro, ampléctere,
30 spés mea. ut me ómnium iám laborúm levas!
PA óccupas práeloqui quáe mea orátiost.
núnc abire hínc decet nós. AM quŏ, amabo, íbimus?
PA lítus hoc pérsequamúr. AM sequór quo lubet.   250
sícine hic cum úvida véste grassábimur?
35 PA hóc quod est, íd necessárium est pérpeti.

They begin to cross the stage.

séd quid hoc, ópsecro, est?
                  AM quid? PA víděn, amábo,
fanum hóc? AM ubi est?
                  PA ad déxteram.
          AM videó decorum dís locum vidérier. 255

They approach the temple.

PA haud lónge abesse opórtet homines hínc, ita hic
lepidúst locus.   *They raise their hands in prayer.*

58

PA *et* AM   quísquis est deus, véneror ut nos éx hac
   aerumna éximat;
míseras, ínopes, aérumnosas út aliquo auxilio ádiuvet.

I v

PTOLEMOCRATIA *appears in the temple doorway.*

PT   Qui súnt qui a patróna precés mea expetéssunt ?
   nam vóx me precántum huc forás excitávit.   260
   bonam átque opsequéntem deam átque hau gravátam
   patrónam exsequóntur benígnamque múltum.

5   PA et AMP   iubémus te sálvere, máter. PT   salvéte,
         puéllae.   sed únd' vos
                 íre cum uvida
            véste dicam, ópsecro,
               tam maéstiter vestítas ?   265
      PA   ílico hinc ímus, hau lóngule ex hóc loco;
10   vérum longe hínc abest únde advectae húc sumus.
      PT   némpe equo lígneo pér vias cáerulas
      éstis vectae ? PA   ádmodum. PT   ergo aéquius vós erat
      cándidatás venire hóstiatásque: ad hoc   270
      fánum ad istúnc modum nón veniri solet.
15   AM   quáene eiectae é mari símus ambae, ópsecro ?
      únde nos hóstias ágere voluístis huc ?

They kneel and clasp PTOLEMOCRATIA'S *knees.*

      PA   núnc tibi ampléctimur génua, egentés opum,
      quae ín locis nésciis néscia spé sumus,   275
      út tuo récipias técto servésque nos,
20   míseriarúmque te ambárum uti mísereat,
      quibús nec locúst ullus néc spes paráta,
      neque hóc quod vidés ampliús nobis quícquamst.
      PT   manús mi date; éxsurgite á genibus ámbae.   280
      miséricordiór nulla mést feminárum.   *The girls rise.*
25   sed háec pauperés res sunt ínopesque, puéllae:
                 égomet vix vitám colo;
               Véneri cibŏ meo sérvio.

AM Venerís fanum, opsecro, hóc est?
PT fateṓr: ego huiius fáni
    sacérdos clùeo.   285
30 verúm quidquid ést comitér fiet á me,
    quó nunc cópiā valébit.
ite hác mecum. PA amíce benígneque honórem,
    máter, nóstrum habes.— PT opórtet.—

Exeunt to temple.

ACT II

Enter fishermen from the town, carrying rods and lines.

PISCATORES

Omníbu' modis qui pauperes sunt homines misere vivont, 290
  praesertim quibu' nec quaestus est nequé didicere artem
    ullam:
  necessitate, quidquid est domi, id sat est habendum.
  nos iam de ornatu propemodum, ut locupletes simus, scitis:
5 hisce hami atque haec harundines sunt nobis quaestu et cultu.
  cottidie ex urbe ad mare huc prodimus pabulatum: 295
  pro exercitu gymnastico et palaestrico hoc habemus;
  echinos, lopadas, ostreas, balanos captamus, conchas,
  marinam urticam, musculos, plagusias striatas;
10 postid piscatum hamatilem et saxatilem adgredimur.
  cibum captamus e mari: si eventus non evenit   300
  neque quicquam captumst piscium, salsi lautique pure
  domum redimus clanculum, dormimus incenati.
  atque ut nunc valide fluctuat mare, nulla nobis spes est:
15 nisi quid concharum capsimus, cenati sumu' profecto.
  nunc Venerem hanc veneremur bonam, ut nos lepide
    adiúerit hodie.   305

They turn to the temple and raise their hands in prayer.

60

II ii   *Enter* Trachalio *from the town.*

TR   Animum advorsavi sedulo ne erum usquam praeterirem;
     nam quom modo exibat foras, ad portum se aibat ire.
     sed quos perconter commode eccos video astare. adibo.

He approaches the fishermen.
5 salvete, fures máritumi, Conchitae atque Hamiotae,   310
     famelica hominum natio. quid agitis? ut peritis?
PI   ut piscatorem aequomst, fame sitique speque falsa.
TR   ecquém adulescentem huc, dŭm hic astatis, expedite,
     vidistis ire strenua facie, rubicundum, fortem,
10 qui tris secum homines duceret chlamydatos cum machaeris?
PI   nullum istac facie ut praedicas venisse huc scimus.   316
                                        TR   ecquem
     recalvom ad Silanum senem, statutum, ventriosum,
     tortis superciliis, contracta fronte, fraudulentum,
     deorum odium atque hominum, málŭm, mali viti probrique
         plenum,
15 qui duceret mulierculas dụas secum sati' venustas?   320
PI   cum istiụsmodi virtutibús operisque natus qui sit,
     eum quídem ăd carnuficem est aequius quam ad Venerem
         commeare.
TR   at si vidistis, dicite. PI   huc profecto nullus venit.
     vale.—
                                   Exeunt to shore.
     TR   valete. credidi: factum est quod suspicabar;
20 data verba ero sunt; leno abit scelestus exsulatum;
     in navem ascendit; mulieres avexit, sceleris semen.
     nunc quid mihi meliust quam ilico hic opperiar érŭm dum
         veniat?
     eadem hanc—sacerdos Veneriá si quidpiam amplius scit,
     si videro, exquisivero: faciet me certiorem.   330

61

II iii

Enter AMPELISCA *from the temple, with a water-pot. She speaks back into the temple.*

AM   Intellego: hanc quae proxumast tu villam Veneris fano
pulsare iussisti atque aquam rogare.   TR   quoia ad áuris
vox mi advolavit?   *He turns.*
                           AM   opsecro, quís hìc loquitur?   *She turns.*
                                     TR   quém ego video?
estne Ampelisca haec quae foras e fano egreditur?   AM   estne
     hic
5 Trachalio quem conspicor, calator Plesidippi?   335
     TR   east.   AM   is est.   Trachalio, salve.   TR   salve,
     Ampelisca.
quid agi' tŭ?   AM   aétatem hau malam mále.   TR   melius
     ominare.
AM   verum omnes sapientes decet conferre et fabulari.
sed Plesidippus tuos erus ubi, amabo, est?   TR   heia vero,
10 quasi non sit intus!   AM   neque pol est neque huc quidem
     ullus venit.   340
     TR   non venit?   AM   vera praedicas.   TR   non est meum,
     Ampelisca.
sed quam mox coctum est prandium?   AM   quod prandium,
     opsecro te?
TR   nemp' rem divinam facitis hic?   AM   quid somnias,
     amabo?
TR   certe huc Labrax ad prandium vocavit Plesidippum
15 erum meum eru' voster.   AM   pol hau miranda facta dicis:
     si deos decepit et homines, lenonum more fecit.   346
     TR   non rem divinam facitis hic vos neque erus?   AM
     hariolare.
TR   quid tu ágis hìc igitur?   AM   ex malis multis metuque
     summo
capitalique ex periculo orbas auxilique opumque huc
20 recepit ad se Veneria haec sacerdos me et Palaestram.   350
     TR   an hic Palaestrast, opsecró, eri mei amica?   AM   certo.

TR inest lepos in nuntio tuo magnus, mea Ampelisca.
sed istúc periclum perlubet quod fuerit vobis scire.
AM confracta est, mi Trachalió, hac nocte navis nobis.
25 TR quid, navis? quaé ístaec fabulast? AM non audivisti,
    amabo,   355
quo pacto leno clanculum nos hinc auferre vóluit
in Síciliam, et quicquid domi fuit ín navem imposivit?
ea nunc perierunt omnia. TR oh, Neptune lepide, salve!
nec te aleator nullus est sapientior; profecto
30 nimi' lepide iecisti bolum: periurum perdidisti.   360
sed nunc ubi est leno Labrax? AM periit potando, opinor:
Neptunus magnis poculis hac nocte eum invitavit.
TR credo hercle anancaeo datum quod biberet. ut ego amo te,
mea Ampelisca, ut dulcis ēs, ut mulsa dicta dicis!
35 sed tu et Palaestra quomodo salvae estis? AM scibis faxo.
de navi timidae ambae in scapham insilúimus, quia videmus
ad saxa navem ferrier; properans exsolvi restim,   367
dum illi timent: nos cum scapha tempestas dextrovorsum
differt ab illis. itaque nos ventisque fluctibusque
40 iactatae exemplis plurumis miserae perpetuam noctem; 370
vix hodie ad litus pertulit nos ventus exanimatas.
TR novi, Neptunus ita solet; quamvis fastidiosus
aedilis est: si quae improbae sunt merces, iactat omnis.
AM vae capiti atque aetati tuae! TR tuo, mea Ampelisca!
45 scivi lenonem faxere hoc quod fecit; saepe dixi;   375
capillum promittam optumumst occipiamque hariolari.
AM cavistis ergo tu atque erus ne abiret, quom scibatis?
TR quid faceret? AM sí amabat, rogas, quid faceret?
    adservaret
dies noctesque, in custodia esset semper. verum ecastor, 380
50 ut multi fecit, ita probe curavit Plesidippus.
TR qur tu istuc dicis? AM res palam est. TR scin tu?
    etiam qui it lavatum
in bálineas, quom ibi sedulo sua vestimenta servat,

tamĕn surrupiuntur, quippe qui quem illorum opservet
    falsust;
fur facile quem opservat videt: custos qui fur sit nescit. 385
55 sed duce me ad illam ubi est. AM i sane in Veneris fanum
    huc intro;
sedentem flentemque opprimes. TR ut iam istuc mihi
    molestumst!
sed quid flet? AM ego dicam tibi: hoc sese excruciat animi,
    quia leno ademit cistulam ej quam habebat ubique habebat
    qui suos parentes nosceré possēt: eam veretur   390
60 ne périerit. TR ubinam ea fuit cistellula? AM íbidem in
    navi.
conclusit ipse in vidulum, ne copia esset eiius
    qui suos parentes noscerēt. TR o facinus impudicum,
    quam liberam esse oporteat servire postulare!
    AM nunc eam cum navi scilicēt abiisse pessum in altum. 395
65 et aurum et argentum fuit lenonis omne ibídem.
    TR credo aliquem immersisse atque eum excepisse. AM id
    misera maestast,
sibi eorum evenisse ínopiam. TR iam istoc magis usus
    factost,
ut eam intro consolerque eam, ne sic se excruciet animi;
    nam multa praeter spem scio multis bona evenisse.   400
70 AM at ego étiam, qui speraverint, spem decepisse multos.
    TR ergo animus aequos optumum est aerumnae condi-
    mentum.
ego eo íntro, nisi quid vis.—AM eas. (*Exit* TRACHALIO *to temple.*)
                           ego quod mihi imperavit
sacerdos, id faciam atque aquam hinc de proxumo rogabo;
    nam extemplo, si verbis suis peterem, daturos dixit.   405
75 neque digniorem censeo vidisse anum me quemquam
    quoi deos atque homines censeam bene facere magi' decere.
ut lepide, ut liberaliter, ut honeste atque hau gravate
timidas, egentis, uvidas, eiectas, exanimatas

accepit ad sese, hau secus quam si ex se simus natae!   410
80 ut eapse sic succincta aquam calefactat, ut lavemus!
nunc, ne morae illi sim, petam hinc aquam unde mi imperavit.
                                                    (*Knocks.*)
heus, ĕcquis in villast? ecquis hoc recludit? ecquis prodit?

II iv

The door is flung open violently, and SCEPARNIO *appears.*

SC   Quís ĕst qui nostris tam proterve foribus facit iniuriam?
AM   ego sum.   SCEPARNIO's *manner changes.*   SC   Hem! quíd
    hŏc boni est? eŭ edepol, specie lepida múlierem! 415
AM   salve, adulescens.   SC   et tu multum salveto, adules-
    centula.
AM   ad vos venio.   SC   (*giggling*) accipiam hospitio, si mox
    venies vesperi,
5 item ut adfectam; nam nunc nihil est qui te mane mulierem . . .
sed quid ais, mea hilara, lepida?   *He makes advances.*   AM   ah!
    nimium familiariter
me attrectas.   SC   pro di inmortales!   Veneris effigia haec
    quidem est.   (*He again makes advances.*)   420
ut in ocellis hilaritudo est! heia, corpus quoiusmodi!
subvolturium—illud quidem, "subaquilum" volui dicere.
10 vel papillae quoiusmodi! tum quae indoles in saviost!
AM   non ego sum pollucta pago. potin ut me apstineas
    manum?
SC   non licet te sic placidule bellam belle tangere?   425
AM   otium ubi erit, tum tibi operam ludo et deliciae dabo:
nunc quam ob rem huc sum missa, amabo, vel tu mi aias vel
    neges.
15 SC   quid nunc vis?   AM   sapienti ornatus quid velim
    indicium facit.
SC   meu' quoque hic sapienti ornatus quid velim indicium
    facit.

AM haec sacerdos Veneris hinc me a vobis iussit petere
    aquam.   430
SC at ego básilicus sum; quem nisi oras, guttam non feres.
    nostro illum puteum periclo et ferramentis fodimus.
20 nisi multis blanditiis a me gutta non ferri potest.
    AM qur tu aquam gravare, amabo, quam hostis hosti
    commodat?
SC qur tu operam gravare mihi quam civis civi commodat?
AM immo etiam tibi, mea voluptas, quae voles faciam omnia.
SC eugepae! salvos sum: haec iam me suam voluptatem
    vocat. (*She lets him kiss her.*)   437
25 dabitur tibi aqua, ne nequiquam mé ames.   cedo mi urnam.
    AM cape.
propera, amabo, ecferre.   SC manta: iam hic ero, volŭptás
    mea.—   *Exit to farm-house with pot, giggling and blowing kisses.*

As soon as he is out of sight, AMPELISCA, *with a grimace, wipes off
traces of his kisses.   Then she turns and looks around.*

AM quid sacerdoti me dicam hic démoratam tam diu? 440
    ut etiam nunc misera timeo ubi oculis intueor mare!
    sed quid ego misera video procul in litore?   442-50
30 meum erum lenonem Síciliensemque hospitem;
    quos periisse ambos misera credebam in mari.
    iam illud mali plus nobis vivit quam ratae.
    sed quid ego cesso fugere in fanum ac dicere haec
    Palaestrae, in aram ut confugiamus priu' quăm huc   455
35 scelestus leno veniat nosque hic opprimat?
    confugiam huc; ita res suppetit subitaria. *Exit hastily to temple.*

II v

Enter SCEPARNIO: *he carries the water-pot before him in a stately
attitude, which interferes with his vision.*

SC Pro di inmortales! in aqua numquam credidi
volŭptátem inesse tantam.   ut hanc traxi lubens!

66

nimio minus altus puteus visust quam prius.   460
ut sine labore hanc extraxi! praefiscine!

5   satĭn néquam sum, utpote qui hodie amare inceperim?
em tibi aquam, mea tu belliata. em, sic volo
te ferre honeste, ut ego fero, ut placeas mihi.
sed ubi tu es, delicata? cape aquam hanc, sis. ubi es? 465
amat hercle me, ut ego opinor. delituit mala.

10   ubi tu es? etiamne hanc urnam accepturá's? ubi es?
commodule meliust. tandem vero serio:
etiam acceptura es urnam hanc? ubi tu es gentium?
    (He lowers the pot.)
nusquam hercle equidem illam video. ludos me facit. 470
adponam hercle urnam iám ego hanc in media via.
                   (Sets it on the ground.)

15   sed autem, quid si hanc hinc apstulerit quispiam,
sacram urnam Veneris? mi exhibeat negotium.
metuo hercle ne illa mulier mi insidias locet,
ut comprehendar cum sacra urna Véneria.   475
nempe optumo me iure in vinclis enicet

20   magĭstrátus, si quis me hanc habere viderit.
nam haec litteratast, eapse cantat quoiia sit.
iam hercle evocabo hinc hanc sacerdotem foras,
ut hanc accipiat urnam. accedam huc ad fores.   480
heus, exi, Ptolemocratia, cape hanc urnam tibi:

25   muliercula hanc nescioquae huc ad me detulit.   *(Pause.)*
intro ferundast. repperi negotium,
siquidem mihi his ultro adgerunda etiam est aqua.—
                Exit to temple, bearing pot.

II vi

Enter from the shore LABRAX, *wet.*

LA Qui homo esse sese miserum et mendicum volet, 485
Neptuno credat sese atque aetatem suam:
nam si quis cúm eo quid rei commiscuit,

ad hoc exemplum amittit ornatum domum.
5 edepol, Libertas, lepida es, quae numquam pedem
voluisti in navem cum Hercule una imponere.   490
sed úbi ïlle meus est hospes, qui me perdidit?

(Enter CHARMIDES, *wet.)*

atque eccum incedit. CH quo, malum, properas, Labrax?
nam equidem te nequeo consequi tam strenue.
10 LA utinam te priu' quăm oculis vidissem meis,
malo cruciatu in Sícilia perbiteres,   495
quem propter hoc mihi optigit misero mali.
CH utinam, quom in aedis me ad te adduxisti domum,
in carcere illo potius cubuissem die:
15 deosque inmortalis quaeso, dum vivas, uti
omnis tui similis hospites habeas tibi.   500
LA Malam Fortunam in aedis te adduxi meas.
quid mihi scelesto tibi erat auscultatio?
quidve hinc abitio? quidve in navem inscensio?
20 ubi perdidi etiam plus boni quam mihi fuit.
CH pol minime miror navis si fractast tibi,   505
scelu' te et sceleste parta quae vexit bona.
LA pessum dedisti me blandimentis tuis.
CH scelestiorem cenam cenavi tuam
25 quam quae Thyestae quondam aut posita est Tereo.
LA perii! animo male fit. contine quaeso caput.   510

CHARMIDES *boxes his ears.* LABRAX *staggers to back-stage and vomits.*

CH pulmoneum edepol nimi' velim vomitum vomas.
LA eheu! Palaestra atque Ampelisca, ubi esti' nunc?
CH piscibus in alto, credo, praebent pabulum.
30 LA mendicitatem mi optulisti opera tua,
dum tuis ausculto magnidicis mendaciis.   515
CH bonam est quod habeas gratiam merito mihi,
qui te ex insulso salsum feci opera mea.
LA quin tu hinc is a me in maxumam malam crucem?
35 CH eas: easque res agebam commodum.
LA eheu! quis vivit me mortalis míserior?   520

68

CH   ego multo tanta míserior quam tu, Labrax.
LA qui? CH quia ego indignus sum, tu dignus qui sies.
LA o scirpe scirpe, laudo fortunas tuas,
40 qui semper servas gloriam aritudinis.
CH equidem me ad velitationem exerceo,   525
nam omnía corusca prae tremore fabulor.
LA edepol, Neptune, es bálineator frigidus:
cum vestimentis postquam aps te ábii al-algeo.
45 CH ne thermipolium quidem ull-ullum instruit;
ita salsam praehibet potionem et frigidam.   530
LA ut fortunati sunt fabri ferrarii,
qui apud carbones adsident! semper calent.
CH utinam fortuna nunc anetina ut-uterer,
50 ut, quom exiissem ex áq-aq-aqua, arerem tamen.
LA quid si aliquo ad ludos me pro manduco locem? 535
CH quapropter? LA quia pol clare crepito dentibus.
CH iure optumo med ela-lavisse arbitror.
LA qui? CH qui-quia auderem tecum in navem
     ascendere,
55 qui a fundamento mi usque movisti mare.
LA tibi auscultavi, tu promittebas mihi   540
illi esse quaestum maxumum meretricibus,
ibi me conruere posse aiebas ditias.
CH iam postulabas te, inpurata belua,
60 totam Siciliam devoraturum insulam?
LA quaenam ballaena meum voravit vidulum,   545
aurum atque argentum ubi omne compactum fuit?
CH eadem illa, credo, quae meum marsuppium,
quod plenum argenti fuit in sacciperio.
65 LA eheu! redactus sum usque ad unam hanc túniculam
                        (*he wrings the water out of it*)
et ad hoc misellum pallium. perii oppido. *Sits down.* 550
CH vel consociare mihi quidem tecum licet:
aequas habemus partis.   *Sits down back to back with* LABRAX.
LA saltem si mihi

mulierculae essent salvae, spes aliquae forent.
70 nunc si me adulescens Plesidippus viderit,
    quŏ ab arrabonem pro Palaestra acceperam,   555
    iam is exhibebit hic mihi negotium.
    CH quid, stulte, ploras? tibi quidem edepol copiast,
    dum lingua vivet, qui rem solvas omnibus.

II vii

Enter Sceparnio *from the temple. He does not see* Labrax *and* Charmides.

    SC quíd illuc, opsecro, negoti, quod duae mulierculae
    hic in fano Veneris signum flentes amplexae tenent,   560
    nescioquem metuentes miserae? nocte hac aiunt proxuma
    se iactatas atque eiectas hodie esse aiunt e mari. Labrax *jumps up.*
5 LA opsecro hercle, adulescens, úbi ïstaec sunt quas memoras
    múlieres?
    SC hic in fano Veneris. LA quot sunt? SC totidem quot
    ego et tu sumus.
    LA nemp' meae? SC nemp' nescio istuc. LA qua sunt
    facie? SC scitula.   565
    vel ego amare utramvis possum, si probe adpotus siem.
    LA nemp' puellae? SC nemp' molestus ēs. i, vise, si lubet.
10 LA meas oportet intus esse hic mulieres, mi Charmides.
    CH Iuppiter te perdat, et si sunt et si non sunt tamen.
    LA intro rumpam iam huc in Veneris fanum.— *Exit to temple.*
    CH in barathrum mavelim.   570
    (*He approaches* Sceparnio).
    opsecro, hospes, da mihi aliquid ubi condormiscam loci.
    SC istic ubi vis condormisce: nemo prohibet; puplicum est.
15 CH at vides me ornatus ut sim vestimentis uvidis:
    recipe me in tectum; da mihi vestimenti aliquid aridi,
    dum arescunt mea; ín aliquo tibi gratiam referam loco.   575
    SC tegillum eccillud (*he points in to the farm-yard*); mihi unum
    id aret: id, si vis, dabo.

 eodem amictus, eodem tectus esse soleo, si pluit.
20 tu istaec mihi dato: exarescent faxo. CH eho an te paenitet
 in mari quod semel elavi, ni hic in terra iterum eluam?
 SC eluas tu an exunguare, ciccum non interduim.   580
 tibi ego numquam quicqum credam, nisi si accepto pignore.
 tu vel suda vel peri algu vel tu aegrota vel vale.
25 barbarum hospitem mi in aedis nil moror. sat litiumst.—
             Exit, slamming door.
 CH iamne abeis? venalis illic ductitavit, quisquis est:
 non est misericors. sed quid ego hic asto infelix uvidus? 585
 quin abeo huc in Veneris fanum, ut edormiscam hanc
  crapulam,
 quam potavi praeter animi quam lubuit sententiam?
30 quasi vinis Graecis Neptunus nobis suffudit mare,
 itaque alvom prodi sperabat nobis salsis poculis.
 quid opust verbis? si invitare nos paullisper pergeret, 590
 ibidem obdormissemus: nunc vix vivos amisit domum.
 nunc lenonem quid agit intus visam, convivam meum.—
             Exit to temple.

ACT III

III i

Enter DAEMONES.

 DA miris modis di ludos faciunt hominibus,
 mirisque exemplis somnia in somnis danunt:
 ne dormientis quidem sinunt quiescere.   595
 velut ego hac nocte quae processit proxuma
5 mirum atque inscitum somniavi somnium.
 ad hirundininum nidum visa est simia
 ascensionem ut faceret admolirier,

    *   *   *   *   *

      neque eas eripere quibat inde. postibi   600
10   videtur ad me simia adgredirier,
      rogare scalas ut darem utendas sibi.
      ego ad hoc exemplum simiae respondeo:
            *   *   *   *   *

      natas ex Philomela ac Progne esse hirundines.
15   agŏ cúm illa, ne quid noceat meis popularibus.   605
      atque illa nimio iam fieri ferocior;
      videtur ultro mihi malum minitarier.
      in ius vocat med. íbi ego nescioquo modo
      iratus videor mediam arripere simiam;
20   concludo in vincla bestiam nequissumam.   610
      nunc quám ad rem dicam hoc attinere somnium,
      numquam hodie quivi ad coniecturam evadere.
           (Screams are heard.)
      sed quíd hĭc in Veneris fano meae viciniae
      clamoris oritur? animus miratur meus.

III ii
Enter TRACHALIO *in great excitement from the temple. He does not notice* DAEMONES, *but addresses the audience.*

  TR Pro Cyrenenses populares! vostram ego imploro fidem!
    agricolae, accolae propinqui qui estis his regionibus, 616
    ferte opem ínopiae atque exemplum pessumum pessum date!
    vindicate, ne inpiorum potior sit pollentia
  5 quam innocentum, qui se scelere fieri nolunt nobilis!
    statuite exemplum inpudenti, date pudori praemium, 620
    facite hic lege potius liceat quam vi victo vivere!
    currite huc in Veneris fanum! vostram iterum imploro fidem,
    qui prope hic adestis, quique auditis clamorem meum!
 10 ferte suppetias qui Veneri Véneriaeque antistitae
    more antiquo in custodelam suom commiserunt caput! 625
    praetorquete iniuriae priu' collum quám ăd vos pervenat!
  DA quíd ístuc est negoti? TRACHALIO *flings himself at his feet and grasps his knees.*
          TR per ego haec genua te optestor, senex,

quisquis es—DA quin tu ergo omitte genua et quid sit mi expedi
15 quod tumultues! TR teque oro et quaeso, si speras tibi
   hoc anno multum futurum sirpe et laserpicium,   630
   eamque eventuram exagogam Capuam salvam et sospitem,
   atque—ab lippitudine usque siccitas ut sit tibi—
   DA sanun' es? TR seu tibi confidis fore multam
   magydarim,
20 ut ne te pigeat dare operam mihi quod te orabo, senex!
          DAEMONES *seizes him by the hair and flourishes his stick over him.*
   DA at ego te per crura et talos tergumque optestor tuom, 635
   ut tibi ulmeam uberem esse speras virgidemiam
   et tibi eventuram hoc annō uberem messem mali,
   ut mi istuc dicas negoti quid sit quod tumultues.
          DAEMONES *releases* TRACHALIO, *who picks himself up.*
25 TR qui lubet maledicere? equidem tíbi bona exopto
   omnia.   639
   DA bene equidem tibi dico, qui te digna ut eveniant precor.
   TR opsecro, hoc praevortere ergo. DA quid negotist?
   TR múlieres
   duae innocentes intus hic sunt, tuí indigentes auxili,
   quibus advorsum ius legesque hic insignite iniuria
30 facta est fitque in Veneris fano; tum sacerdos Veneria
   indigne adflictatur. DA quis homo est tanta confidentia 645
   qui sacerdotem violare aúdeat? séd eae múlieres
   quae sunt? aut quid is iniqui? TR si das operam,
   eloquar.
   Veneris signum sunt amplexae. nunc homo audacissumus
35 eas deripere volt. eas ambas esse oportet liberas.
   DA quís ístic est qui deos tam parvi pendit? TR vis
   dicam tibi?   650
       (*All in one breath.*)
   fraudis, sceleris, parricidi, peiiuri plenissumus,
   legerupa, inpudens, inpurus, inverecundissumus:
   uno verbo apsolvam, lenost: quíd illum porro praedicem?
40 DA edepol infortunio hominem praedicas donabilem.
                        73

TR   qui sacerdoti scelestus faucis interpresserit.   655
DA   at malo hercle cum magno suo fecit.
                              (*Shouts*)   ite istinc foras,
Turbalio, Sparax!   ubi estis?   TR   i, opsecro, intro, subveni
illis.   DA   (*shouting*) iterum haud imperabo.
          (*Enter from the farm-house* TURBALIO *and* SPARAX)
                              séquimini hac.   TR   age nunciam,
45 iube oculos elidere, itidem ut sepiis faciunt coqui.
   DA   proripite hominem pedibus huc itidem quasi occisam
       suem.—   660
          Exeunt DAEMONES, TURBALIO, SPARAX *to the temple.   A din is heard
          within.*
TR   audio tumultum.   opinor, leno pugnis pectitur.
nimi' velim inprobissumo homini malas edentaverint.
séd ĕccas ipsae huc egrediuntur timidae e fano múlieres.

          Enter hastily, from the temple, PALAESTRA *and* AMPELISCA.   *They
          do not observe* TRACHALIO; *they sing.*

III iii
          PA *et* AM núnc id est quom ómnium cópiarum átque
              opum,
          aúxili, práesidi víduitas nós tenet.   665
          néc salus, néc viast quaé salutem ádferat,
          néc quam in partem íngredi
                        pérsequamur
          scímus: tanto ín metu
      5   núnc sumus ambae.
          tánta inportúnitas tántaque iniúria
          órta in nos ést modo hic íntus ab nóstro ero.   670
          quín scelestús sacerdótem anum práecipes
          réppulit, própulit pérquam indignís modis,
      10 nósque ab signo íntumo ví deripuít sua.
          sed núnc sese ut fĕrŭnt res fortúnaeque nóstrae,
          nos pár est moríri; neque ést melius mórte in   675
          malís rebus, míseris.
                          74

TR quid ést? quae illaec oratiost? cesso égo illas
    consolari?

15 heús, Palaestra! PA   quí vocat?

TR Ámpelisca! AM ópsecro, nám quis est quí vocat?

PA quís is est qui nóminat? TR sí respexis, scies.

The girls see TRACHALIO, *rush to him, and fling their arms round him.*

PA ó salutís meae spés. TR   tace ac bóno animo es.

(He shakes off their embrace and strikes an attitude)

    mé vide! PA sí modo id líceat, vis ne ópprimat;   680

20 quaé vis vim mi ádferam ipsa ádigit. TR ah, désine!
                    nímis inepta es.

PA desiste dictis nunciam miseram me consolari.

AM nisi quid re praesidi apparas, Trachalio, acta haec res est.

PA certumst moriri quam hunc pati saevire lenonem in me.

sed muliebri animo sum tamen: miserae quom venit in
    mentem   685

25 mihi mortis, metu' membra occupāt. edepol diem hunc
   acerbum!

TR bonum animum habete. PA nam, opsecro, unde iste
    animus mi invenitur?

TR ne, inquam, timete; adsidite hic in ara. AM quíd
    ístaec ara

prodesse nobis plus potest quam signum in fano hic intus

Veneris, quod amplexae modo, unde abreptae per vim
    míserae?   690

30 TR sedete hic modo; égo hínc vos tamen tutabor. aram
    habete hanc

vobis pro castris; moenia haec; hinc ego vos defensabo:

praesidio Veneris málitiae lenonis contra incedam.

PA *et* AM tibi auscultamus. *(They kneel at the altar)*

                et, Venus almă, ambae te opsecramus,

aram amplexantes hanc tuam, lacrumantes, genibus nixae, 695

35 in custodelam nos tuam ut recípias et tutere.

PA illos scelestos, qui tuom fecerunt fanum parvi,

                        75

fac ut ulciscare, nosque ut hanc tua pace aram opsidere
patiare.   AM   lautae ambae sumus opera Neptuni noctu,
ne indignum id habeas neve idcirco nobis vitio vortas,   700
40   si quippiamst minu' quod bene esse lautum tu arbitrare.
   TR   Venus, aequom has petere intellego: decet aps te id
       impetrari;
   ignoscere his te convenit: metus has id ut fáciant súbigit.
   te ex concha natum esse autumant: cávĕ tu harum conchas
       spernas.
   sed optume eccum exit senex patronus mihique et vobis.   705

III iv

Enter DAEMONES *from the temple; then* LABRAX, *violently propelled
by* TURBALIO *and* SPARAX.

   DA   exi e fano, natum quantumst hominum sacrilegissume!
   vos in aram abite sessum.   sed ubi sunt?   TR   huc respice.
   DAEMONES *looks round, and sees the girls at the altar.*
   DA   optume: istuc volueramus.   iúbĕ modo accedat prope.
   LABRAX *rashly accepts the invitation and moves to lay hands on
   the girls.*
   DA   tun legérupionem hic nobis cum dis facere postulas?
   (*To one of the* lorarii) pugnum in os impinge.
                                    (*Lorarius punches* LABRAX)
5   LA   iniqua haec patior cum pretio tuo.   710
   DA   at etiam minitatur audax?   LA   ius meum ereptum est
       mihi;
   meas mihi ancillas invito me eripīs.   TR   habe iudicem
   de senatu Cyrenensi quemvis opulentum virum,
   si tuas esse oportet nive eas esse oportet liberas,
10 neu te in carcerem compingī aequom est aetatemque ibi 715
   te usque habitare, donec totum carcerem contriveris!
   LA   non hodie isti rei auspicavi, ut cum furcifero fabuler.
   (*To* DAEMONES) tḗ ego appello.   DA   cum istoc primum qui
       te novit disputa.
   LA   (*again to* DAEMONES) tecum ago.   TR   atqui mecum
       agendumst.   suntne illae ancillae tuae?

76

15 LA sunt. TR agedum ergo, tange utramvis—digitulo
  minimo modo.   720
  LA quid si attigero? TR extemplo hercle ego te follem
  pugilatorium
  faciam, et pendentem incursabo pugnis, peiiurissume.
  LA mihi non liceat meas ancillas Veneris de ara abducere?
  DA non licēt: ita est lex apud nos. . . . LA mihi cum
  vostris legibus
20 nihil est commercí. equidem istas iam ambas educam foras.
  tu senex, si istas amas, huc arido argentost opus;   726
  si autem Veneri complacuerunt, habeat, si argentum dabit.
  DA di tibi argentum? nunc adeo, méam ŭt scias sententiam,
  occipito modo illis adferre vim ioculo pauxillulum,
25 ita ego te hinc ornatum amittam, tu ipsus te ut non noveris. 730
  (*To the lorarii*) vos adeo, ubi ego innuero vobis, ni ei caput
  exoculassitis,
  quasi murteta iunci, item ego vos virgis circumvinciam.
  The lorarii acknowledge their instructions with a grin.
  LA ví agis. TR etiam vim proportas, flagiti flagrantia?
  LA tun, trifurcifer, mihi audes inclementer dicere?
30 TR fateor, ego trifurcifer sum, tu 's homo adprime probus:
  numqui minus hasce esse oportet liberas? LA quid, liberas?
  TR atque eras tuas quidem hercle, atque ex germana
  Graecia;   737
  nam altera haec est nata Athenis ingenuis parentibus.
  DA quid ego ex te audio? TR hanc Athenis esse natam
  liberam.
35 DA mea popularis, opsecro, haec est? TR non tu
  Cyrenensis es?   740
  DA immo Athenis natus altusque educatusque Atticis.
  TR opsecro, defende civis tuas, senex. DA (*staring at*
  PALAESTRA) o filia
  mea, quom hanc video, mearum me apsens miseriarum
  commones;
  trima quae periit mi, iam tanta esset, si vivit, scio.

77

40 LA argentum ego pro istisce ambabus quoiiae erant domino
    dedi;   745
    quid mea refert, Athenis natae haec an Thebis sient,
    dum mihi recte servitutem serviant? TR itane, inpudens?
    tune hic, feles virginalis, liberos parentibus
    sublectos habebis atque indigno quaestu conteres?
45 nám huïc alterae quae patria sit, profecto nescio—   750
    nisi scio probiorem hanc esse quam té, ínpuratissume.
    LA túaĕ ïstae sunt? TR contende ergo, uter sit tergo
    verior;
    ni offerrumentas habebis pluris in tergo tuo
    quam ulla navis longa clavos, tum ego ero mendacissumus:
50 postea aspicito meum, quando ego tuom inspectavero: 755
    nĭ erit tam sincerum, ut quivis dicat ampullarius
    optumum esse operi faciundo corium et sincerissumum,—
    quid caussaest quin virgis te usque ad saturitatem sauciem?
    quíd ïllas spectas? quas si attigeris, oculos eripiam tibi.
55 LA atqui, quia votas utramque iam mecum abducam
    semul. . . .   *He moves towards the farm-house.* 760
    DA quid facies? LA Volcanum adducam; is Venerist
    advorsarius.
    TR qúo ïllic ït? LA heus, ecquis hic est? heus! DA si
    attigeris ostium,
    iam hercle tibi mergis in ore fiet messis pugneis.
                        The lorarii threaten LABRAX.
    LORARIUS nullum habemus ignem; ficis victitamus aridis.
60 TR ego dabo ignem, siquidem in capite tụo conflandi
    copiast.   765
    LA ibo hercle aliquo quaeritatum lignum. DA quid,
    quom inveneris?
    LA ignem magnum hic faciam. DA quin inhumanum
    exuras tibi?
    LA immo hasce ambas hic in ara ut vivas comburam, id volo.
    TR iam hercle ego te continuo barba arripiam, in ignem
    cóniciam,

65 teque ambustulatum obiciam magnis avibus pabulum.   770
  DA (*to himself*) quom coniecturam egomet mecum facio,
    haec illast simia,
  quaé hăs hirundines ex nido volt eripere ingratieis,
  quod ego in somnis somniavi.   TR scin quid tecum oro,
    senex?
  út íllas serves, vim defendas, dúm ego erum adducam meum.
70 DA quaere erum atque adduce.   TR at hic ne. . . .
                 DA maxumo malo suo,   775
  si attigerit sive occeptassit.   TR cura.   DA curatumst; abi.
  TR hunc quoque adserva ipsum ne quo abitat; nam
    promissimus
  carnufici aut talentum magnŭm aút hunc hodie sistere.
  DA ábĭ modō; ego dum hoc curabo recte.   TR iam ego
    revenero.—
                        Exit TRACHALIO *towards shore.*

III v

  DA utrum tu leno, cum malo lubentius   780
  quiescis, an sic sine malo, si copiast?
  LA ego quae tu loquere flocci non facio, senex.
  meas quidem té invito et Venere et summo Iove
5 de ara capillo iam deripiam.   DA tangedum.
  LA tangam hercle verō.   DA ágedum ergo, accede huc
    modo.   785
    LABRAX *moves towards the girls: the lorarii close in towards him.*
  LA iubĕdum recedere istos ambo illuc modo.
  DA immo ad te accedent.   *The lorarii close in further.*
    LA (*hesitating*) non hercle equidem censeo.
  DA quid ages si accedent propius?
                    The lorarii come closer still.
    LA ego recessero.   (*He retreats*)
10 verum, senex, si te umquam in urbe offendero,
  numquam hercle quisquam me lenonem dixerit,   790
  si te non ludos pessumos dimissero.

DA facito istuc quod minitare; sed nunc interim,
si illas attigeris, dabitur tibi magnum malum.

15 LA quam magnum vero? DA quantum lenoni sat est.
  LA minacias ego flocci non faciam tuas: 795
  equidem has te invito iam ambas rapiam. DA tangedum.
  LA tangam hercle vero. DA tanges? at scin quo modo?
  i dum, Turbalio, curriculo, adferto domo
20 duas clavas. LA clavas? DA (*ignoring* LABRAX *and speaking
  to* TURBALIO) sed probas. propera cito.
                    (*Exit* TURBALIO *to farm-house*)
  (*To* LABRAX) ego te hodie faxo recte acceptum ut 800
  dignus es.
  LA eheu! scelestus galeam in nave perdidi;
  nunc mi opportuna hic esset, salva si foret.
  licet saltem istas mi appellare? DA non licet.
      (*Re-enter* TURBALIO *with two cudgels*)
25 ehem! optume edepol eccum clavator advenit. 804-5
  LA illud quidem edepol tinnimentum est auribus.
  DA age accipe illinc alteram clavam, Sparax.
  age, alter istinc, alter hinc adsistite.
  adsistite ambo. (*The lorarii flank* LABRAX) sic. audite
  nunciam:
30 si hercle illic illas hodie digito tétigerit 810
  invitas, nei istunc istis invitassitis
  usque adeo donec qua domum abeat nesciat,
  periistis ambo. si appellabit quempiam,
  vos respondetote istinc istarum vicem;
35 sin ipse abitere hinc volet, quantum potest 815
  extemplo amplectitote crura fustibus.
  LA etiam me abire hinc non sinent? DA dixi satis.
  et ubi ille cúm ero servos huc advenerit,
  qui erum accersivit, itote extemplo domum.
40 curate haec, sultis, magna diligentia.— 820
                    Exit to farm-house.
  LA heu hércle! né ístic fana mutantur cito:

iam hoc Herculēi est, Veneris fanum quod fuit;
ita duo destituit signa hic cum clavis senex.
non hercle quó hǐnc nunc gentium aufugiam scio;
45   ita nunc mi utrumque saevit, et terra et mare.   825
Palaestra! LO quid vis? LA apage, controvorsia est;
haec quidem Palaestra quae respondit non mea est.
heus, Ampelisca! LO cávě, sis, infortunio.
LA (*aside*) ut potis est, ignavi homines satis recte monent.
50   (*Aloud*) sed vobis dico—heús vos! num molestiaest   830
me adire ad illas propius? LO nil, nobis quidem.
LA numquid molestum mihi erit? LO nil, si caveris.
LA quid est quod caveam? LO (*making a feint with his
cudgel*) ém! a crasso infortunio.
LA quaeso hercle abire ut liceat. LO abeas, si velis.
55   LA bene hercle factum. habeo vobis gratiam   835
(*He starts to go, and the lorarii raise their cudgels*)
non cedam potius. illic astate ilico.
(*He resumes his position, and the lorarii resume theirs*)
(*aside*) edepol proveni nequiter multis modis.
(*He squats down*)
(*aloud*) certumst hasce hodie usque opsidione vincere.

III vi

Enter PLESIDIPPUS *and* TRACHALIO *from the shore.   They pause at
the side of the stage.*

PL meamne ille amicam leno vi violentia
de ara deripere Veneris voluit? TR admodum.   840
PL quin occidisti extemplo? TR (*after a slight hesitation*)
gladius non erat.
PL caperes aut fustem aut lapidem. TR (*with a virtuous
air*) quid? ego quasi canem
5   hominem insectarer lapidibus? nequissumum.
LABRAX *sees them, and uneasily gets to his feet.*
LA (*aside*) nunc pol ego perii: Plesidippus eccum adest.
convorret iam hic me totum cum pulvisculo.   845
PL etiamne in ara tunc sedebant mulieres,

quom ad me profectu's ire? TR ibídem nunc sedent.

10 PL quis íllas nunc illic servat? TR nescioquis senex,
vicinus Veneris; is dedit operam optumam;
is nunc cum servis servat: ego mandaveram.   850
PL duc me ad lenonem recta. (*He strides with* TRACHALIO
on to mid-stage, and glares around) úbi íllic est homo?
LA salve. PL salutem nil morōr. opta ocius:

15 rapi te optorto collo mavis, an trahi?
utrumvis opta, dum licet. LA neutrum volo.
PL abí sane ad litus curriculo, Trachalio;   855
iube íllos in urbem ire obviam ad portum mihi,
quos mecum duxi, hunc qui ad carnúficem traderent.

20 post huc redito atque agitato hic custodiam.
ego hunc scelestum in iús rapiam, exigam exulem.
(*Exit* TRACHALIO; PLESIDIPPUS *lays hands on* LABRAX)
age, ambula in ius. LA quid ego deliqui? PL rogas?
quin arrabonem a me accepisti ob múlierem   861
et eam hinc abduxti? LA non avexi. PL qur negas?

25 LA quia pol provexi: avehere non quivi miser.
equidem tibí me dixeram praesto fore
apŭd Veneris fanum. numquid muto? sumne ibi?   865
PL in iure caussam dicito; hic verbum sat est.
sequere. *With the help of the lorarii,* PLESIDIPPUS *begins to hustle*
LABRAX *off.* CHARMIDES *strolls out of the temple.*
LA opsecro te, subveni, mi Charmides.

30 rapiōr optorto collo. CH (*ostentatiously uninterested*) quis
me nominat?
LA viden me ut rapior? CH video, atque inspecto
lubens.
LA non subvenire mi audes? CH quis homo te rapit?
LA adulescens Plesidippus. CH ut nanctu's habe.   871
bono animo meliust te in nervom conrepere:

35 tibi optigit quod plurumi exoptant sibi.
LA quid id est? CH ut id quod quaerant inveniant sibi.
LA sequere, opsecro, me. CH pariter suades qualis es.

82

tu in nervom rapere; eo me opsecras ut te sequar?   876
PL etiam retentas? LA perii! CH verum sit velim.
40 PL tu, mea Palaestra, et Ampelisca, ibidem ilico
manete dŭm ego huc redeo. LO équidem suadeo
ut ad nos abeant potius, dum recipis. PL placet;   880
bene facitis. LA fures mi estis. LO quid, fures? rape.
LA oro, opsecro, Palaestra. PL sequere, carnufex.
45 LA hospes— CH non sum hospes: repudio hospitium
        tuom.
LA sicine me spernis? CH sic ago. sat sémĕl bibo.
LA di te infelicent!— *He is haled off towards the town.*
        CH isti capiti dicito. (*Turns to audience*)   885
credo alium in aliam beluam hominem vortier:
illĭc in columbum, credo, leno vortitur;
50 nam collus in colŭmbári haud multo post erit.
in nervom ille hodie nidamenta congeret.
verum tamen ibo, ei advocatus ut siem,   890
si qui mea opera citius—addici potest.—
Exeunt, CHARMIDES *to the town, lorarii with girls to the farm-house.*

ACT IV

IV i

Enter DAEMONES *from the cottage; he soliloquises.*

Bene factum et volup est mḗ hodie his mulierculis
tetulisse auxilium. iam clientas repperi,
atque ambas forma scitula atque aetatula.
séd ŭxor scelesta me omnibus servat modis,   895
5 ne quid significem quippiam mulierculis.
        (*He shrugs his shoulders, and looks around*)
sed Gripus servos noster quid rerum gerat

83

miror, de nocte qui abiit piscatum ad mare.
pol magi' sapisset si dormivisset domi;
nam nunc et operam ludos facit et retiam,   900
10   ut tempestas est nunc atque ut noctu fuit:
in digitis hodie percoquam quod ceperit;
ita fluctuare video vehementer mare.   (*Voice within.*)
séd ăd prandium uxor me vocat.   redeo domum.
iam meas opplebit auris vaniloquentia.—   905

IV ii

Enter GRIPUS *from the shore. He carries in a fishing-net a heavy*
trunk; from the net a long rope trails. He sings.

Neptúno has agó gratiás meo patróno,
qui sálsis locís incolít pisculéntis,
quom me éx suis locís pulchre ornátum expedívit,
templís redducém, plurumá praeda onústum,
5   salúte horiaé, quae in marí fluctuóso   910
piscátu novó me uberí compotívit.
miróque modo atque incrédibili hic piscátu' mihi lepide évenit;
neque píscium ullam unciam hodié pondo cepí, nisi hŏc quod
fero hĭc ín rete.
nam ut dé nocte múlta inpigréque exsurréxi,   915
10   lucrúm praeposívi sopóri et quiéti,
tempéstate saéva experíri expetívi
paupértatem erí qui et meám servitútem
tolerárem—opera háu fuĭ parcu' mea.
nimis hómŏ nihilist quist píger, nimi'que id genus ódi ego
male: 920
vigiláre decēt hominém qui volt sua témperí conficere ófficia;
non énim íllum expectare íd oportet dum eru' se ád suom
suscitet ófficium.
                    nám qui dormiúnt lubenter,
                    síne lucro et cum málŏ quiescunt.
                              năm ego nunc mihi,
                              qui ínpiger fui,

répperi ut piger,
sí velim, siem.   925
20   hóc ego in mari,
quidquíd inĕst, repperi.
quidquíd inĕst, grave quidemst.

(Sets down the trunk)

aurum híc ego inesse reór, nec mihi
conscíus est ullus homó.   nunc haec
occásiọ tibi, Gripe, óptigit ut
libéret extemplo praétor te.
nunc síc faciam, sic cónsilium est:
ad erúm veniam docte átque astu;
25   pauxíllatim pollícitabor
pro cápite argentum, ut sím liber.
iam ubi líber erō, igitúr demum   930
instrúam agrum ătque aedis, máncupia;
navíbu' magnis mercáturam
faciam, ápŭd reges rex pérhibebor;
post ánimi caussa míhi navem
faciam átque imitabor Strátonicum:
30   oppída circumvectabor, ubi
nobílitas mea erit clára.
ŏppidúm magnum commúnibo:
ei ego úrbi Gripo indám nomen,
monuméntum meạe famae ét factis;   935
ibi régnum magnum instítuam.
35   magnás res hic agito ín mentem
instrúere.   hunc nunc vidlúm condam.

(He picks up the trunk, still in the net.)

sed hĭc réx cŭm aceto pránsurust
et sále sine bónŏ pulménto.

85

IV iii

He crosses the stage towards the farm-house, carrying the net and trunk, and trailing the rope behind him. Enter TRACHALIO *from the shore; he seizes the rope and pulls* GRIPUS *back.*

TR Heus, mánĕ. GR quid máneam?

                         TR *(coiling the rope)* dum hánc tibi
quam tráhi' rudentem complico.
GR mitté modo. TR at pól ego te adiuvo;
nam bónĭs quod bene fit haud perit.
GR turbída tempestas hérĭ fuit;   940
nil hábeo, aduléscens, piscium;
ne tú mihi esse postules.
5   non vídĕs referre me uvidum
retém sine squamoso pecu?
TR non édepol piscis expeto
quam tui̯ sermonis sum indigens.
GR enícăs iam me odio, quisquis es. *Turns to go.*
TR non sínam ego abire hinc te. mane.
                              Jerks him back.
GR cávĕ, sis, malo. quid tú, malum,
nám me retrahis? TR aúdi.   945
GR nón audio. TR *(still holding the rope tight)* at pol
qui áudies
póst. GR *(resignedly)* quin loquere quídvis.
TRACHALIO *beckons him mysteriously.*
10   TR ého modo est operaé pretium
quód tibi egō narráre volo.
               GRIPUS, *in spite of himself, is impressed.*
GR éloqueren quid id ést? TR vidĕ num
quíspiam consequitúr prope nos.
                         Both look round.
GR écquid est quód mea réferat? TR scílicet.
séd boni cónsilĭ écquid in té mihi est?   950
GR quíd negoti ést modō díce. TR dicám, tace,
15   sí fidem modŏ dás mihi te
nón fore infidum. GRIPUS *is now very curious.*

86

GR   dó fidem tibi; fídus ero,
      quísquis ēs.   TR   audi.   955
furtum égo vidi qui fáciebat;
norám dominum, id quoi fíebat;
post ád furem egomet dévenio,

20   ferŏque   éi condicionem hóc pacto :
"ego ĩstúc furtum scio quoí factum est;
nunc sí mihi vis dare dímidium,
indícium domino nón faciam."
is míhi nihil etiam réspondit.

25   quid ĩnde aéquom est dárĭ mihi? dímidium   960
volo ŭt dícas.   GR   (*with enthusiasm*) immo hercle
      étiam plus;
nam nísi dat, domino dícundum
censéo.   TR   tuo consilió faciam.
nunc ádvorte animum; námque hoc omn'

30   attínet ad te.   GR   quid fáctumst ?

TR   vidulum istum quoius est novi ego hominem iam
    pridem.   GR   quid est ?

TR   et quo pacto periit.   GR   (*setting down the trunk and
firmly placing a foot on it*) at ego quo pacto inventust scio,
et qui invenit hominem novi, et dominus qui nunc est scio.
nihilo pol pluris tua hoc quam quanti illud refert mea.   966

35 égo ĩllum novi quoiius nunc est, tu illum quoius antehac fuit.
hunc homō feret a me nemo, ne tu te speres potis.

TR   non ferat, si dominus veniat ?   GR   dominus huic, ne
    frustra sis,
nisi ego nemo natust, hunc qui cepi in venatu meo.   970

TR   itane vero?   GR   ecquem esse dices in mari piscem
    meum ?

40 quos quom capio, siquidem cepi, mei sunt; habeo pro meis;
nec manu adseruntur, néque ĩllinc partem quisquam postulat :
in foro palam omnis vendo pro meis venalibus.
mare quidem commune certost omnibús.   TR   adsentio:

    qui minus hunc communem, quaeso, mǐhi ĕsse oportet
      vidulum?   976
45 in mari inventust communi. GR esne inpudenter inpudens?
    nam si istuc ius sit quod memoras, piscatores périerint.
    quippe quom extemplo in macellum pisces prolati sient,
    nemo emat, suam quisque partem piscium poscant sibi; 980
    dicant in mari communi captos. TR quid ais, inpudens?
50 ausu's etiam comparare vidulum cum piscibus?
    eadem tandem res videtur? GR in manu non est mea.
    ubi demisi retem atque hamum, quidquid haesit extraho.
    meum quod rete atque hami nancti sunt, meum potis-
      sumumst.   985
    TR immo hercle haud est, siquidem quod vas excepisti.
    GR phǐlosophe!
55 TR sed tu enumquam piscatorem vidisti, venefice,
    vidulum piscem cepisse aut protulisse ullum in forum?
    non enǐm tu hic quidem occupabis omnis quaestus quos
      voles:
    et vitorem et piscatorem te esse, inpure, postulas.   990
    vel te mihi monstrare oportet piscis qui sit vidulus,
60 vel quod in mari non natum est neque habet squamas ne
      feras.
    GR quid? tu numquam audisti esse antehac vidulum
      piscem? TR scelus,
    nullus est. GR immo est profecto; ego qui sum piscator scio;
    verum rare capitur, nullus minu' saepe ad terram venit. 995
    TR nil agis; dare verba speras mihi te posse, furcifer.
65 quo colore est? GR hoc colore capiuntur pauxilluli;
    sunt alii puniceo corio, magni autem; atque atri. TR scio.
    tu hercle, opino, in vidlum piscem te convortes, nisi caves:
    fiet tibi puniceum corium, postea atrum denuo.   1000
    GR quod scelús hodie hic inveni! TR verba facimus; it
      dies.
70 vide, sis, quoiius arbitratu nos vis facere. GR viduli

arbitratu. TR itane? GR ita enim vero. TR stultus es.
GR salve, Thales.
TR   tu istunc hodie non feres, nisi das sequestrum aut
arbitrum,
quoiius haec res arbitr atu fiat. GR quaeso, sanun' es ?
TR elleborosus sum. GR ego cerritus; hunc non amittam
tamen.   1006
75 TR verbum etiam adde unum; iam in cérebro colaphos
apstrudam tuo (adopts a pugnacious posture);
iam ego te hic, itidem quási peniculus novos exurgeri solet,
ni hunc amittis, exurgebo quidquid umoris tibist.
GR (similarly pugnacious) tange: adfligam ad terram te
itidem ut piscem soleo polypum.   1010
vis pugnare? TR (dropping his fists) quid opust? quin tu
potius praedam divide.
80 GR hinc tu niseĭ malum fruniscei nil potes; ne postules.
(Picks up the trunk)
abeo ego hinc. He turns and starts to go. TRACHALIO, by a
jerk of the rope, swings him round again.
TR   at ego hinc offlectam navem, ne quo abeas. mane.
sei tu proreta isti navi es, ego gubernatōr ero.
GR mitte rudentem, sceleste. Tug-of-war.
TR   mittam: omitte vidulum.   1015
Renewed tug-of-war. At last by mutual consent both cease their
efforts and stand upright again.
GR numquam hercle hinc hodie ramenta fies fortunatior.
85 TR non probare pernegando mihi potes, nisi pars datur
aut ad arbitrum redeitur aut sequestro ponitur.
GR quemne ego excepi in marī? TR at ego inspectavi e
litore.
GR mea opera, labore, et rete et horia? TR numqui
minus,   1020
si nunc veniat dominus quoiiust, ego, qui inspectavi procul
90 te hunc habere, fur sum quam tu? GR nihilo. TR mánĕ,
mastigia:

89

quo argumento socius non sum et fur sum? facdum ex te
sciam.
GR nescio, neque ego istas vostras leges urbanas scio,
nisi quia hunc meum esse dicō. TR ét ego item esse aio
meum. *Pause.* 1025
GR mánĕ, iam repperi quo pacto nec fur nec socius sies.
95 TR quo pacto? GR sine me hinc abire; tú abi tacitus
tuam viam;
nec tu me quoiquam indicassis, neque ego tibi quicquam
dabo;
tu taceto, ego mussitabo: hoc optumum atque aequis-
sumum est.
TR ecquid condicionis audes ferre? GR iam dudum
fero: 1030
ut abeas, rudentem amittas, mihi molestus non sies.
100 TR mánĕ, dum refero condicionem. GR te, opsecro
hercle, aufer modo.
TR ecquem in heis locis novisti? GR oportet vicinos
meos.
TR ubi tu hic habitas? GR *(waving his arm vaguely round)*
porro illíc longe usque in campis ultumis.
TR vin qui in hac villa habitat, eiius arbitratu fĭeri? 1035
GR paullisper remitte restem, dum concedo et consulo.
105 TR fiat. *He slacks off the rope.* GRIPUS *turns away from him,
and speaks aside.* GR eugae! salva res est: praeda haec
perpetua est mea.
ad meum erum arbitrum vocat me hic intra praesepis meas:
numquam hercle hodie abiudicabit ab suo triobolum.
ne iste hau scit quam condicionem tétulerit. eo ad arbitrum.
Turns back.
TR quid igitur? GR quamquam istuc esse ius meum
certo scio, 1041
110 fiat istuc potius quam nunc pugnem tecum. TR nunc
places.

90

GR *(sanctimoniously)* quamquam ad ignotum arbitrum me
     adpellis, si adhibebit fidem,
etsi ignotust, notus; si non, notus ignotissumus.

*The pair are about to approach the farm-house, when the door
suddenly opens. Enter hurriedly* PALAESTRA *and* AMPELISCA,
amid a hail of domestic missiles; DAEMONES; *and* TURBALIO *and*
SPARAX.

IV iv

DA serio edepol, quamquam vobis volo quae voltis, mulieres,
    metuo propter vos ne uxór mea med extrudat aedibus,   1046
    quae me paelices adduxe dicet ante oculos suos.
    vos confugite in aram potius quám ego. PA *et* AM
    (kneeling at the altar) miserae périimus.
5 DA ego vos salvas sistam, ne timete. *(To* TURBALIO *and* SPARAX*)*
    sed quid vos foras   1049
    prosequimini? quoniam ego adsum, faciet nemo iniuriam.
    ite, inquam, domum ambo nunciam ex praesidio praesides.

Exeunt TURBALIO *and* SPARAX.   GRIPUS *and* TRACHALIO
approach DAEMONES.

GR o ere, salve. DA salve, Gripe. quid fit? TR
    (surprised) tuŏ'ne hic servos est?
GR hau pudĕt. TR níl agŏ tecum. GR ergo ábi hĭnc,
    sis. TR quaeso, responde, senex:
10 tuos hic servost? DA meus est. TR em, istuc optume,
    quando tuost.
   iterum te saluto. DA et ego te. tune es qui hau multo
    prius   1055
   abiisti hinc erum accersitum? TR ego is sum. DA quid
    nunc vis tibi?
   TR nempe hic tuos est? DA meus est. TR istuc
    optume, quando tuost.
   DA quid negotist? TR vir scelestus íllĭc est. DA quid
    fecit tibi
15 vir scelestus? TR homini ego isti talos subfringi volo.

DA quíd ĕst? qua de re litigatis nunc inter vos? TR
eloquar.   1060
GR immo ego eloquār. TR ego, opinor, rem facesso.
GR si quidem
sis pudicus, hinc facessas. DA Gripe, animum advorte ac
tace.
GR utin ĭstic priu' dicat? DA audi. (*To* TRACHALIO)
loquere tu. GR alienon prius
20 quam tuo dabis orationĕm? TR (*in a superior tone*) ut
nequitur comprimi!
ita ut occepi dicere, illum quem dudum e fano foras   1065
lenonem extrusisti, hic eiius vidulum eccillum tenet.
GR (*vainly trying to screen the trunk from view*) non habeo.
TR negas quod oculis video? GR at ne videas velim.
habeo, non habeo: quid tu me curas quid rerum geram?
25 TR (*impressively*) quo modō habeas, id refert, iurene anne
iniuria.
GR (*to* DAEMONES) ni istum cepi, nulla caussa est quin
me condones cruci.   1070
(*To* TRACHALIO) si in marī rétia prehendi, qui tu͜om potiust
quam meum?
TR (*to* DAEMONES) verba dāt. hoc módŏ res gesta est ut ego
dico. . . . GR quid tu ais?
TR quod primarius vir dicat. (*To* DAEMONES) comprime
hunc, sis, si tuost.
30 GR quid? tu idem mihí vis fieri quod erus consuevit tibi?
si ille te comprimere solitust, hic noster nos non solet. 1075
DA (*to* TRACHALIO) verbo illo modo ille vicit. quid nunc tu
vis? dic mihi.
TR equidem egō neque partem posco míhi ĭstinc de istoc
vidulo,
neque meum esse hodie umquam dixi; séd ĭsti inest cistellula
35 huiius mulieris, quam dudum dixi fu͜isse liberam.
DA nemp' tu hanc dicis quam esse aiebas dudum popularem
meam?   1080

92

TR admodum; et ea quae olim parva gestavit crepundia
istic ín ïsta cistula insunt, quae isti inest in vidulo.
hoc neque isti usust et illi miserae suppetias feret,
40 si id dederit qui suǫs parentes quaerat. DA faciam ut det.
tace.
GR nihil hercle ego sum isti daturus.   TR nil peto nisi
cistulam   1085
et crepundiá. GR quid si ea sunt aureá? TR quid
ïstúc tua?
aurum auro expendetur, argentum argento exaequabimus.
GR fac, sis, aurum ut videam; post ego faciam ut videas
cistulam.
45 DA (*To* GRIPUS) cávĕ malo ac tácĕ tu. (*To* TRACHALIO) tu
perge ut occepisti dicere.
TR unum te opsecro, ut ted huiius commiserescat mulieris—
si quidem hic lenonis eius est vidulus quem suspicor;   1091
hic nisï de opinione certum nil dico tibi.
GR vídĕn? scelestus aucupatur. TR sine me ut occepi
loqui.
50 si scelesti illius est hic quoiius dico vidulus,
haec poterunt novisse: ostendere his iube. GR ain?
ostendere?   1095
DA haud iniquom dicit, Gripe, ut ostendatur vidulus.
GR immo hercle insignite inique. DA quidum?
GR quia, si ostendero,
continuo hunc novisse dicent scilicet.   DAEMONES *nods.*
TR scelerum caput,
55 ut tute ēs, item omnis censes esse, peiiuri caput?
GR omnia istaéc ego facile patior, dum hic hinc a me
sentiat.   1100
TR atqui nunc aps te stat, verum hinc cibit testimonium.
DA Gripe, advorte animum. (*To* TRACHALIO) tu paucis
expedi quid postulas.
TR dixi equidem; sed si parum intellexti, dicam denuo.
60 hasce ambas, ut dudum dixi, ita esse oportet liberas:

93

haec Athenis parva fuit virgo surrupta. GR dic mihi, 1105
quid id ad vidlum pertinet, servae sint istae an liberae?
TR omnia iterum vis memorari, scelus, ut defiat dies.
DA apstine maledictis, et mihi quod rogavi dilue.
65 TR cistellam isti inesse oportet caudeam ín ísto vidulo,
ubi sunt signa qui parentes noscere haec possit suos,   1110
quibu'cum periit parva Athenis, sicuti dixi prius.
GR Iuppiter te dique perdant! quid ais, vir venefice?
quíd, ístae mutae sunt, quae pro se fabulari non queant?
70 TR eo tacent, quiá tacitast bona mulier semper quam
loquens.
GR tum pol tu pro portione nec vir nec mulier mihi es. 1115
TR quidum? GR quia enim neque loquens es neque
tacens umquam bonus.
TR (to DAEMONES) quaeso, enumquam hodie licebit mihi
loqui? DA (to GRIPUS) si praeterhac
unum verbum faxis hodie, egó tibi comminuam caput.
75 TR ut id occepi diceré, senĕx, éam te quaeso cistulam
ut iubeas hunc reddere illis; ob eam si quid postulat   1120
sibi mercedis, dabitur: aliud quidquid est habeat sibi.
GR nunc demum istuc dicis, quoniam ius meum esse
intelligis:
dudum dimidiam petebas partem. TR immo etiam nunc
peto.
80 GR vidi petere miluom, etiam quom nil auferret tamen.
DA (shaking his stick at GRIPUS) non ego te comprimere
possum sine malo? GR si istic tacet,   1125
ego tacebo; si iste loquitur, sine me pro parti loqui.
DA cedo modō mihi istum vidlum, Gripe. GR concredam tibi:
ac, si istorum nil sit, ut mihi reddas. DA reddetur. GR
tene.

GRIPUS *lays the trunk at* DAEMONES'S *feet.*

85 DA audi nunciam, Palaestra, atque Ampelisca, hoc quod
loquor.

94

estne hic vidlus ubi cistellam tuam inĕsse aiebas ? PA is est.
GR perii hercle ego misér. uti priusquam plane aspexit,
  ilico   1131
eum ĕsse dixit! PA faciam ego hanc rem ex ardua planam
  tibi.
cistellam isti inesse oportet caudeam ín ĭstoc vidulo.
90 ibi ego dicam quidquid inerit nominatim : tu mihi
  nullum ostenderis; si falsa dicam, frustra dixero,   1135
  vos tamen istaec quidquid isti inérĭt, vobis habebitis.
  sĭ erunt vera, tum opsecro te ut mea mi reddantur.
  DA placet.
ius merum oras meo quidem animō. GR at meo hercle
  iniuriam.
95 quid si ista aut superstitiosa aut hariolast, atque omnia
  quidquid insit vera dicet ? idne habebit hariola ?   1140
DA non feret nisi vera dicet: nequiquam hariolabitur.
solve vidulum ergo, ut quid sit verum quam primum sciam.
    As GRIPUS *unties the rope round the trunk,* TRACHALIO *jeers.*
TR hoc habet. GR (*to* DAEMONES) solutum est. DA aperi.
    GRIPUS *obeys.* PA video cistellam. DA (*holding it up*)
  haecinest ?
100 PA istaec est. (DAEMONES *lets her handle it, but does not let go*)
  o meï parentes, hic vos conclusos gero;
  huc opesque spesque vostrum cognoscendum condidi.   1145
  GR tum tibi hercle dĕos iratos esse oportet, quisquis es,
  quae parentes tãm in angustum tuọs locum compegeris.
  DA Gripe, accede huc; tua res agitur. (GRIPUS *comes and*
    stands at DAEMONES'S *elbow, to look at the casket. Then*
    DAEMONES *motions to* PALAESTRA *to stand back*) tu, puella,
  istinc procul
105 dicito quid insit et qua facie: memorato omnia.
  si hercle tantillum peccassis, quod posterius postules   1150
  te ad verum convorti, nugas, mulier, magnas egeris.
  GR ius bonum oras. TR edepol hau ted orat, nam tu
  iniuriu's.

DA loquere nunciam, puella. (*To* GRIPUS, *who is defying*
   TRACHALIO.) Gripe, animum advorte ac tace.
110 PA sunt crepundia. DA ecca video. GR perii in primo
   proelio. (*Seizes* DAEMONES'S *hand.*)
mánĕ, ne ostenderis. DA (*ignoring* GRIPUS, *and speaking to*
   PALAESTRA) qua facie sunt? responde ex ordine.   1155
PA énsiculust auréolus primum litteratus. DA dicedum,
in eo ensículo litterarum quíd ĕst? PA mei nomen patris.
post altrinsecust secúricula ancipes, itidem aurea,
115 litterata; ibi matris nomen in securiculast. DA mane.
dic, in énsiculo quid nomen est paternum? PA Daemones.
         DAEMONES *gasps;* TRACHALIO *and* PALAESTRA *stare at him;*
         GRIPUS *stares at* PALAESTRA.
DA di inmortales, ubi sunt spes meae? GR (*bitterly*)
   immo edepol meae?   1161
TR pergite, opsecro, continuo. GR (*with a snarl*) placide,
   aut ite in malam crucem.
DA (*agitated*) loquere matris nomen hic quid in securicula
   siet.
120 PA Daedalis. *The casket drops from* DAEMONES'S *hands; the*
         necklace remains in his fingers.
      DA di me servatum cupiunt. GR at me perditum.
DA filiam meam ĕsse hanc oportet, Gripe. GR sit per me
   quidem. (*He turns on* TRACHALIO)   1165
qui te di omnes perdant, qui me hodie oculis vidisti tuis,
meque adeo scelestum, qui non circumspexi centiens
priu' me, nequis inspectaret, quam rete extraxi ex aqua!
125 PA post sicílicula argentéola et duaç conexae mániculae et
   sucula. . . .   GR quin tu i díerecta cum sucula et cum
   porculis.   1170
PA et bulla aurea est, pater quam dédĭt mi natali die.
DA éa ĕst profecto. contineri quin complectar non queo.
      (*He rushes to embrace* PALAESTRA)
filiá mea, salve. (*She shrinks back in alarm and incredulity*)
   ego is sum qui te produxi pater,

130 ego sum Daemones; et mater túa ĕccam hic intus Daedalis.
PA (*flinging herself into his arms*) salve, mi pater insperate.
          DA salve. ut te amplector lubens! 1175
They remain hugging each other; GRIPUS *spits furiously and glares*
at TRACHALIO, *who makes insulting gestures at him. Then* TRACHALIO
deferentially approaches DAEMONES.
TR volup est quom istuc ex pietate vostra vobis contigit.
DA (*recollecting himself and releasing* PALAESTRA) capedum;
     hunc, si potes, fer intro vidulum. PA age, Trachalio.
TRACHALIO *takes the trunk, and on his way into the farm-house pauses*
to jeer again at GRIPUS.
TR ecce Gripi scelera! quom istaec res male evenit tibi
     Gripe, gratulŏr.— *Exit.*
135   DA age, eamus, mea gnata, ad matrem tuam,
quae ex te poterit argumentis hanc rem magis exquirere, 1180
quae te magi' tractavit magi'que signa pernovit tua.
PA intro eamus omnes, quandŏ (*she stretches out her hands*)
     óperam promiscam damus.
sequere me, Ampelisca. AM quom te dí amant, vólŭptati
     est mihi.—
          Exeunt DAEMONES, PALAESTRA *and* AMPELISCA *to farm-house.*
140 GR sumne egŏ scelestus, qui illunc hodie excepi vidulum?
aut, quom cepi, qui non alicubi in solo apstrusi loco? 1185
credebam edepol turbulentam praedam eventuram mihi,
quia illa mihi tam turbulenta tempestate evenerat.
credo edepol ego illic inesse argenti et auri largiter.
145 quid meliust quam ut hinc intro abeam et me suspendam
     clanculum—
saltem tantisper dum apscedat haec a me aegrimonia? 1190
Exit to farm-house with net, wrapping the rope round his neck.

IV v

          Enter DAEMONES; *he soliloquises.*
DA Pro di inmortales! quis me est fortunatior,
qui ex inproviso filiam inveni meam?
satin si quoii homini dí ĕsse bene factum volunt,

97

aliquo illud pacto optingit optatum piis?
5 ego hodie qui neque speravi neque credidi,   1195
   is inproviso filiam inveni tamen.
   et eam de genere summo adulescenti dabo
   ingenuo, Atheniensi et cognato meo.
   ego eum adeo arcessi huc ad me quam primum volo,
10 iussique exire huc eiius servom, ut ad forum   1200
   iret; nondum egressum esse eum, id miror tamen.
   accedam, opinor, ad fores. (*He looks in through the door*)
      quid conspicor?
   uxor complexa collo retinet filiam.
   nimi' paene inepta atque odiosa eius amatiost.

IV vi

DA (*shouting*) aliquando osculando meliust, uxor, pausam
   fíeri;   1205
atque adorna, ut rem divinam faciam, quom intro advenero,
   Laribus familiaribus, quom auxerunt nostram fámiliam.
   sunt domi agni et porci sacres. sed quid istum remoramini,
5 mulieres, Trachalionem? atque optume eccum exit foras!
      Enter TRACHALIO, *speaking back through the door.*
TR ubi ubi erit, iam investigabo et mecum ad te adducam
   simul   1210
Plesidippum. DA eloquere ut haec res optigit de filia;
   eum roga ut relinquat alias res et huc veniat. TR licet.
DA dicito daturum méam illi filiam uxorem. TR licet.
10 DA et patrem eiius me novisse et míhi ésse cognatum. TR
   licet.
DA sed propera. TR licet. DA iam hic fac sit, cena ut
   curetur. TR licet.   1215
DA omnian licet? TR licet. sed—scin quid est quod te
   volo?
quod promisisti ut memíneris, hodie ut liber sim. DA licet.
TR fac ut exores Plesidippum ut me manu emittat. DA
   licet.

15 TR et tua filiá facito oret: facile exorabit. DA licet.
   TR atque ut mi Ampelisca nubat, ubi ego sim liber. DA
       licet.   1220
   TR atque ut gratum mi benefícium factis experiar. DA
       licet.
   TR omnian licet? DA licet: tibi rusum refero gratiam.
   sed propera ire in urbem actutum et recipe te huc rusum.
       TR licet.
20 iam hic ero. tu interibi adorna ceterum quod opust. DA
       licet.   *Exit* TRACHALIO *towards town.*
   DA Hercules istum infelicet cum sua licentia!   1225
   ita meas replevit auris: quidquid memorabam, "licet".

IV vii

Enter GRIPUS. *He looks round to make sure he is alone with*
DAEMONES.

   GR quam mox licet (DAEMONES *winces*) te compellare,
       Daemones?
   DA quid est negoti, Gripe? GR de illo vidulo:
   si sapias, sapias; habeas quod di dánŭnt boni.
   DA aequom videtur tibi, ut ego álienum quod est 1230
 5 meum esse dicam? GR quodne ego inveni in mari?
   DA tanto illi melius optigit qui perdidit;
   tuom esse nihilo magis oportet vidulum.
   GR isto tu pauper es, quom nimi' sancte piu's.
   DA o Gripe, Gripe, in aetate hominum plurumae 1235
10 fiunt transennae, úbi decipiuntur dolis;
   atque edepol in eas plerumque esca imponitur:
   quam si quis avidus poscit escam avariter,
   decipitur in transenna avaritia sua.
   ïlle qui consulte, docte atque astute cavet,
                          (with much self-approval)   1240
15 diutine uti bene licet partum bene.
   mihi ïstaéc videtur praeda praedatum irier,
   ut cum maiore dote abeat quam advenerit.

99

egone ut quod ad me adlatum esse alienum sciam
celem? minume istuc faciet noster Daemones.   1245
20 semper cavere hoc sapientis aequissumumst,
ne conscii sint ipsi málefici suis.
ego mihi conlusim nil morōr ullum lucrum.
GR spectavi ego pridem comicos ad ĭstúnc modum
sapienter dicta dicere, atque is plaudier,
                                  (glaring at the audience)
25 quom illos sapientis mores monstrabant poplo: 1251
sed quom inde suam quisque ibant divorsi domum,
nullús erat illo pacto ut illi iusserant.
DA abi intro, ne molestu's, linguae tempera.
ego tibi daturus nil sum, ne tu frustra sis.   1255
30 GR at ego deọs quaeso ut, quidquid ín illo vidulost,
si aurum, si argentum est, omne ut id fiat cinis. *Exit.*
DA illuc est quod nos nequam servis utimur.
nam illic cum servo si quo congressus foret,
et ipsum sese et illum furti astringeret;   1260
35 dum praedam habere se censeret, interim
praeda ipsus esset, praeda praedam duceret.
nunc ibo hinc intro, et sacruficabo; postibi
iubebo nobis cenam continuo coqui.
                                  Exit to farm-house.

IV viii
   Enter TRACHALIO *and* PLESIDIPPUS *from the town, in high spirits.*
PL Iterum míhi ĭstaec omnia itera, mi anime, mi Trachalio,
mi liberte, mi patrone potius, immo mi pater.   1266
repperit patrem Palaestra suom ắtque matrem? TR repperit.
PL et popularis est? TR opino. PL et nuptura est mi?
   TR suspicor.
5 PL censen hodie despondebit ẹam mi, quaeso? TR censeo.
PL quid? patri etiam gratulabor quom illam invenit?
   TR censeo.   1270
PL quid matri eiius? TR censeo.... PL quid ergo
censes? TR quod rogas

100

censeo. PL dic ergo quanti censes. TR egone? censeo....
PL adsum equidem, ne censionem semper facias. TR censeo.
10 PL quid si curram? TR censeo. PL an sic potius
    placide? TR censeo.
PL etiamne eam adveniens salutem? TR censeō.
   PL etiam patrem?   1275
TR censeo. PL post eiius matrem? TR censeo.
   PL quid postea?
etiamne adveniens complectar eius patrem? TR non censeo.
PL quid, matrem? TR non censeo. PL quid, eampse
   illam? TR non censeo.
15 PL perii! dilectum dimisit. nunc non censet quom volo.
   TR sanus non es. sequere. PL duc me, mi patrone, quo
      lubet.   1280

Exeunt to farm-house.

ACT V

V i

Enter LABRAX *from the town, disconsolate.*

LA Quis me est mortalis míserior qui vivat alter hodie,
   quem ad récuperatores modō damnavit Plesidippus?
   abiudicata a me modo est Palaestra. perditus sum.
   nam lenones ex Gaudio credo esse procreatos;
5   ita ŏmnés mortales, si quid est mali lenoni, gaudent.   1285
   nunc alteram illam, quae mea est, visam huc in Veneris
      fanum,
   saltem ut eam abducam, de bonis quod restat réliquiarum.

Enter GRIPUS, *polishing a spit.* *He soliloquises gloomily.*

101

V ii

GR Numquam edepol hodie ad vesperum Gripum inspicietis
    vivom,
nisi vidulus mihi redditur.   LA (*aside, startled by the word*)
perii! quom mentionem
fieri audio usquam viduli . . .
                        . . . quasi palo pectus tundat. 1290
GR (*still unaware of* LABRAX'S *presence*) istic scelestus liber est:
    ego, qui in mari prehendi
5 rete atque excepi vidulúm, ei dárei negatis quicquam?
    LA (*aside*) pro di inmortales! suo mihi hic sermone arrexit
    auris.
GR cubitum hercle longis litteris signabo iam usquequaque:
si quis perdiderit vidulum cum auro atque argento multo, 1295
ad Gripum ut veniat.   non feretis istum, ut postulatis.
10 LA meum hercle illíc homo vidulum scit quí habet, ut ego
    opinor.
adeundus míhi íllic est homó. di, quaeso, subvenite.
GR quid me intro revocas? hic volo hoc ante ostium
    extergere.
nam hoc quídĕm pol e robiginé, non est e ferro factum; 1300
ita quanto magis extergeo, rutilum atque ténuius fit.
15 nam quídem hŏc venenatumst verúm; ita ĭn mánibus
    consenescit. LABRAX *approaches* GRIPUS.
LA adulescens, salve. GR di te amant cum inraso capite.
    LA quid fit?
GR verum extergetur. LA ut vales? GR quid tu?
num medicus, quaeso, es?
LA immo edepol una littera plus sum quam medicus.
    GR tum tu   1305
mendicus es? LA (*wincing*) tetigisti acu. GR videtur digna
    forma.
20 sed quid tibi est? LA hac proxuma nocte in mari mi et álii
confracta est navis; perdidi quidquid erắt míser ibi omne.

GR quid perdidisti? LA vidulum cum auro atque argento
multo.

GR ecquid meministi, in vidulo qui periit quid ibi infúerit?

LA quid refert, qui periit? GR tamen.... LA sine hŏc;
aliud fabulemur.   1311

25 GR quid si ego sciam qui invenerit? volo ex te scire signa.

LA nummi octingentī—aurei—in marsuppio infuerunt,
praeterea centum mínariá Philĭppa in pascéolo sorsus.

GR (aside) magna hercle praedast; largiter mercedis
indipiscar.

dí homines respiciunt: bene hercle ego hinc praedatus ibo.

30 profecto est huiius vidulus. (Aloud) perge alia tu expedire. 1317

LA talentum argenti commodum magnum inerit in crumina,
praeterea sinus, cantharús, epíchysis, gaulus, cýathus.

GR papae! divitias tu quidém habuisti luculentas.   1320

LA miserum istuc verbum et pessumum est, "habuisse" et
nihil habere.

35 GR quid dare velis, qui istaec tibi investiget indicetque?
eloquere propere celeriter. LA nummos trecentos. GR tricas.

LA quadrigentos, GR tramas putidas. LA quingentos.

GR cassam glandem.

LA sescentos. GR curculiunculos minutos fabulare. 1325

LA dabŏ séptingentos. GR os calet tibi; nunc id frige-
factas.

40 LA mille dabŏ nummum. GR somnias. LA nihil addo.

GR abi igitur. LA audi:
si hercle ábiero hinc, hic non ero. vin centum et mille?

GR dormis.

LA eloquere quantum postules. GR quo nihil invitus
addas:

talentum magnum. non potest triobolum hinc abesse. 1330
proin tu vel aias vel neges. LA quid ĭstíc? necessum est,
video.

45 dabitur talentum. GR (going over to the altar) accededum
huc: Venus haec volo adroget te.

LA   quod tibi lubēt, id mi impera.   GR   tange aram hanc
Veneris.   (LABRAX *obeys*)   LA   tango.
GR   per Venerem hanc iurandum est tibi.   LA   quid iurem?
GR   quod iubebo.
LA   prae͡i verbis quidvis.   quod domist, numquam ulli
supplicabo.   1335

      GRIPUS *notices that* LABRAX *has let go of the altar.*

GR   tene aram hanc.   LA   (*obeying*) teneo.   GR   deiera te mi
argentum daturum
50 e͡odem die, tu͡i vidulí ubi sis potitus.   LA   fiat.
     Venu' Cyrenensis, testem te testor mihi:
     si vidulum illum, quém ego in navi perdidi,
     cum auro atque argento salvom investigavero,   1340
     isque in potestatem meam pervenerit,
55   tum ego huic . . . (*He lays his hand on his breast, but* GRIPUS
     firmly takes it and lays it on himself)
      GR   "tum ego huíc Gripo", inquito, et me tangito.
     LA   tŭm égo huïc Grípo, dico, Venus, ut tu audias,
     talentum argenti magnum continuo dabo.

     He is about to leave the altar, but GRIPUS *detains him.*

     GR   si quid fraudassis, dic ut te in quaestu tuo   1345
     Venus eradicet, caput atque aetatem tuam.

     (*He detaches* LABRAX's *hand from himself.*)

60   tecum hoc habeto tamen, ubi iuraveris.
     LA   illaec advorsum si quid peccasso, Venus,
     veneror te ut omnes miseri lenones sient.
     GR   tamĕn fíet, etsi tu fidem servaveris.   1350
     tu hic opperire; iam ego faxo exibit senex:
65   e͡um tu continuo vidulum reposcito.
                              Exit to farm-house.

LA   si maxume mihi íllŭm reddiderit vidulum,
non égo ïllic hodie debeo triobolum.
meus arbitratust lingua quod iuret mea.   1355
sed conticiscam: eccum exit et ducit senem.

V iii

Enter GRIPUS *and* DAEMONES.

GR   sequere hac.   DA   úbi ĭstic lenost?   GR   heus tū!
ém tibi, hic habĕt vídulum.

DA   habeo, et fateor esse apúd me, et, si tuos est, habeas tibi.

(*At a sign from* DAEMONES, GRIPUS *goes in*)
omnia, ut quídquid infuere, ita salva sistentur tibi.

(GRIPUS *reappears with the trunk*)
ténĕ, si túŏst.   GRIPUS *delivers the trunk into* LABRAX'S *embrace*.

LA   o di inmortales!   meus est.   salve, vidule.   1360
5 DA   tuo'ne est?   LA   rogitas?   si quidem hercle Iovi' fuit,
meus est tamen.

DA   omnia insunt salva; una istinc cistella excepta est modo,
cum crepundiis, quibu'cum hodie filiam inveni meam.

LA   quam?   DA   tua quae fuit Palaestra, ea filia inventast
mea.

LA   (*swallowing hard*) bene mehercle factum est.   quóm
ĭstaec res tibi ex sententia   1365
10 pulchre evenit, gaudeo.   DA   istuc facile non credo tibi.

LA   (*with an air of great generosity*) immo hercle, ut scias
gaudere me, mihi triobolum
ob eam ne duis: condono te.   DA   (*ironically*) benigne edepol
facis.

LA   (*with great civility, as he edges away*) immo tu quidem hercle
verō.   GR   heús tu!   iam habĕs vídulum.

LA   habeo.   GR   propera.   LA   quid properabo?
GR   reddere argentum mihi.   1370
15 LA   neque edepol tibi do neque quicquam debeo.   GR   quaé
haĕc factio est?
non debes?   LA   non hercle vero.   GR   non tu iuratus
mihi es?

LA   iuratus sum et nunc iurabo, si quid vólŭptati est mihi:
ius iurandum rei servandae, non perdendae conditum est.

GR   cedo, sis, mihi talentum magnum argenti, peiiurissume.

20 DA Gripe, quod tu istum talentum poscis? GR iuratust
 mihi   1376
dare. LA lubet iurare. tun meo pontifex peiiurio es?
DA (*to* GRIPUS) qua pro re argentum promisit hic tibi?
GR si vidulum
hunc redegissem in potestatem eiius, iuratust dare
mihi talentum magnum argenti. LA (*to* GRIPUS) cedo
 quicum habeam iudicem,   1380
25 ni dolo malo instipulatus sis, sive etiamdum siem
 quinque et víginti annos natus. GR (*pointing at* DAEMONES)
 hábĕ cŭm hóc. LA aliost opus.
iăm ab istoc auferre haud ausim, si istunc condemnavero.
DA promisistin huic argentum? LA (*cheerfully*) fateor.
 DA quod servo meo (LABRAX's *cheerfulness vanishes*)
promisisti, méum ĕsse oportet, ne tu, leno, postules 1385
30 te hic fide lenonia uti: non potes. GR iam te ratu's
nactum hominem quem defrudares? dandum huc argentum
 est probum:
id ego continuo huic dabo adeo, mé ut hic emittat manu.
DA (*To* LABRAX) quando ergo erga te benignus ego fui, atque
 opera mea
haec tibi sunt servata. . . . GR immo hercle mea, ne tu
 dicas tua.   1390
35 DA (*to* GRIPUS) si sapies, tacebis. (*To* LABRAX) tum te mihi
 benigne itidem addecet
bene merenti bene referre gratiam. LA nemp' pro meo
iure oras? DA mirum quin tuom ius meo periclo aps te
 expetam. LABRAX *hesitates.*
GR salvos sum: leno labascit; libertas portenditur. 1394
DA vidulum istunc ille invenit; illud mancupium meum est;
40 ego tibi hunc porro servavi cum magna pecunia.
           LABRAX *gives in.*
LA gratiam habeo, et de talento nulla caussa est quin feras,
 quód ïsti sum iuratus. GR heus tu! mihi dato ergo, si sapis.

DA tácĕn an non? GR tu meam rem simulas agere, tibi
   munis viam.

non hercle istoc me intervortes, si aliam praedam perdidi. 1400

45 DA vapulabis, verbum si addes isto unúm. GR (*quite
   out of control*) vel hĕrcle énica:

non tacebo umquam alio pacto nisi talento comprimor.

LA (*to* GRIPUS) tibi operam hicquidem dat.   tace.

DA concede hoc tu, leno. LA licet.

   DAEMONES *and* LABRAX *go to the other side of the stage.*

GR palam age; nolo ego murmurillum neque susurrum
   fíeri.

DA (*to* LABRAX) dic mihí: quanti illam emisti tuam alteram
   mulierculam?
                                                  1405

50 LA Ampeliscam? mille nummum denumeravi. DA vin
   tibi

condicionem luculentam ferre me? LA sane volo.

DA dividuom talentum faciam. LA bene facis. DA pro
   illa altera,

libera ut sit, dimidium tibi sume, dimidium huc cedo.

LA maxume. DA pro illo dimidiō égo Gripum emittam
   manu,   1410

55 quem propter tu vidulum et ego gnatam inveni. LA bene
   facis;

gratiam habeo magnam.   *They return towards* GRIPUS.

   GR quam mox mi argentum ergo redditur?

DA res soluta est, Gripe: ego habeō. GR át ego mé
   hĕrcle mavolo.

DA nihil hercle hic tibi ĕst, né tu speres. iuris iurandi volo
gratiam facias. GR perii hercle! nisi me suspendo, occidi.

60 numquam hercle iterum defrudabis me quidem post hunc
   diem.   1416

DA hic hodie cenato, leno. LA fiat, condicio placet.

DA sequimini intro. (*He turns to the audience*) spectatores,
   vos quoque ad cenam vocem,

ni daturus nil sim neque sit quicquam pollucti domi,

nive adeo vocatos credam vos esse ad cenam foras.   1420
65 verum si voletis plausum fabulae huic clarum dare,
   comissatum omnes venitote ad me ad annos sedecim.

       (*He turns back to* LABRAX *and* GRIPUS)

vos hic hodie cenatote, ambo.

       He offers GRIPUS *his hand.* GRIPUS *recognises the implied offer of freedom, and drops on his knee to receive the traditional box on the ear.*

    LA *et* GR fiat. OMNES plausum date.

Notes

PROLOGUE. *Arcturus introduces himself, preaches a short sermon, and then explains the situation at the outset of the play. In his speech the dignity of a divine personage is tempered by a condescending jocularity appropriate to an address to a holiday crowd.*

METRE: six-beat iambics.

1. qui: the antecedent is *eiius* in the next line; Jupiter of course is meant. **gentis omnis** is accusative plural: if the reader is not familiar with this form, from 3rd declension *i*-stem nouns, which is used in many editions of classical authors, he had better familiarise himself.

2. civitate caelitum: "by fellowship with the gods in the sky", Arcturus being himself a constellation. **civis civitate:** The use of two cognate words in a construction is called *figura etymologica*. It is a trick of style much beloved by Plautus. In this first paragraph its purpose is to add dignity by suggesting ancient legal phraseology; cf. 14: there is an ordinary specimen of it at 747. Elsewhere it is used merely for emphasis, tragic at 187, comic at 977.

3. stella candida: ablative.

4-5. He is as punctual in the theatre as in the sky, because he never misses his cue.

7. Hiatus after *ambulo*; the god pauses slightly, that we may not fail to notice his pun between *interdius* and *inter deos*.

9. divom = *divum*, genitive plural; on the spelling, see p. 43.

10. aliā: adverb.

11. qui: adverb or conjunction, equivalent to *ut*; it is in origin the instrumental case of the relative pronoun.

12. ut here means "how": the celestial investigators are to report on two things: how men are behaving (11), and how they are prospering ("how success is helping each"), in order that Jupiter may redress the balance.

14. abiurant: "deny the receipt of". *abiūrant pecuniam:* Plautus has an uneasy conscience about using a stressed heavy

NOTES

syllable for a light in the fourth foot (cf. p. 22); and when he does, he usually makes amends by using a four-syllable word for the fifth and sixth foot, which gives a perfect correspondence of stress and metrical beat. Cf. 89, 91, and (similar in principle) 93.

16. quaerat malum: is deliberately ambiguous: "makes ill-gotten gains" or "is looking for trouble".

17. postulo means "demand", but in many contexts a better translation is "hope". **peiiurio** = *periurio*; it is Plautus's normal form.

20. multa: ablative of the noun *multa*, "fine", "punishment". Again we have *figura etymologica*.

22. atque here and in some other passages, *e.g.* 1128, has almost the same meaning as *atqui*, "and yet". **scelesti:** though the full meaning of the word is appropriate here, it often has a weaker meaning in colloquial speech, something like "bloody fool"; cf. 1184, where Gripus applies it to himself.

23. donis, hostiis: the omission of "and" is old-fashioned and dignified; cf. 675 *malis rebus, miseris*.

24. eo: adverb, like *ideo*, referring forward to *quia*.

25. supplici: genitive, depending on *nihil*.

26. si qui: strictly speaking, *qui* is the adjective, *quis* the pronoun; so this should mean "if any sort of man" rather than "if any man". But practically the difference is not great. Cf. the use of *qui* interrogative, 98 and note.

27. inveniet veniam: another of the god's puns.

29-30. Between these two lines the palimpsest had another, which presumably contained something like *morem bonum* as object of *retinete* in 30.

30. post factum ut laetemini may be construed in two ways: 1. "that you may rejoice after the deed" (*factum* noun), 2. "that you may afterwards rejoice that it was done" (*factum = factum esse*). The general effect is the same.

31. qua caussa: "for the sake of which", the antecedent being *argumentum*. *qua caussa*, not *cuius caussa*, is normal Latin.

32-82. *The god explains that Daemones lives on a sea-side farm near Cyrene. His long-lost daughter, in slavery to a leno, has attracted a lover, who had arranged to buy her; but her owner attempted to break this contract and sell her at a higher price in Sicily. He sets sail, having given the young lover a bogus invitation to lunch with him at Venus's temple. Arcturus himself has frustrated this scheme by wrecking the ship, and its occupants are now coming ashore.*

NOTES

32. primumdum: "Well, to begin with". From its meaning "just so long" (which is found at 779), *dum* comes to mean "just a moment", and then little more than an emphasising particle; cf. its use with imperatives, 720, 784, 785, and often. In this sense it is enclitic (i.e. attached to the preceding word, which it emphasises). **huic:** the god's gesture indicates the district in general. **Diphilus** of Sinope, writer of Greek comedies, flourished around 290 B.C. One of his plays bore the title *Epitrope*, "The Arbitration"; and as such a title would suit Act IV of *Rudens* very well, Marx supposes that this was the play which Plautus was adapting.

33. Cyrenas: *Cyrene* or *Cyrenae* was the name of a thriving Greek colony on the coast of North Africa; it was famous for the export of the products of the *silphium* plant, for which see 630-3 and notes. **illic:** The door which the god indicates is to be thought of as opening rather into the walled farm-yard than into the house: the well is within, and the farm-workers go in and out on their errands (83, 184, 414, 657).

36. adeo: This word, from *ad* + *eo*, "to this", diverges into two main senses: 1. "in addition", 2. "to this extent". Students are probably more familiar with the latter meaning, introducing a consecutive clause; but both are good Latin: it is the former that we have here.

38. rem bene paratam: "his well-earned fortune"; the god is refuting the thought that the proverb *male parta male pereunt* might apply to Daemones.

39. periit: not "died", but "was lost"; *perire* serves as passive to *perdere*, cf. 964.

41. leno: on his business, see p. 35.

42. civis huiius: "fellow-citizen of this gentleman", viz. of Daemones.

45. minis: on the monetary system, see p. 41. **destinat:** "books", by paying a first instalment.

46. adligat: sc. *lenonem*.

47. ut se aequomst: *se* is ablative, *aequom* being given the same construction that *dignus* normally has; cf. *Bacchides* 488, *me atque illo aequom*. Cf. also the treatment of *decorus* in 255. By rule we should have not *se*, but *eo*, since the pronoun does not refer to the subject of the clause (there is none), nor is it in indirect speech. Such uses of *se* and *suus* are found even in the most correct authors, for no other reason than temporary forgetfulness that the person who is referred to, and who is very much in the writer's thoughts, is not in fact the grammatical subject; cf. *sui* in 49, *ex se* in 410, *sua* in 1225.

NOTES

50. scelestus: cf. note on 22. **Agrigentinus:** *Agrigentum,* the Greek *Acragas,* Italian *Girgenti,* was a Greek colony near the south coast of Sicily; it has fine remains of temples. **urbis proditor:** not that he had betrayed a city, but that he would. "The sense of *habit,* which attaches to nouns in -*or,* easily passes into that of tendency" (Sonnenschein).

51. infit: there is no first person *infio.*

52. eius: sc. *lenonis.* **mulierculae,** in the relative clause as nominative, needs to be taken in translation outside, along with *aliarum.* The diminutive, as in German, is not an exact description of size, but a piece of familiarity, friendly or contemptuous.

58. quidquid erat: "all his property"; cf. 1308.

61. id fanum is the subject; *hic,* adverb, is predicate. Hiatus at the pause after *fanum;* similar pauses and hiatus at 63, 65. **eo:** "there", "to the aforementioned temple": the word is then picked up in the next line by *huc,* "here", "to the place that I'm showing you"; a good illustration of the difference between unemphatic *eo* and emphatic *huc,* which the common translation "to this place" might conceal.

62. ilico: "on the spot" (from *in* + *loco*), whether of time, as here, or of place. The word is strangely absent from Smith's Dictionary. Do not confuse it with *ilicet.*

64. ut: "how".

66. apscesserat: *aps-* is Plautus's normal spelling of *abs-.*

67. quoniam here, and in some other passages, means "when": it is derived from *quom* + *iam.* **asportarier** = *asportari.*

68. tetuli is from *fero.*

69. hibernum: neuter of the adjective used adverbially, "roared wintry", i.e. "gave a wintry roar".

70. unum: Seyffert's conjecture to mend the metre; it emphasises the superlative.

71. He rises in September and sets in November.

75. desuluerunt = *desiluerunt.*

77. illius: sc. *senis.* Plautus has instead put *senex* into the relative clause; cf. his treatment of *mulierculae* in 52.

78. quoius = *cuius.* On its scansion, see p. 30.

79. servos: nominative singular. **qui** "refers to *illic,* not to *eiius*" (Sonnenschein).

82. ut introduces a wish, like *utinam* (which, of course, is only *uti* + *nam* for emphasis). **vostri** = *vestri.*

ACT I

Act I, Scene i, 83-147. *Sceparnio and his master Daemones, surveying their storm-damaged roof, are accosted by Plesidippus, who is in search of Labrax; but they can give him no information.*

83. pro: interjection, not preposition.

86. Alcumena = *Alcmene*, the mother of Hercules: the Romans found the combination *-lcm-* hard to pronounce. This play by Euripides does not survive: it must have contained a vivid description of a storm.

87. ita ... deturbavit: not "so it blew down", which would require *itaque*, but "it so blew down", giving the reason for the last remark, not its consequence. The heavy stress on *ita* has resulted in the shortening of *omn-* by *breves breviantes*.

88. inlustriores fecit: If the object to be supplied is *tegulas*, Sceparnio's language is careless: some scholars suppose a line has been lost, containing the word *aedis*. **fenstras** = *fenestras* (which the MSS have); this form, or something like it, is known to have been used by Plautus's contemporary Cato, and is required here by the metre.

89. et is co-ordinate with *neque* in 90 and 91; but it is better omitted in translation.

90. qua ... gratia: "for the sake of which", like *qua caussa*, line 31.

93. eo: ablative neuter, with *diutius*, "that much longer"; it refers back to the previous line.

94. venio visere: infinitives of purpose are quite common in Plautus with verbs of motion.

96. si sapiam ... concinnem: literally, "If I were wise, I should fix"; i.e. "I'd better fix" (Sonnenschein). **mactat:** The verb *mactare* can either mean "to sacrifice (an offering)", or "to present (someone with something)": in the latter sense it is often used ironically, e.g. *mactare infortunio*. But in the present passage neither the former sense, nor, in default of a suitable ablative, the latter, seems appropriate. Lindsay, in a footnote, writes *alludit, credo, ad* maccare *lutum concinnare*; but I do not know this verb *maccare*, nor do dictionaries, though *maceria* is a mud wall.

98. qui nominat me ?: *qui* is the interrogative adjective, *quis* the pronoun. Sceparnio demands, not the identity of the person

113

who calls him, but his quality: is he entitled to give orders? (Of course he really knows.) So at 677, *qui vocat?*, Palaestra wants to know, not "Name and address?", but "Friend or foe?". But the difference is not always significant: *e.g.* in *Epidicus* I, *Heus adulescens!—Quis properantem me reprehendit pallio?*, the *quis* is spoken in the same spirit as Sceparnio's *qui*. Cf. the note at 26 on *qui* and *quis* indefinite.

99. quasi dicas: literally, "As if you meant", i.e. "I suppose you mean". The line ("intended for the benefit of the audience", Sonnenschein) should be spoken in a tone of resignation. **Daemones**: Though polite forms of address existed (e.g. *pater*, 103), and a slave might say *ere* (1052), it was not impolite to name one's superior directly; cf. 481, 1227.

100. usust = *usus est*: *usus* is noun, not participle, and *usus est* is similar in meaning and construction to *opus est*.

101, 102. Daemones puns with *integundam intellego* and *cribrum crebrius*.

103. Hiatus in the pause after *salveto*: Plesidippus, after a moment, notices Sceparnio and includes him in the greeting. **adeo**: cf. line 36 and note.

103-7. pater is a polite form of address to elderly men—not of course necessarily priests! But since, in the literal sense, Daemones was *pater* only to a girl, Sceparnio chooses to take the word so, hinting broadly to Plesidippus that he is not welcome. Then, because without an explanation Sceparnio's words sound, and were probably meant to sound, like an accusation of effeminacy, Daemones hastens to explain.

105. voces: subjunctive because the relative clause is causal, "since you call". **porro** here and at 1034, but not at 30, has its literal meaning of "further off".

107. sexus is usually masculine, here neuter: this line is quoted by the Latin grammarian Priscian to illustrate this fact. The common phrase later was *virile secus*, used as a "limiting accusative" (practically an adjectival phrase); so *virile sexus* is no doubt also such a phrase, and consequently *ullum* is masculine: "any child of male sex". **at di dabunt** is polite sympathy; Plesidippus is not claiming the gift of prophecy.

108. tibi: sc. *dabunt*. Presumably Sceparnio's rudeness is not quite audible to Plesidippus, who endeavours to ignore him.

111. quon = *quo* + *-ne*: it is the *-ne* that makes the sentence interrogative; *quo* is relative adverb, whose antecedent is *loca*; *furatum* is supine of purpose. A similar remark is made about a

NOTES

shady character in *Trinummus* 864: *quo mox furatum veniat, speculatur loca.*

112-23. *Plesidippus can ignore Sceparnio no longer, and speaks with severe irony, probably not directly to him, but to his master. Sceparnio is unabashed, until his master checks him, and even then still mutters rudely.*

112. peculiosum: it is assumed that a slave whose earnings are large is a reliable and trusted servant, entitled to take occasional liberties. **addecet:** "must be", and similarly in **115**; in a similar exchange in *Poenulus* 1030-3, *oportet* is used.

113-23. Observe the subjunctives in relative clauses in these lines: *praetereat* and *praefestinet* (113, 119) are causal, "since he insists on speaking", "since he hurries"; *debeatur* and *adsit* (117, 119) are concessive, "though nothing is owed", "though his master is present"; *pertegamus* (123) is final, "to thatch".

113. quem . . . haud praetereat oratio: i.e. "who does not fail to speak". *haud* is a conjecture.

114. inclementer dicere is the ordinary Latin for "be rude"; cf. 734.

115. Literally, "It befits an impudent man to . . .", i.e. "And *you* must be an impudent man to . . ."

117. *If they owed him money, there might be some excuse for his visit. A similar point is made in Menander's* Dyscolus, 469 seq., *also by a surly rustic:*

CNEMON Why, did I ever make a contract with you,
You rascal? *GETAS* Contract? No, sir; so I haven't
Come to present a bill, nor brought the bailiffs:
I simply want a cauldron.

The passage also illustrates Daemones's remarks at 133-6 *about borrowers.*

118. opust: *opus est* can take accusative as well as ablative or genitive. *istic*: dative; sc. *opus est*, "He needs...". **infortunium:** almost a technical term for a thrashing; cf. 828, 833.

120. paucis: sc. *verbis*; cf. 1102.

121. atque in negotio: "*and* when I'm busy"; the *atque* is emphatic, almost equivalent to "even".

122. quin, used with the present indicative interrogatively, is virtually a command: "Why don't you . . . ?" (for *quin = qui + nĕ*); hence it was also used with an imperative, *e.g.* at line 628. **exsicas** either = *exsecas*, "cut out", as is usually assumed; or Plautus could have meant *exsiccas*, "dry out", since double consonants were not usually written in his time: either makes good sense.

115

NOTES

123. qui: see note on 11.

125. This of course describes Labrax's mask; more details of it are given in 317-18.

126. plurumos: see stage direction. The audience received similar compliments from Aristophanes.

127. vivo: here means little more than *sum*; cf. 290.

128. hic dico: "I mean here."

129. adduxit: The indicative is rather surprising; it wrongly implies that Labrax *had* taken the girls to the temple. Plesidippus, it seems, still believes what Labrax had said: Trachalio at line 320 is less naive, and uses the subjunctive of virtual indirect speech ("would, according to his account, be bringing"). Plesidippus does use the subjunctive in *adornaret*.

130. rem divinam: i.e. a sacrifice, with a meal to follow. "Divine Service" had different implications for the ancients and for us.

133-5. See extract quoted in note on 117, and p. 35.

135. aulam: "pot", different from the word meaning "court-yard"; its later form was *olla*.

138. ut verba praehibes: i.e. "to judge by what you say". For this use of *ut*, cf. 303; *praehibes* is the older form of *praebes*, and perhaps already so pronounced, cf. 530; **praedicas** is from *praedicare* (not *praedicere*). The whole line is rather a long way round of saying "If that's the case, I've had it".

139. mea . . . caussa salvos sis licet: literally, "So far as I'm concerned you may be in good health". The line is, however, polite and apologetic, meaning something like "I'm sorry; I didn't mean to distress you".

140-6. Plesidippus is too concerned with losing Labrax to notice Sceparnio's further impertinences.

140. "Going round to pick up scraps from the altars" was a regular term of abuse among the Greeks. For a poor man it was a real temptation, as St Paul found with his Corinthians, see I Corinthians viii and x. 20-1.

143. nullus venit: "didn't put in an appearance". This is a colloquial use of *nullus*, meaning not "no" or "none", but simply "emphatically not". Other examples at 323, 1135, 1253, and *neque ullas* at 340. **admodum:** "Exactly!" Plesidippus is laconic in his fury.

144. nullumst periclum: i.e. "It won't hurt you".

146. Sceparnio's explanation of his own witticism falls very flat. Perhaps Plautus had translated the previous line exactly from Diphilus, and feared that the Roman audience might not see the point. Or perhaps there is a special sting in *tritico*: that if Plesidippus were not greedy, he would have been content with bread or porridge at home, instead of hoping for a meat meal at a temple. For the datives, see note on 182.

147. indignis modis: "outrageously". The plural is common in such phrases; cf. 593, 672.

148-84. *Daemones suddenly sees some of the survivors of the shipwreck coming ashore: Plesidippus hurries off with his friends to see if these include Labrax. Then Sceparnio sees two more coming ashore, girls this time: both are seen to reach land safely, though separately. After this excitement Daemones recalls Sceparnio to work.*

148. illuc: pronoun, neuter of *illic*; *hominum* depends on it.

149. secundum: preposition, "along".

150-1. There was a sacrifice, undertaken before a journey, known as *propter viam*, but nothing that is known of it is particularly apposite here, except that the shipwrecked persons are travellers. Sceparnio affects to think that they are merely having the usual bath before attending a sacrifice and lunch—the same non-existent lunch that Plesidippus had missed. His enigmatic words prompt Daemones to ask for an explanation; and he affects to misunderstand the request: he offers an explanation not of *propter viam*, but of *prandium*, viz. that it must be *prandium*, not *cena*, because they had their bath after their *cena* last night, and one has a bath before, not after, the meal to which one is invited.

151. qui: adverb.

153. at hercle, etc.: sc. *confractae sunt*.

154. homunculi: on the effect of the diminutive, see note on 52. **quanti:** "genitive of value, here = 'how little worth'" (Sonnenschein). **ut:** exclamatory, "How . . . !".

158. sacerrumus: like the French *sacré*, not "sacred", but "damned".

159. si non moneas: "without your advice". **meminimus:** sc. *valere*. Present subjunctive in the "if" clause, present indicative in the main clause, is a common form, in Plautus, for open conditionals.

161. Herculei (so Lindsay, for MSS *herculi* or *hercule* or *herculis*): genitive of *Hercules*.

162: facinus: "deed", "action" not necessarily wicked.

162. (mulierculas) -177: This is all given to Sceparnio in most editions. Marx divided the speech between him and Daemones, which certainly enlivens the scene: both watch what is happening, and speak excitedly. Sceparnio is much more excited about the girls than about the other survivors at 148-53.

NOTES

164. ut: cf. 154.

169. alteram: Ampelisca, as we learn from 200-1.

171. This line was deleted by Sonnenschein, because it repeats the sense of 169. With Marx's division of speakers we may suppose that Sceparnio, having paid no attention to Daemones in 169, now tells him in 171-2 what he already knows. **foras:** merely "out", "away", not "out of doors"; cf. 725.

172. salva res: Contexts in which this phrase and others like it, such as *salvos sum*, are used, show that they had a less final and emphatic meaning than "Saved!" or "All's well!": something like "So far, so good!": cf. 442, 1037, 1394.

176. in malam crucem: the Latin equivalent for "to the devil".

177. hem, or *ehem*, in Latin is not a clearing of the throat, but an exclamation of surprise or uncertainty, and its English equivalents are "Ha!", "Oho!"; cf. 415, 804. A special use of it, for which the English equivalent is "Eh?", is when the speaker thinks he has misheard or misunderstood something; cf. 237. **hodie** is often a mere expletive in colloquial Latin, virtually meaningless.

178. ad saxum: not "to the rock", but "at the cliff".

180. This line, of course, means "she'll break her neck". *In reading and performance, care must be taken to speak the line as callously as possible, and 176-7 rather as amorous disappointment than as anxious sympathy. Otherwise we shall get the impression that Sceparnio is more humane than his master, which Plautus certainly did not intend. Gestures and voice must make it clear that at 175 the girls are out of trouble, and too far off for immediate help.*

181. vesperi is noun, ablative, governed by *de*.

182. illis is not dative of *agent*; *curo* can take a dative in early Latin: "attend to them"; cf. 146.

183. essuru's = *esurus es*, from *edo*.

ACT I, SCENE iii. *Palaestra, entering from the shore, wet and miserable, laments her fate:—Human life is bitterer than one could have supposed, and it is a cruel injustice that the gods should lay misfortune on her, who has never done any wrong; her plight is not due to her wickedness but her master's. Her comrade has disappeared, and she is herself lost, hungry, and destitute, cast away, so far as she can see, on a desert shore; and her fondly remembered parents have had no joy of her. Finally, it seems, she collapses from exhaustion.*

118

NOTES

For a discussion of the special problems with which this scene and the next confront the producer, see Appendix A.

METRE: see Appendix B.

185. nimio goes with *minus miserae*; the phrase is predicative: "are said to be much less wretched".

186. in usu experiundo: "in experiencing practice". Or, as OCT, *in usu, experiundo:* "in experience, in practice". In either case pleonastic. **is** = *eis,* dative, i.e. *hominibus.* **acerbum:** neuter adjective used as a noun (cf. 767, *inhumanum*), subject of *datur:* "than bitterness is given to them . . ."; but English would rather say, "than the bitterness which is given to them in reality is".

187. satin (*satisne*): cf. 462, 1193: literally, "has it sufficiently pleased . . . ?". Practically the word is a colloquial way of introducing a question which invites the answer "Yes". It is "Yes" in this case because her present plight shows that a god has indeed willed it.

Palaestra is confronted with Problem of Evil: why, if the world is controlled by just gods, does evil come upon the good? It is one of the world's great commonplaces, of which Plautus, like many another poet, makes use in a serious mood. The claim in 190, pietatem praecipuam, and in 193, is not for derision: Palaestra is represented as a good, seriously minded girl, and Plautus's audience at any rate would have accepted her as such.

ornatu ornatam: *figura etymologica;* see note on 2. **eiectam,** sc. *esse,* is accusative and infinitive; so is *natam* in 189.

191. laborist = *laboris est.* **potiri:** note: 1. the verb can take an accusative in ante-classical Latin; 2. its meaning is not confined to getting something that one wants; it may be something unpleasant (cf. 205).

193. parate is adverb.

194. The emphasis is on the adverbs: translate, "It is improper, unfair, indecent of you to . . ."

195. signi depends on *quid.* **inpii** is nominative. It is to be scanned *inpiĭ,* by analogy with *piĭ,* though as a single word it would properly be pronounced *ĭnpii;* cf. 944 *e-nĭcas.*

196. honor is not so much "honour" as "consideration", "decent treatment". Cf. 288, and *Captivi* 392, *qui me honore honestiorem semper fecit et facit,* said by a slave of a considerate master. Translate the present passage, "if that is the way you treat. . . ."

119

NOTES

197. miserer: from *miseror*.

199. She is not pitying Labrax, but blaming him as a Jonah, as Charmides later does, II, vi.

203. opera: ablative, "by her doing", "because of her". For similar phrases cf. 1020, 1329.

204. consili depends on *quid*.

205. ita: "so lonely are the places in which . . ." See line 87, note on *ita*. **compotita:** sc. *sum*. The MSS indeed have *sum*, but it spoils the metre.

207. hoc is subject, *opes* complement; the verb "to be" is to be supplied. **sim:** deliberative question. **oppido:** adverb.

208. There is a zeugma here: *loco* suits *tecta*, but *cibo* does not.

212. ita: cf. 205. **eam:** deliberative subjunctive.

216. me nunc miseram esse is in apposition to *haec*, and explains it.

217. leibera is the old form of *libera*, which happens to be here preserved in the MSS.

218. qui is interrogative adverb; *serva* is ablative.

219. This, Palaestra's final line in the scene, is a plain seven-beat iambic, as though, collapsing from sheer weariness, she could no longer sing. **quicquam:** adverbial; *profuit* is impersonal.

ACT I, SCENE iv. *Ampelisca enters as Palaestra had done, and laments that she is lost herself and has lost her friend. Her lament is shorter than Palaestra's, and metrically simpler.*

METRE: anapaests.

220. in rem: "to the point".

221. ita: cf. 87, 205 and notes. But in the next line, 222, *ita* refers forward. **male** of course means "unhappily", not "wickedly"; cf. 337, where there is a play on the two senses.

222. perdídi: cf. 195, *inpii*, and note.

224. quaerere: cf. 94, *visere*, and note.

225. neque . . . consultumst: "and I haven't thought".

227. The subject is *terrae solae*; the first *solae* is predicative.

228. eam is object of *inveniam*; *viva* agrees with the subject of *desistam*.

NOTES

229-58. *Palaestra revives; the girls hear each other's voices, and meet; they turn to go, notice the temple, and appeal to its deity for protection.*

METRE: see Appendix B.

229. quoia is the old interrogative possessive adjective, "whose?"; cf. 332, and the relative possessive at 745. *Quoia* appears to be either one heavy or two light syllables; cf. *quoius* at 78 and elsewhere.

233. As the girls settle down to seek each other the metre changes. At the half-line pause, the light last syllable of *muliebris* stands where there should be a heavy one.

235. tĕn = *tē-nĕ*.

237. hem: cf. 177 and note.

238. For such a ruefully humorous reply, cf. 337: it is true in a sense, but not what the questioner had asked.

242. The metre throws the stress on to *ac-* and *ad*: "Come *on*, come *to* me!".

243. cĕdŏ (not *cēdō*) is an interjection, meaning "Here!", "Give me . . . !", "Tell me . . . !". The hiatus after *manum*, and the short *e* of *accipe* standing for a heavy syllable (cf. 233 and note) are both explicable by the pauses in speech as the girls run together and meet.

244. me is anticipated from the subordinate clause (the "I-know-thee-who-thou-art" construction): the English of course is "make me wish".

245. licet: Plautus does not feel bound to use a subjunctive after causal *quom*; cf. 908, 1178.

246. te is object of *tenere*; *me* is to be understood as subject.

247. laborum: the ablative is the normal classical construction with *levare*.

248. occupas: "you get in first"; it governs *praeloqui*. As antecedent of *quae* understand *eam orationem*.

249. amabo was one Latin word for "please"; cf. 253. As might be guessed from its derivation, it was affectionate and friendly: it is used between the girls and Trachalio and by Ampelisca in coaxing Sceparnio. The most frigid term was *sis*, plural *sultis*, used for example between Daemones, his *lorarii*, and Labrax, 820, 828.

251. hic . . . grassabimur: not "go along here" (which would require *hac*, not *hic*), but "tramp around here (in this desolate *district)"*. Ampelisca names *two* hardships: this is one, her wet dress is the other.

252 hoc quod est: "this present state of things", picked up by *id* as object of *perpeti*.

253. The metre changes with the new development of the scene.

254. ad dexteram: As the girls are going towards the shore, stage right (cf. 156), it follows that the temple is back stage right.

255. dis depends on *decorum*; it is ablative, the case it would have after *dignum*; cf. *Miles Gloriosus* 619, *te decora*, "befitting you". Cf. also *se aequom*, 47. **locum viderier** (*viderier* = *videri*): indirect statement; **decorum** is complement after *viderier*.

256. ita: cf. 87 and note.

257. The girls are now standing at the temple door—not kneeling; for the ancients stood for prayer, and *ire* in line 265 implies that they are on their feet. Ampelisca joins in the prayer; cf. the plurals in the Priestess's opening words.

quisquis est deus: "a common formula, to avoid blundering when the name of the god was unknown" (Sonnenschein).

ACT I, SCENE v. *The Priestess appears at the door of the temple: she is to be thought of as having a small apartment at the back of it. At first sight of the ragged and dripping girls her sense of propriety is outraged, but on understanding their plight she offers them what hospitality she can.*

METRE: see Appendix B.

259. preces expetessunt: is a slightly illogical phrase, a cross between "seek favours from" and "make prayers to". *mea* is contracted by *synizesis* and then elided, so that here it is metrically non-existent; cf. 352.

260. precantum = *precantium:* this form of the genitive plural of the participle is common in verse in classical Latin.

262. multum: adv. with *benignam*.

265. und': on the form, see p. 31.

267. Understand *locus* as subject of *abest* and antecedent of *unde*.

268. nempe: "presumably", "I take it", to verify that one has understood his information correctly; for scansion, see p. 31.

NOTES

268-9. The Priestess speaks in exalted tragic diction; Palaestra understands her, but does not venture to vie with her.

269. erat: we should say "would have been", but the Latin idiom is that it *was* the proper thing to do, whether they did it or not.

271. veniri solet: impersonal passive: "people do not come", "it is not done to come".

272. quaene: cf. note on 111; *-ne* asks the question. The implied antecedent of *quae* is *nos*: "Do you mean us, who . . ." *The slightly cheeky tone of these lines seems to me to fit Ampelisca better than Palaestra, and I have assigned them accordingly.*

273. voluistis (Hermann's emendation for the less metrical *voluisti* of the MSS) is generalising plural, meaning "you and others like you": cf. 728, *di*, though only Venus is concerned; 748, *liberos*, though only Palaestra is meant.

275. nesciis . . . nescia: passive in both cases, "unknown".

279. hoc: ablative of comparison, depending on *amplius*.

282. haec: feminine plural.

283. cibo meo: "at my own expense"; the Priestess condescends to be colloquial. And the metre changes accordingly. **servio:** she is not of course literally a slave; see p. 34.

285. clueo is an old and dignified word: the Priestess cannot unbend for long.

286. quidquid est: "all I have"; cf. 58.

287. quo: adverb, "so far as". Lindsay understands *copiā* as nominative, though this termination was normally short in Plautus's time, as later. But perhaps it is ablative, in which case the subject is "it", viz. the *quidquid est* of the line before.

288. amice benigneque: on the emphatic adverbs, cf. 194 and note. **honorem:** cf. 196 and note.

289. nostrum: adjective (the objective genitive of *nos* would be *nostri*); but translate "of us", or rather "for us".

123

ACT II

ACT II, SCENE i. *Local fishermen, on their way to the shore, bemoan their over-worked and ill-rewarded trade, and pause at the temple to pray for good luck.*

METRE: seven-beat iambics.

It is possible that in Diphilus's play the fishermen were the chorus, and performed between all the acts. So far as Plautus is concerned, they do not appear again. In a modern production they may very well sing their lines: the tune of "Little Bo Peep" fits them nicely.

290. omníbu' modis is accented as if it were a single word like *multimodis.* **vivont:** cf. 127. Its subject is *ei* understood as antecedent to *qui.*

291. Again understand *ei* before *quibus.*

293. de: "from". **ut locupletes:** "how rich", meaning in this context "how poor".

294. hisce is nominative plural masculine, **haec** nominative plural feminine, of *hic;* of these old forms, *hisce* is rare, *haec* fairly common. **quaestu, cultu** are datives, predicative.

295. pabulatum: supine.

296. exercitu: "training".

297-8. Perhaps the fishermen shout the names of these creatures as if crying their wares.

297. captamus: not "catch", but "try to catch", "fish for."

299. postid = *post id.* **adgredīmur,** as if 4th conjugation; cf. *moriri,* 675.

300. si eventus non evenit: "if no results result"; *figura etymologica.*

301. salsi lautique: being soaked to the skin in sea-water is ironically presented as an advantage: *salsi,* "briny", also means "witty" (cf. 517); *lauti,* "washed clean", also means "luxurious".

303. ut is used as in 138.

304. capsimus is old future or future perfect of *capere;* cf. 365, *faxo.* **cenati:** ironical; they mean, "We shall get no dinner". (The MSS give *incenati,* which does not scan.) **profecto** is adverb, not a part of *proficisci.*

NOTES

305. Venerem . . . veneremur: a favourite pun of Plautus; cf. 1348-9.

ACT II, SCENE ii. *Trachalio, Plesidippus's man, arrives to look for his master, and enquires of the fishermen.*

306. animum advorsavi means the same as *animum advorti* (*animadverti*).

307. aibat: as usual, two syllables.

309. quos perconter: "to ask", depending on *eccos*. **eccos:** a contraction of *ecce* and *hos* or *ecce* and *eos*. The accusative is used even when the persons indicated are to be subjects of finite verbs; cf. 663, 705, 804.

310. Trachalio's greeting to the fishermen is humorously grandiloquent. *-itae* and *-otae* are typical Greek endings for nouns denoting nationality.

311. natio: "tribe" (not "nation", which is *populus*). **quid agitis?** and *ut valetis?* were common phrases for "How do you do?", "How's life?" For the second Trachalio facetiously substitutes *ut peritis?*

312. aequomst: sc. *perire.* **siti:** ablative.

313. As the line stands, there is hiatus after *ecquem* and after *dum*. But the MSS text is confused. **expedite:** imperative.

314. facie: "appearance" rather than "face"; cf. 1155.

315. duceret: for the subjunctive, cf. 320.

317-18. Cf. note on 125.

317. ad: "in the fashion of". **Silanum:** Silenus was the drunken old companion of Bacchus.

320. duceret: on the subjunctive, cf. note on 129.

321. cum . . . natus of course belongs inside the *qui* clause.

323. profecto: cf. 304. **nullus:** cf. 143 and note.

325. data verba: *verba dare* was colloquial Latin for "cheat"; cf. 996. **abit:** i.e. *abiit.* **exulatum:** supine.

327. sceleris semen: a term of abuse for Labrax; cf. 1098, *scelerum caput.*

328. ilico: cf. 62 and note. **opperiar:** "that I should wait for": *ut* is not needed. Cf. pp. 43-4.

329-30. eädem hanc . . . exquisivero: Plautus begins with two accusatives, as if *rogabo* was to follow: *hanc* by a gesture indicates the inmate of the temple. Then, to specify the Priestess

125

NOTES

more precisely, he breaks off the sentence, and constructs a new one. Or *eādem* may be an adverb, "at the same time", "by the way". **Veneriá:** light syllable at the mid-verse pause.

ACT II, SCENE iii. *Trachalio and Ampelisca meet, with mutual delight. Each hears the other's story; and Ampelisca adds the information that Palaestra has, in the wreck, lost the box of baby-trinkets by which she had hoped one day to discover her parents. Finally Trachalio goes in to console Palaestra, and Ampelisca goes to the farm-house for water.*

Though nothing much happens in this scene, it is important in the play's structure. It brings together the girls and Trachalio who is to be in some sort their champion, and so prepares for Acts III and IV. For the same purpose it gives us our first news of the vidulus, *on which the plot will turn. It also conveniently fills in our knowledge of the night's events. But observe that the dramatist (probably Plautus owes this to Diphilus) is careful to spare us a second account of the girls' adventures after they got ashore, and does this naturally and unostentatiously: in some plays such problems are solved more crudely, e.g. Pseudolus 720-1:* horum caussa haec agitur spectatorum fabula; hi sciunt, qui hic adfuerunt; vobis post narravero. *"This play is for the amusement of the spectators: they know, because they were here; I'll tell you later".*

The lively banter of the slaves carries the scene well, and there is also room for business: Trachalio whirls Ampelisca round in a dance at 352, is perhaps allowed a kiss at 363, and nearly gets his ears boxed at 374. The meeting at 332-6 is pleasantly symmetrical; gestures and movements, at opposite sides of the stage, should match, as the words do.

332-3. quoia ad auris vox mi advolavit?: The language is mock-tragic. For *quoia* see 229 and note.

337. quid agi' tu?: cf. 311 and note. But Ampelisca answers, by giving *ago* a more precise sense, *aetatem hau malam male,* i.e. "I am leading an innocent life in misfortune", "I'm having a bad time, though I'm not a bad girl". **melius ominare** (*ominare* is imperative of a deponent): "God forbid!", "Don't say that!".

338. verum: "the truth", neuter of the adjective.

339. tuos = *tuus*. **amabo:** cf. 249 and note; so again in 343.

126

heia: the ejaculation (otherwise *eia*) has two distinct uses: one is an exhortation to action, the other expresses incredulity, as here: "Come off it!"

340. neque . . . ullus: cf. 143, *nullus*, and note.

341. non est meum: "It (telling the truth) is not a habit of mine." A facetious claim to rascality is conventional among the slaves of comedy.

342. quam mox: "always takes the present, not future, tense, *e.g.* 1227, 1412" (Sonnenschein).

343. nempe: cf. 268 and note. **rem divinam:** cf. 130 and note.

344. certe always has in it something of the meaning of "at least"; *certo* (351) has not.

347. hariolare (second singular present indicative): "You guess right!"

348. quid tu agis . . . ?: This, unlike 337, is a request for information; Ampelisca had been waiting for it, and takes the chance to impress Trachalio with her story: she begins it with full solemnity.

349. orbas governs *auxilique opumque*.

351. Hiatus at the mid-verse pause, and again at 354. And very likely the last words of this line scan *ĕrĭ mĕĭ amīca*.

356-7. voluit . . . imposivit: indirect question, despite the indicative. *Posivi*, not *posui*, is Plautus's regular form (Sonnenschein).

359. nec . . . nullus: the double negative, strengthening, not cancelling, is "quite Plautine" (Sonnenschein); as it is good Greek, though bad Latin, it may be due to translation. **profecto:** cf. 304.

360. bolum: is a Greek word, a "throw" at dice. Note: 1. Gambling and drinking terms in Latin are largely borrowed from Greek; 2. the remark would be more pointed in Greek, with the double meaning of "cast", referring also to shipwreck. Cf. 373, where Plautus has found the joke easier to translate.

362. magnis poculis: ablative, though the English would say "to".

363. datum: sc. *esse*. **anancaeo:** another Greek word, meaning "under compulsion", obviously a technical term for having to drink up a big bowl without stopping for breath. **ut ego amo te!** "Lovely girl!" The literal "How I love you!" is misleadingly passionate; for although Trachalio is to marry Ampelisca in the end, the Latin need mean no more than "Thank you!" But the phrase is ambiguous, and Ampelisca perhaps permits him a kiss at this point.

364. mulsa: "sweet". Plautus refers frequently and appreciatively to the drink *mulsum,* sweet wine.

365. scibis faxo: "You will know; I will make you"; i.e. "I'll tell you". For the syntax, cf. p. 43.

370. iactatae: sc. *sumus*; cf. 205, *compotita*; 453, *ratae.* **exemplis plurumis:** "in all sorts of ways". "Examples" would be misleading; cf. 594; but at 620 "example" is appropriate.

372. novi: verb. **quamvis** here only modifies *fastidiosus:* translate "ever so".

373. The duties of the aedile, as of his Greek counterpart the *agoranomus,* included the inspection of markets, and he could throw out sub-standard goods; hence the joke, picking up *iactatae* of 370.

374. vae + dative: the conventional translation, "Woe to" is inappropriate; the expression is colloquial and impatient: "Damn your eyes!" or some such phrase. **tuo:** sc. *vae capiti tuo*; "Same to you!" Neither of the two is really angry, as the affectionate *mea* shows.

376. faxere is Sonnenschein's emendation, to mend metre and sense: this infinitive is not found elsewhere, but cf. *faxo* at 365.

377. promittam: for the syntax, cf. note on *opperiar,* 328.

379. faceret . . . servaret: past jussive subjunctives; "What was he to do?"—"He should have kept watch". Similarly *esset* in 380.

381. ut . . . ita: "in proportion as . . . , so . . ." The implication here is "Not at all". **multi** is genitive of value.

382. scin tu? (*scin = scisne*): This phrase introduces what is to follow: "Look here!" or "You know". **it** is probably perfect (Marx). **lavatum:** supine. The antecedent of *qui* is the owner of the clothes: "A man who . . ."

384. quippe qui: "inasmuch as". To judge from other Plautine examples, *qui* is the conjunction, not the pronoun. **falsust:** "he is unaware"; so *Aulularia* 123, *hau falsa sum,* with accusative and infinitive, where the meaning "am deceived" is inappropriate.

385. quem opservat: relative clause, unlike *quem opservet* in the preceding line. **qui:** cf. 98 and note.

386. duce: imperative; to be avoided in classical composition: cf. 951, *dice.* **ubi est** might be punctuated separately as a question. **i sane:** "All right, go!" *sane* with imperatives implies that the recipient of the command is itching to carry it out; cf. 855. Here there is the further implication, "I'm not stopping you, but neither am I coming with you".

387. opprimes: merely "You'll come upon her". Cf. 789, *offendero*, "bump into", similarly used in the weaker sense of "meet".

388. animi: locative case.

389. ei: dative is normal with *adimere*, not ablative or *ab*. **ubique** = *ubi* + *que*, not the adverb *ubique*.

390. qui: instrumental case; sc. *aliquid* as antecedent; similar expressions at 393, 1084, 1110. **noscere:** light syllable at the mid-line pause; cf. 329. **eam** is anticipated from the subject of *perierit*; cf. 244, *me*, and note.

392. copia . . . eiius: "chance to get at it".

394. For antecedent of *quam*, sc. *eam* as subject of *servire*.

395. eam . . . abiisse: the accusative and infinitive depends on *scilicet*.

397. credo: Trachalio is of course merely trying to say something cheerful; but from the dramatist's point of view, it helps to soften the audience's incredulity for the events of Act IV. **id misera maestast:** "This is what she's sad about"; *id* anticipates the following accusative and infinitive.

398. eorum: sc. *crepundiorum*, though they have not yet been mentioned; we find out about them in detail in Act IV. **istoc magis:** "all the more"; *istoc* is ablative. **usus factost:** on *usus*, see 100 and note: *facto* is superfluous, literally, "there is need of this done".

399. eam . . . eam: the pun is not subtle, but Plautus despises none; he uses it again at 519. **animi:** cf. 388.

401. qui: the antecedent is *multos*, object of *decepisse*.

402. aequos: nominative singular.

403. nisi quid vis and *num quid vis?* are polite formulas for leave-taking. **eas:** verb.

404. proxumo: probably neuter.

405. verbis suis: "in her name".

406. quemquam: feminine.

408. honeste: cf. 196, *honor*, and note.

410. ex se: cf. note on 47; but *se* is more defensible here as virtual indirect speech, in the Priestess's mind.

411. eapse: old form of *ipsa*.

412. morae: predicative dative.

NOTES

Aст II, Scene iv. *Sceparnio, who answers Ampelisca's knocking, is much taken with her; it requires all her tact to avoid his amorous advances and at the same time persuade him to get her the water.*

Metre: seven-beat trochaics. On the change, Beare says, "The door bursts open and the angry Sceparnio appears with an explosive trochaic line".

415. hem: cf. 237 and note. **mulierem:** exclamatory accusative.

418. item ut adfectam: "like a sick person", i.e. with all possible comfort (and in bed?). **qui:** neuter of the pronoun instrumental case. After *mulierem*, if this is the correct reading, some verb is to be supplied; I fear, an unseemly one.

419. sed quid ais? usually leads up to a question or request: either Sceparnio translates his request at once into action, or, if he was going to make it verbally, it is interrupted by Ampelisca's protest.

421. ut: exclamatory; "What a ... !". **heia:** cf. note on 339; again the second sense of the word.

422. The word *subaquilus*, which meant "darkish", "brunette", had nothing to do with eagles, but sounded as though it had; hence Sceparnio's blunder about "vultures".

424. pollucta: from *pollucere*, "dish up" (as a feast for the gods—the worshippers, as usual, would get the leavings); *pago* is dative. **potin** = *potisne*: "Is it possible?", "Would you mind ... ?".

425. sic is illustrated by action. **bellam belle:** *figura etymologica.*

426. deliciae: dative singular; in classical Latin the word is always plural.

427. quam ob rem: "About the reason why ...". **aias ... neges:** equivalent to imperatives; cf. 1331.

428-9. ornatus is noun: in the former line it means the waterpot; in the second it is *sensu obsceno*.

430. Ampelisca ignores line 429, and, to discourage any further ambiguity, speaks as nearly in words of one syllable as Latin permits. **hinc** is to be taken with *haec sacerdos*, "the priestess who lives here".

431. basilicus: "Venus" was a good throw at dice; *basilicus*, "the king's", was even better: another Greek gambling term; it also occurs at *Curculio* 359. Apart from meaning that his will prevailed over Venus and her priestess's, Sceparnio has no reason for claiming to be *basilicus*.

NOTES

432. nostro . . . periclo: "by our own effort", rather than "peril"; cf. 1393.

434. gravare: 2nd singular present indicative deponent. **hostis hosti** in the older sense of "stranger", "foreigner".

435. civis, feminine; **civi,** masculine.

436. immo etiam: "Oh yes, I will...". Ampelisca in desperation decides to let Sceparnio have his way, up to a point, and changes her tone accordingly.

437. salvos sum: cf. 172, *salva res,* and note.

438. cedo: cf. 243 and note.

439. ecferre: old form of *efferre.*

440. quid: "Why . . . ?", with *demoratam.*

ACT II, SCENE V. (*Technically the new scene only begins at 458, with the entry of a character, and after the stage has been left empty; practically it begins at 450, as the metre shows.*) *Left alone, Ampelisca catches sight of the detested Labrax and Charmides, and runs away into the temple. Sceparnio, returning, at first thinks she is playing hide-and-seek; then to his disgust, he finds he can only get rid of the temple water-pot by carrying it into the temple.*

METRE: six-beat iambics. Beare notes the dramatic effect of the sudden change, as the figure of Labrax casts a blight over the scene.

453. "That's more trouble alive than we had reckoned on"; **ratae** = *ratae sumus,* cf. 370 *iactatae.*

457. ita res suppetit subitaria: "so (sc. and no more) the emergency affords"; i.e. "that's all I can do in the circumstances".

461. praefiscine: "be it said without offence", "in a good hour be it spoken", "touch wood!". The word (derived from *fascinum*) was used to avert divine jealousy or the evil eye, when something boastful was said; it might be accompanied by various gestures, the least offensive of which was to spit three times on oneself.

462. nequam: "naughty"; this is "merely an expression of complacency . . . Sceparnio is filled with self-satisfaction at having fallen in love" (Sonnenschein). **utpote qui** is like *quippe qui,* equivalent to a causal clause.

463. em: "Here you are!", "Take this!". The word is an old imperative of *emo* (in its old sense, *take*), and must not be

131

confused with *hem.* **belliata:** "'Beautified' is a vile phrase!"—
Polonius in *Hamlet.*

465. sis is contraction of *si vis* (it is not from *esse*); see note on
249, *amabo.*

467, 469. etiam is not to be translated, either as "even" or
as "also"; it is merely a colloquial expletive in questions: here
the tone is impatient, but at 1275, 1277, merely lively.

468. commodule meliust: "Better not go too far!" Some
vague prolate infinitive dependent on *melius*, and modified by
commodule is to be understood. The meaning of *commodulus*,
diminutive of *commodus*, "suitable", is shown in *Miles Gloriosus*,
750, *commodulum opsona, ne magno sumptu:* "Do your buying
within reason, don't be extravagant." **tandem vero:** "Really
though".

469. ubi . . . gentium: "where in the world"; *gentium* is partitive
genitive.

470. ludos: "a laughing-stock".

473. exhibeat negotium: "make trouble".

478. eapse: cf. 411. **quoiia:** cf. 229 and note.

ACT II, SCENE vi. *Labrax, the* leno, *and his partner Charmides,
wet, cold, and dispirited, exchange recriminations.*

*The scene introduces us to the two villains, and allows us to get to
know them and to enjoy their discomfort. It is on the one hand a
companion piece to the scene in which we meet and pity the other
castaways, Palaestra and Ampelisca, and, on the other, balances, by
the savage wrangling of the rascals, the friendly chaff of Trachalio
and Ampelisca.*

METRE: six-beat iambics.

485. qui homo: "whoever".

486. aetatem: "life"; cf. 337, 1346.

488. ad hoc exemplum: "like this".

489-90. quae voluisti: Since this gives the reason for *lepida es*,
in classical Latin we should expect a subjunctive.

492. eccum: cf. 309, *eccos.* The accusative is used even when
the person indicated is to be subject of a verb, cf. 803. **quo,
malum:** "where the devil . . . ?". For the expletive *malum* in
impatient questions, cf. 945.

495. perbiteres: *bitere*, equivalent to *ire*, was an old verb,
which dropped out of use soon after Plautus's time. If the imper-
fect subjunctive of *perbiteres* is pressed, it will mean "had been

perishing", and on the other hand, *cubuissem* in 493 will mean, not "lain", but "gone to bed".

500. tui similis: i.e. bringing bad luck.

501. malam fortunam: in apposition to *te*.

502. Literally, "Why was there to me a listening to you?", i.e. "What possessed me to listen to you?". In Plautine colloquial Latin, a verbal noun in *-io* often takes the same construction as the verb from which it is derived, especially in indignant questions; cf. *hinc* and *in navem* in the next line, and *Curculio 626, quid tibi istum tactio est?* **scelesto:** cf. note on 22. It might agree either with *mihi* or with *tibi*.

504. A mere hyperbole, I think, but Sonnenschein says, "i.e. Palaestra, who had been sold to Plesidippus".

506. scelus: concrete, "rascal", in apposition to *te*. **parta** is in form the perfect participle of *parere*, but in use it serves as the participle of *parare*, in the sense of "got", leaving *paratus* for the sense "prepared" (though *paratus* can mean "got" too, cf. 38).

508. scelestiorem: again see note on 22. **cenam cenavi:** *figura etymologica.*

509. Both Thyestes and Tereus in mythology were tricked into eating their own children. The unpleasant allusion is too much for Labrax's still queasy stomach.

510. animo male fit (or *est*) is a common phrase for "I feel ill". The belief that holding a patient's head would ease vomiting is illustrated by a vase-painting.

511. "I only hope you vomit up your lungs." The Latin circumlocution is chosen for the sake of *figura etymologica.*

516. est quod habeas: "There is reason for you to feel".

517. ex insulso salsum: a more explicit version of the joke in 301.

518. quin: cf. 122. **in maxumam malam crucem:** One would expect *malam crucem* to become ⌣⌣⌣⌣, by Breves Breviantes: since this shortening has not occurred, we can presume this phrase, and a similar one at 775, was pronounced with slow emphasis.

519. eas (verb); **eas** (demonstrative pronoun): cf. the similar pun in 399. **easque res agebam commodum:** "I was just thinking about (*or* going to say) that".

521. Here and in similar passages in Plautus, MSS vary between *multo tanto* and *multo tanta*. If *tanta* is right, it is presumably an adverb like *ea, hac, istac, qua,* and so on. In any case, the expression means "this much", looking forward to the reason which Charmides gives in the next line.

523-4. Perhaps a parody of a couplet in Greek or Latin tragedy, for the verse is unusually regular and dignified. A modern stage setting may include the bulrushes which Labrax apostrophises.

525-6. ad velitationem: *velitatio* is "skirmishing", the activity of the light-armed troops called *velites*; the word was also used of verbal skirmishing, "wrangling", but there seems to be no point in that here. Apparently the point is simply in *corusca*, comparing Charmides's jerky utterance to the rapid movements of the *velites*; it does not seem to us a very witty point, but perhaps we should appreciate it more if we knew more about the training of the *velites*.

528-38. These lines contain, according to the MSS, an unusual number of hiatus which are not explicable on normal grounds. The suggestion was made by Seyffert, and adopted by Sonnenschein and in this edition, that chattering teeth filled up the missing syllables.

530. ita: cf. note on 87. **praehibet:** cf. 138 and note.

534. The onomatopoeia of *aqu-aqu-aqua* makes Seyffert's suggestion of stammering particularly persuasive here.

535. me pro manduco locem: "hire myself out as the manducus". Manducus was a traditional character in the "Atellan" farces, whose mask had huge movable jaws; see Beare, pp. 131-2.

537. The MSS give the unmetrical and seemingly pointless *lavisse*. *Elavare*, intransitive, like its doublet *eluere* (579) has the colloquial meaning of "be cleaned out, robbed". Even so, the remark does not lead to any very clever repartee in the next line; so perhaps the true reading is lost.

541. illi: adverb. Note the tense of *esse*, "that there was": *promittere* does not *necessarily* take a future infinitive.

542. conruere: "shovel together", since "dig" was one of the meanings of the verb *ruo*; the noun *rutrum* means a spade.

543. postulabas: cf. 17 and note. Here it actually has the construction of verbs of hoping.

549-50. On the effect of the diminutives, cf. note on 52.

550. oppido: adverb.

551. vel: "if you like". It was originally an imperative of *velle*: hence are derived its two main uses, viz. "even", to give an extreme example (cf. 566), and "or" in unrestrained choice, see 582 and note. **consociare** is usually transitive, here intransitive.

555. quo ab: this order of words is normal with two-syllable prepositions, but not with monosyllabic.

558. qui: instrumental case of the relative pronoun; the antecedent is *lingua*.

ACT II, SCENE vii. *Labrax learns from Sceparnio that the girls are in the temple, and dashes in to recapture them. Charmides vainly begs Sceparnio for shelter.*

METRE: eight-beat trochees.

559. quid: sc. *est.*

563. istaec: nominative plural feminine.

565. nempe: on its meaning, see note on 268; on its scansion, p. 31.

566. vel: see note on 551. Sceparnio, who is actually of a distinctly amorous disposition, represents himself as one unlikely to be stirred by female charms. **amare possum, si . . . siem:** the infinitive with the modal verb *possum* is regarded as equivalent to a conditional subjunctive: this is normal classical Latin.

568. mi Charmides: "Joy makes Labrax affectionate" (Sonnenschein).

570. mavelim: old form of *malim.*

571. loci depends on *aliquid.*

576. tēgillum: it was made of rushes; perhaps "mat", rather than "hood" which the dictionaries give, and used as farmlabourers use a sack over their shoulders against the rain. **eccillud** = *ecce* + *illud.* To judge from the pronoun, the mat was not within Sceparnio's reach; perhaps he points in to the farmhouse door, which was left open after line 414.

578. dato: imperative. **eho** is used in "vehement questions, commands, remonstrances" (Smith): "Here, I say!" "Hey!" **an te paenitet:** "Aren't you content . . . ?" As Sonnenschein says, "Charmides is dissatisfied with the proposed exchange of garments."

579. elavi . . . eluas: see note on 537.

580. eluas tu an exunguare: "washed out or oiled out", "soaked or soaped". Oiling was part of the routine at the baths, but the compound *exunguere* is coined by Plautus merely to correspond to *eluere.* **ciccum non interduim:** i.e. "I couldn't care less"; *interduim* is an old subjunctive of *interdare*; cf. *duis,* 1368.

NOTES

581. nisi si is pleonastic but idiomatic: "except".

582. vel: cf. note on 551. It is used here to produce an effect of indifference; Charmides may do any or all of these things, *if he pleases*; Sceparnio could not care less.

583. barbarum hospitem: An infinitive such as *venire* is to be supplied; the accusative and infinitive depends on *nil moror*: the latter is a colloquial understatement for "I don't want": so, too, at 852, 1248. Charmides, though a Sicilian, is not, so far as we know, non-Greek: Sceparnio is offensive. **litium:** from *lis*.

584. abeis: old form of *abis*. **venalis ductitavit:** i.e. "he has been a slave-dealer". (*Venalis* is accusative plural.)

587. quam potavi is a compendious expression for "which I got by drinking". **praeter animi quam lubuit sententiam** is a compound of two phrases, both of which mean "contrary to my inclinations", viz. *praeter quam lubuit* and *praeter animi sententiam*.

588-91. Charmides combines and confuses two similes: 1. Neptune, as *arbiter bibendi* at a party, orders the guests to mix their wine and drink it up—the same figure as at lines 362-3; and 2. Neptune, as a physician, prescribes a dose of salts to be taken in wine. *Suffundere* was a technical term for mixing a dose; thus at *Curculio* 160, after the old duenna has said, *mane, suffundam aquolam* ("pour in a little water"), to keep the pivot of the door from squeaking), an onlooker says, *viden ut anus . . . medicinam facit?* A link between the two similes was that cheap Greek wines were mixed with sea-water, as to-day they are mixed with resin.

589. itaque: not "therefore", but "and in this way". **alvom prodi:** "that our constipation would be relieved". Plautus is often content to use accusative and present infinitive (or even the bare infinitive) with *sperare*, especially in the passive, where Latin had no genuine future infinitive.

590. pergeret: on the tense, cf. 495 and note.

ACT III

ACT III, SCENE i. *Daemones relates in soliloquy a strange dream which he had the night before. The dream obviously anticipates the events to come; but the practical purpose of the scene is to give an actor time to change from Charmides to Trachalio.*

METRE: six-beat iambics, appropriately quiet between the lively trochees which have preceded and which are to follow again at Trachalio's entry.

593. miris modis: on the plural, see 147 and note. **ludos faciunt hominibus:** *ludos facere alicui* means to give somebody trouble, "play him up", cf. *Truculentus* 759, *ego tibi ludos faciam clamore in via* ("make a scene outside the house"). Contrast *ludos facere aliquem*, "make somebody a laughing-stock", e.g. *Rudens* 470.

594. exemplis: on the meaning, see 370 and note.

597. inscitum: "uncanny" (Sonnenschein).

599a. The palimpsest has traces of a line which the other MSS omit.

600. eas: the swallows, perhaps mentioned in the missing line.

602. scalas . . . utendas: A gerundive implies a transitive verb, taking the accusative: Plautus does use an accusative sometimes with *utor*; but even Cicero uses its gerundive.

603a. Again the palimpsest has traces of a missing line.

604. Daemones's dream-mythology is not quite correct: Progne (Procne) was indeed turned into a swallow, but her sister Philomela became a nightingale; they were daughters of Pandion, king of Athens.

605. ago cum: "plead with", "argue with", a regular classical usage.

606. nimio goes with *ferocior.* **fieri:** historic infinitive. Or it could be punctuated to depend on the following *videtur.*

612. coniecturam: this was the technical name for interpreting dreams. There were even professional *coniectores* (*Curculio* 249).

613. meae viciniae: locative case.

NOTES

Act III, Scene ii. *Trachalio rushes out of the temple, bawling for help, and it is some time before Daemones can get any coherent statement from him. Once he does understand that the sanctuary of the temple has been violated and the priestess herself assaulted, he summons two muscular assistants and goes in to effect a rescue, while Trachalio offers encouragement from without.*

Trachalio's opening speech is a parody of tragic and oratorical diction: observe its heavy alliteration.

Metre: eight-beat trochaics: on the effect, see p. 24.

615. Pro: the interjection. **Cyrenenses** is adjective; **populares,** "fellow countrymen" (cf. 605, 740, 1080), is the noun. Even apart from being a slave, it is not clear what claim Trachalio had to be a Cyrenaean: his master was an Athenian (42).

617. pessum: see 395 and note.

619. nobilis (accusative plural): not "noble", but "famous", even "infamous"; the adjective is derived from *nosco.*

621. facite . . . liceat: On the omission of *ut*, see p. 43. **vi** depends on *victo; victo,* masculine dative, depends on *liceat.*

624. Supply *eis* as antecedent to *qui.*

625. suom . . . caput: "themselves"; cf. 886, *isti capiti,* "yourself".

626. pervenat = *perveniat:* "perhaps from an old present *venere"* (Sonnenschein).

627. per governs *haec genua;* but in urgent appeals a confused order is common; *per* is put first, and the word that it governs follows any time later; e.g. *per te deos oro* is normal.

628. quin with imperative has much the same meaning as *quin* with interrogative indicative (as, *e.g.,* in 122).

629. si speras: "if (*or* as) you hope". The idea of this formula is, "If you do this, I will pray the gods to reward you by granting your dearest wish, which I know is . . ." A comic turn is given to it here by the assumption that dearest to all Cyrenaean hearts is the *silphium* crop.

630. sirpe represents an early Latin attempt at pronouncing and spelling the Greek word σίλφιον, *silphium.* The exact connection between *sirpe, laserpicium,* and *magydaris* (633) is not clear ("*laserpicium* was probably a product of the plant *silphium,* . . . *magydaris* probably a name of the seed or seed-vessel", Sonnenschein); but anyway *silphium* or *laserpicium* "was grown in great abundance in the neighbourhood of Cyrene, and was the principal source of its wealth: hence it was frequently represented on its coins" (Sonnenschein). From it was produced asafoetida, which was used both in cooking and as a drug.

631. exagogam: "export", a Greek word, presumably known through international use in trade. **Capuam,** "to Capua", depends on the phrase *eventuram exagogam*, as though it were a verb "that it will be exported".

632. ut sit is a wish, as a variant of the *si speras* formula; it is not the object of *oro et quaeso*, which is *ut ne te pigeat* in 634.

633. magydarim: see note on 630.

634. quod: "as to what . . ."

635-8. *Daemones, brandishing his stick, now makes a parody of Trachalio's appeal, equally full of alliteration.*

636. Elm-wood was the traditional material of sticks used for beating; cf. *Epidicus* 27, *lictores duo, duo ulmei fasces* ("two lictors, two bundles of elm-wood"), and 626, *pingent pigmentis ulmeis* ("they'll paint me with paints of stick"), both being facetious references to a flogging. **virgidemiam:** coined from *virga,* "a stick", and *vindemia,* "vintage".

638. negoti depends equally upon *istuc* and *quid*. Hiatus at mid-line, while Daemones flourishes his stick.

639. qui: adverb.

640. te: ablative, depending on *digna*.

641. praevortere: imperative passive or deponent.

642. tui, like *mea* in 259, vanishes in scansion.

643. insignite: adverb; cf. 1097.

644. tum: "and then", i.e. "moreover".

646. Hiatus after *violare*, at mid-line; as Daemones gasps with horror.

647. is: dative plural. **iniqui** depends on *quid*.

650. parvi: genitive of value; cf. 697.

652. legerupa or *legirupa* is a rather rare word in Latin; and from its appearance here and at *Pseudolus* 364 merely as one term of abuse in a string of them, I suspect that it had a narrower meaning than the comprehensive and common English term "law-breaker". At line 709 the offence described by *legerupionem* is in fact interference with the right of sanctuary.

654. infortunio: cf. 118 and note. It is ablative, depending on *donabilem*.

655. qui: the antecedent is *hominem* in the previous line; the clause is causal, "Yes, because he . . .", hence the subjunctive *interpresserit*.

656. ite: in this context "come", not "go".

658. illis, emphatic, and with a gesture: "they're over there".

660. Cuttle-fish, like steak, need to be knocked about to soften them before cooking.

661. pugnis pectitur: *pectere* was slang for "beat up"; cf. *Menaechmi* 1017, *pecte pugnis,* and *Captivi* 896, *fusti pectito.* **pugnis:** from *pugnus.*

662. edentaverint depends on *velim;* for the omission of *ut,* see p. 43.

663. eccas: cf. 309, *eccos,* and note.

ACT III, SCENE iii.   *The girls rush out of the temple in alarm and despair; Trachalio persuades them to take sanctuary at the altar, and promises to defend them.*

METRE of lines 664-81, see Appendix B

The girls' alarm and distress is to be played quite seriously: Trachalio is stirred by it, though he deprecates their wild outbursts. The first twelve lines are usually assigned to Palaestra, but they are more naturally shared by both girls, sometimes speaking together, sometimes in turns.   I take lines 684-6, the thought of suicide, to be the free-born Palaestra's, like line 681; to Ampelisca I give lines 680 (her relations with Trachalio are warmer than Palaestra's), 683 (as being more matter-of-fact), and the rather flippant 699-701, perhaps with the two lines before.   Finally, at line 704, Trachalio's lewd joke brings the play back from tragedy to comedy.

664. nunc id est: "now's the time . . .". *id* anticipates the *quom* clause, just as in line 680 it anticipates the *ne* clause.   The genitives *omnium,* etc., depend on *viduitas.*

667. ingredi persequamur: "attempt to go"; Sonnenschein quotes Horace Odes I, xxiii, 10, *te persequor frangere.*

669. inportunitas is a stronger word than the English "importunity".

671. quin: "Yes, and . . .", going beyond what has just been said.   Compare and contrast *immo* (*e.g.* at 436, 741, 1305), which *corrects* what has just been said.   The old-fashioned translations, *quin* = "Nay more", *immo* = "Nay rather", are still useful memoranda.

672. reppulit, propulit: the two cognate words are used without a conjunction, one capping the other, for rhetorical emphasis; cf. 839, *vi violentia.*   Perhaps here one girl speaks one, and the other comes in with the other. **modis:** on the plural, see 147, note.

673. intumo: not that there was more than one statue; but because it was right inside the temple, the sacrilege seemed worse.

675. par: "right", taking accusative and infinitive. Supply "anything" for *melius* to agree with.

676. For the omission of the *et* which would normally connect the two adjectives *malis* and *miseris*, cf. *Captivi* 406, *rebus in dubiis, egenis*, and see note on line 23: it is a different effect from that aimed at in *reppulit propulit* above.

677. qui: cf. 98 and note.

678. nam quis = *quisnam*; *nam* does not mean "for", but adds urgency to the question: cf. 687, *nam . . . unde.*

679. respexis: for this form of the future perfect, cf. 365, *faxo*; also 731, 776.

680. me vide: "Watch me!", i.e. "Trust me!", a colloquial phrase. **si modo** may be a wish-clause, "Oh, if only . . ."; or we may supply as apodosis *bono animo sim*: the general effect is much the same. **id:** see note on 664; it is subject of *liceat* (neuter pronouns as subjects of impersonal verbs are not uncommon).

681. quae vis: "This force"; *quae* is connecting relative. **vim mi adferam ipsa** depends on *adigit*; for the omission of *ut*, cf. 662 and see pp. 43-4.

682-705. METRE: seven-beat iambics.

682. nunciam is merely *nunc iam*, but scans as three syllables.

683. re: "in action", as opposed to *verbo* or *oratione*. **praesidi** depends on *quid*. **acta haec res est:** "all is lost"; so, commonly, *actum est*: here there is a word-play between *re* and *res*.

684. quam = *potius quam*: for the omission of the comparative, cf. 1114.

685. venit in mentem (mihi) + genitive: "I remember", "I think of".

686. diem hunc acerbum: exclamatory accusative.

687. nam: cf. 678 and note.

688. hic . . . istaec: Trachalio has moved towards the altar; the girls are some way from it, but (to judge from *hic* in the next line) near the temple door.

690. With **amplexae** and **abreptae** supply *sumus*; cf. 205, *compotita* for *compotita sum*.

NOTES

691, 692 hinc: i.e. from Trachalio's position on or behind the altar.

692. hanc...haec: the altar is to be their camp and ramparts, almost a hendiadys for "your camp's ramparts"; *haec*, referring to the altar, is attracted (normally) into the gender and number of *moenia*. The word *haec* is missing in the MSS; if they are right, then, for the scansion of the half-line ending *Veneriă*, see p. 23; and in that case Trachalio describes himself as the wall, *moenia hinc ego*; but surely he is part of the garrison.

693. praesidio Veneris: "under Venus' protection". Though it is often used in the concrete sense of "garrison", *praesidium* is properly abstract.

694. alma: hiatus at this pause.

697. fecerunt . . . parvi: "estimated at a low value", "despised"; cf. 650, **parvi pendit.**

698. fac + subjunctive, with or without *ut*, "take care that". **tua pace:** "by your leave", "under your favour". The phrase was used both in religious and secular contexts, and last century *pace* found its way into English.

699. lautae not only in the sense of respectably dressed and clean (cf. the Priestess's rebuke at 269-71), but also because of the need for *ritual* cleanliness in a religious matter: bloodshed or sexual intercourse, however legitimate, was a disqualification till formal ablution in running water. For the former matter, cf. *Iliad VI*, where Hector will not pour a libation with bloody hands (he has been fighting for his country); for the latter, cf. *Poenulus* 350, *pura sum; comperce, amabo, me attrectare, Agorastocles;* also Exodus XIX. 15, I Samuel XXI. 4. These lines, with their innuendo, are surely not spoken by the virginal Palaestra.

700. id and **idcirco** both refer forward to the *si* clause. **vitio vortas:** "hold it against us"; *vitio* is predicative dative.

701. minus goes with *bene lautum*, and, as often, is virtually a negative.

704. conchas: (*sensu obscoeno*).

705. eccum: cf. 309, *eccos*, and note.

Act III, Scene iv. *Labrax is ejected from the temple by Daemones's servants. A long altercation ensues, Labrax claiming the right to remove his property, and Trachalio claiming that one at least of the girls is a free-born Athenian. This arouses Daemones's*

*sympathy for the girls, and Trachalio goes off to fetch his master,
leaving Labrax to the charge of Daemones and his servants.*

METRE: eight-beat trochaics: once again, as at lines 414 and
615, the change to it marks an explosion into violence.

706. natum belongs inside the *quantum* clause, with *est:* "most
irreligious of all men ever born". Cf. the similar line, *Pseudolus*,
351, *quid ais, quantum terram tetigit hominum peiiurissume?* and
Catullus III 2, *quantum est hominum venustiorum.*
707. vos is addressed to the girls; **sessum** is supine.
708. iube may be addressed to Trachalio or to one of the slaves.
prope: sc. to the girls. For the absence of *ut* with the indirect
command, cf. p. 43.
709. legerupio only occurs here, and was perhaps coined by
Plautus from *legerupa* for the occasion. It is surely intended as an
abstract noun, though Smith gives it as masculine and meaning
the same as *legerupa*. On the meaning, cf. note on 652.
nobis is dative. **cum dis:** "with the blessing of the gods", i.e.
"with impunity". **postulas:** cf. 17 and note.
710. *For stage business, Labrax may come on with scraps of chalk
in his mouth, and appear to spit broken teeth; if he has a little red
grease-paint in his palm, he can make his nose seem to bleed; and if
he is careful to show only one side of his face until this line, he may
now turn his head and reveal a black eye. What Plautus's actors
did, we can only guess.* **iniqua** is emphatic and predicative:
"This is an outrage". **cum pretio tuo:** i.e. "and you shall pay
for it".
712. eripīs, as though 4th conjugation; cf. line 299, *aggredimur,*
line 675 *moriri.* **habe iudicem:** on arbitration, see pp. 39-40.
713. de: "from" (not "about"). **opulentum:** it is assumed
that a wealthy man will also be respectable.
714. nive = *ni + ve. si* and *ni* (*nisi*), rather than an indirect
question, was the regular way of stating the point at issue in a
dispute; cf. 753, 1381. *si* states what the speaker denies,
nisi what he claims to be true.
715. neu here = *nive.* This clause is facetiously added to the
terms of the dispute.
717. non hodie isti rei auspicavi: i.e. "I have no intention
of...", "I've got better things to do than...". On *hodie* see note
on 177.

NOTES

719-20. Assertion of ownership, and formal laying of hands on property claimed, would be the procedure for opening a trial.

720. agedum: for appended *-dum*, see on *primumdum*, 32.

721-2. Trachalio delivers his threats secure in the presence of the *lorarii*. **pugnis:** cf. 661.

723. liceat: indignant deliberative question: "Am I not to be allowed . . . ?".

724. ita est lex apud nos . . . : Daemones, apparently about to explain the correct legal procedure, is interrupted by Labrax.

725. foras: cf. 172 and note.

726. huc: "here", i.e., "into my hand", with a suitable gesture. **arido argento:** "hard cash". The epithet, merely an emphatic expletive, is chosen almost at random; cf. 833, *a crasso infortunio*.

727. Not a purely absurd notion, though this little country shrine could not be staffed like the wealthy and infamous one at Corinth. See p. 34.

728. di tibi argentum?: sc. *dent*. **adeo:** see note on 36; the first sense.

729. modo . . . ioculo: "even as a joke"; cf. *Mostellaria* 923, *egone te ioculo modo ausim dicto aut facto fallere?* *ioculo* is ablative.

730. ita . . . ornatum: "in such a state"; cf. 187.

731. vos adeo: the *lorarii* are addressed. **adeo** as in 728. **exoculassitis:** old future or future perfect; cf. 679, 776, *respexis, occeptassit*.

732. murteta literally means "myrtle-groves"; here apparently "bunches of myrtle-sprays", tied up by rushes: in **virgis circumvinciam** a thrashing is threatened with canes as pliant as the rushes tied round the bunches.

733. proportas presumably means "put forward", as a grievance; but the word is not found elsewhere. **flagiti flagrantia:** literally "blaze of villainy", i.e. "outrageous scoundrel". The Latin metaphor of *flagrare* is not always similar to the English "blaze": one of its meanings is "to be an extreme specimen" of such and such a bad quality or action. E.g. *consules flagrabant invidia* ("had a very bad press") and *quae domesticis flagitiis flagrabat* ("the scene of shocking immorality"); in the latter example Cicero, like Plautus, seizes the chance of word-play.

734. inclementer dicere: cf. 114.

736. numqui: *-qui* is the indefinite adverb.

737. Though *ex germana Graecia* depends grammatically on *esse* in the previous line, what Trachalio means is "and they *are* genuine Greeks".

144

NOTES

742-3. *Daemones, even as he stares at Palaestra, speaks to his long lost daughter as far away, and present only to his imagination. The dramatic effect is obvious.*

744. With *tanta esset* the regular apodosis would be *si viveret* "if she were alive". Naturally her father is unwilling to use that hopeless phrase, and changes it to the open condition, *si vivit*.

745. quoiiae: the old relative possessive adjective; cf. the interrogative at 229, 332: the antecedent is *domino*.

747. servitutem serviant: cf. note on 2 *civis civitate*. **recte:** Labrax means "regularly", "legally"; but the word had various senses, which could be used for quibbling, *e.g.* Terence, *Andria* 955, *Pater, non recte vinctust.—Haud ita iussi.* ("Father, he isn't rightly tied up", i.e. "shouldn't be".—"That wasn't what I ordered", i.e. "I told them to make a good job of it").

748. feles virginalis: not "virginal cat"! *feles* did not suggest to the Romans female spitefulness, but theft; and the phrase means a thief who steals girls: at *Persa* 750 Plautus uses the similar *feles virginaria.* **parentibus** is dative of disadvantage, depending on *sublectos*, "stolen *from*".

750. huic, two syllables; cf. 39, 1342. **alterae:** in classical Latin *alteri.* **profecto:** adverb. The sentence is concessive: Trachalio was going to say, "I don't know where this one comes from, but I do know that the other is a true Athenian"; but in altercation with Labrax he loses the gist.

751. nisi: "except that".

752. tuae istae sunt?: Perhaps Labrax is trying to ignore Trachalio, and addresses the question to Daemones. If it is addressed to Trachalio, who obviously could not own them, it merely means, "This is not your business". **verior:** the question of veracity might be settled by inspecting the two backs, on the ground that the bigger rogue's would show the more whip-marks. Trachalio implies that Labrax has been subject to whippings, i.e. a slave.

753. offerrumentas is only found here; but since *ferrumen* means "cement" or "solder", *offerrumentas* presumably means "joints", "marks of repairing".

755. quando: "when"; not used with temporal clauses in classical Latin.

756-8. The *ni*-clauses, though they are meant to have a legal ring, are not like the clauses in 714-15, virtual indirect questions depending on the previous line, but have their own conditional apodoses, *tum ego te . . .*, and *quid caussae est . . . ?* The latter of these is comically the reverse of what would be expected, for one would expect "then you may flog me". **ad saturitatem**: "till I'm tired".

760. The main clause of this sentence is (I think) *adducam* in 761; *abducam* depends on *votas* (= *vetas*), "forbid me to remove". The subjunctive with *veto*, though uncommon, is not unknown; cf. Horace *Odes* III, ii, 26-8, *vetabo sub isdem sit trabibus*, "I will not let him be under the same rafters". The line is usually punctuated as a complete sentence, with *abducam* as the main verb; as such it seems pointless.

761. Venus, according to mythology, was married to Vulcan, but preferred Mars; Vulcan trapped the pair in bed by a steel drop-net of his own manufacture; hence their enmity. Allegory apart, Labrax states his intentions clearly at 766-8; but the *lorarii* and Daemones already understand him. Smoking or scorching out a suppliant was probably not illegal: in *Mostellaria* 1114, the respectable Theopropides threatens his naughty slave Tranio with it.

762. Labrax does not yet know that the farm-house is Daemones's.

763. mergis is from *mergae*, not from *mergus*. **pugneis**: the adjective is formed, from *pugnus*, for the occasion.

764. Dried figs would need no cooking. The *lorarii* are facetious.

765. *OCT gives this line and 769-70 to Daemones, but they seem better suited to Trachalio's tongue-valour. I assign them as Sonnenschein does.* **copia**: "opportunity"; so too in 781.

766. quaeritatum: supine.

767. Apparently *ignem magnum* (pronounced *ingnem mangnum*) sounded something like *inhumanum*, and Daemones quibbles on it. **inhumanum**, neuter adjective, is used as an abstract noun, "inhumanity"; cf. 186, *acerbum*. **quin** = *qui* + *ne* (where *qui* is the conjunction = *ut*): "So that you may . . . ?" Cf. 111, *quon*, and note.

768. id refers to *lignum* in 766: if, with OCT, we there retain the MSS's *ignem*, *id* will refer to the preceding *ut*-clause.

769. On the question of speaker, see note at 765. **coniciam**: scan ‿‿‿, the consonantal *i* after *con-* (in any case unwritten) being here omitted in pronunciation: a similar pronunciation of *abicio*, *obicio*, *reicio*, and *subicio* is occasionally found, but in 770 we have the normal *ob(i)iciam*.

771. coniecturam: see note on 612.

772. has is the object; **hirundines** is in apposition to it: "these girls, the swallows".

NOTES

773. **oro** usually takes the accusative of the person; but *cum* is found in early Latin and once in Caesar, like the English "plead with" and the Latin *ago cum*.

774. **defendas:** "keep off"; this is as frequent a meaning as "defend".

775. **hic** is Labrax, and Trachalio intends some such verb as *attingat*, but Daemones cuts him short. **maxumo malo suo** literally "with his own very great misfortune", i.e. "He'll be sorry if he does!" On the rhythm, see note on 518.

776. **occeptassit:** for the form, cf. 731 *exoculassitis*.

777. **abitat:** subjunctive of *a-bitere*; cf. *perbiteres*, line 495, and note.

778. This line is pure brag; cf. p. 36. **talentum magnum:** see pp. 41-2.

779. Hiatus after *modo*, in a pause, while Trachalio hesitates. **dum** is demonstrative, "so long"; cf. Catullus, LXII, 45, *virgo dum intacta manet*, dum *cara suis est*, "as long as . . . , so long is she dear . . .". It is from this sense of *dum* that its use as an emphasising enclitic is derived; see note on 32, *primumdum*. But the text of 779, preserved only in the palimpsest, is uncertain.

ACT III, SCENE v. *Daemones leaves Labrax in the custody of the two* lorarii: *he may neither go away, nor molest the suppliants, even verbally. The* lorarii *faithfully carry out their instructions.*

METRE: six-beat iambics. On the effect of the change at this point, see p. 24.

781. **sic:** "as you are". **copia:** cf. 765.

783. The metre throws a rhetorical stress on to the *in-* of *invito* and on to the two *ets*.

784-5. **tangedum . . . agedum . . . iubedum:** cf. 720, *agedum*, and note on 32, *primumdum*.

785. **hercle vero:** "I certainly will . . ."

786. **non equidem censeo:** "No, I think not", said to himself, and meaning "No, after all I won't touch them".

It is not very plausible that after his rough handling in scene iv Labrax should have decided again to defy Daemones and the lorarii; *still less that he should renew his defiance at lines 795-7, though there the defiance is merely verbal. But Plautus knows his audience is enjoying the scene, and he is more than willing to prolong their enjoyment; moreover,* something *must happen on stage to cover the time of Trachalio's absence.*

788. offendero: "run into", i.e. "meet", like *opprimes* in 387.

790. dixerit: "call me"; jussive subjunctive.

791. ludos: cf. 470. **dimissero** = *dimisero*.

797. quo modo: the answer is "at the cost of a thrashing".

798. i dum: like *tangedum*, etc., in 784-5.

799. sed: "And what's more". This is an idiomatic use of *sed*; cf. Martial, I, cvii, 7, *et scalis habito tribus, sed altis,* ". . . up three staircases, long ones too".

801. scelestus: cf. note on 50. **galeam in navi perdidi** appears to be a proverb; for civilians did not really travel with helmets.

804. clavator is apparently to be pronounced as two syllables; cf. such contracted forms as *amaram, amasse,* for *amaveram, amavisse.* At *Miles Gloriosus* 675, Plautus uses *dinis* for *divinis.*

811. nei: old form of *ni.* **invitassitis:** cf. 731, *exoculassitis.* There is a pun between *invitas* and *invitassitis.*

813. periistis is equivalent to a threatening future.

814-20. respondetote ... amplectitote ... itote: formal or emphatic imperatives.

820. sultis = *si vultis,* plural of *sis;* cf. note on 249, *amabo.*

821. ne is not the negative, but an affirmative particle; cf. 1040. To avoid this trap for the unwary, observe that this *ne* (1) does not (normally) take a subjunctive, (2) is always closely followed by a personal or demonstrative pronoun, adjective, or adverb.

823. ita: cf. note on 87. **signa:** the *lorarii* look like statues.

825. ita: again see the note on 87.

826. controvorsia est: "I protest".

In playing or reading the scene, one lorarius *may speak in a deep voice and the other falsetto for contrast.*

829. ut potis est: "so far as possible"; for in the circumstances no advice could be very good. But why does he call the *lorarii "ignavi"?* They were to his cost only too active. The line is marked as corrupt in OCT.

830. Hiatus in the pause after *dico:* the *lorarii* at first ignore the appeal. **molestiae** is predicative dative: "Is it (for) an inconvenience (to you)?" i.e. "Do you mind?"

833. em: cf. 463 and note. Observe that *cavere* can take either a direct object *(quod),* or *a* with ablative, or plain ablative. **crasso:**

148

NOTES

cf. note on 726, *arido*; in *Pseudolus* 1143, *a curvo infortunio* is similarly used. **infortunio:** cf. note on 118.

835. *Plautus repeats the stage-business of 785-8.*

836. non cedam potius: "No, after all I won't retreat." Finding that he cannot safely go away, Labrax speaks in this line and 838 with humorous irony as though he were determined to stay and besiege the altar till the girls surrendered. In parenthesis 837 expresses his real feelings.

837. proveni nequiter: "I've made a mess of it."

ACT III, SCENE vi. *Plesidippus arrives and hales Labrax off to court: Charmides refuses to help his partner: the girls are temporarily sheltered in the farm-house.*

839. meam, emphasised by its position and by the attached *-ne*, is amusingly characteristic of the young lover's egoism. **vi violentia:** for the omission of "and", cf. 676, *reppulit propulit*, and note.

840-2. *More characterisation: the lover hot-headed, the slave ingeniously excusing his timidity.*

842-3. caperes . . . insectarer: past jussive subjunctives: "You should have taken . . .", "Was I to chase . . . ?" **nequissumum:** "That would be most improper".

844. eccum: cf. 492.

850. ego mandaveram: "*I* told him to" (English would not use the pluperfect here); *more characterisation, the self-important slave.*

851. Hiatus after *recta*, in the pause.

852. nil moror: cf. 583 and note.

853. The second alternative would normally be "or to go quietly", cf. 781; but to the young hot-blood this is too mild.

855. abi sane: "Yes, go along . . . !", cf. 386, *i sane*, and note.

857. ad carnuficem is a hyperbole; cf. 778 and note.

859. exulem is predicative; "drive him into exile".

861. quin = *qui* (nominative singular) + *-ne*; the antecedent of *qui* is Labrax, subject of *deliqui* and *of rogas*: "You, who . . . ?"

862. abduxti = *abduxisti*.

863. provexi . . . avehere: "'got her off, but could not get her away'. The terms are nautical" (Sonnenschein).

865. verbum: if nominative singular, "a single word", as

149

opposed to a speech; but it might be genitive plural, depending on *sat*; if so, cf. 583, *sat litium*.

870. audes is here nearer to its older meaning of "desire" (*avideo* from *avidus*) than to "dare"; cf. 1030.

871. ut nanctu's habe: "You've made your bed: lie on it."

872. nervom: This is the same word as *nervus*, "sinew", taken, in the sense of "string", first to mean "cord", and then even "chain", and so "gaol". But it is not a public gaol that is meant, but a private lock-up, where a defaulter could be kept by the plaintiff till trial, or after trial till his debt was discharged: it is quite often mentioned in comedy in this sense.

875. pariter suades qualis es: i.e. "bad advice from a bad man".

876. rapere: 2nd singular present indicative passive.

877. verum sit (depending on *velim*): sc. "that you *had* met your death".

878. ilico: see 62 and note.

879. Hiatus after *redeo*, in the pause between speakers.

880. dum recipis: "till you get them back".

882. *It is comical that the leno should appeal to the victim of his villainies to intervene on his behalf; the same situation and incident occurs at* Curculio 697, *where the appeal is actually successful.*

884. sat semel bibo: "one drink is enough", i.e. "I don't want another shipwreck". *sat* is conjecturally inserted on metrical grounds; but the general meaning is the same without it.

885. isti capiti: "yourself"; cf. 625, *suom . . . caput.*

888. The exact form, scansion and meaning of this line are uncertain. There is a pun on *collus*, "neck", and *columbus*, "pigeon"; *columbar* is "dove-cote" or "pigeon-hole", obviously in this context a pillory or chained collar. Marx suggests that Plautus is trying to render a Greek pun of Diphilus on κολοιός, "jackdaw", and κλοιός, "collar", "pillory". The MSS give *collum* here, the normal classical form, but the grammarian Priscian (cf. note on 107) quotes the passage as having *collus*.

889. nidamentum: "material for a nest", seems to be Plautus's invention: it looks as though here again he had a Greek pun to cope with, but I cannot reconstruct it.

890. An **advocatus** was not a lawyer in any specialist sense, but came to court to support his friend by advice, or by giving evidence as to fact or character, or merely by his presence.

891. qui: indefinite adverb.

NOTES

ACT IV

ACT IV, SCENE i. *Daemones has come out of doors to escape his wife, who is not satisfied with his proximity to two pretty girls. From his soliloquy we also hear for the first time of Gripus and his fishing.*

METRE: six-beat iambics.

893. clientas: cf. p. 35; it is a technical term, though Daemones does mean it technically; do not translate it as "clients".

894. scitula qualifies both *forma* and *aetatula*, and the phrase is an ablative of description. On the effect of the diminutives, see note on *mulierculae*, line 52.

895. The lightening of the first syllable of *uxor* by *breves breviantes* indicates that there was a heavy stress on *sed*; cf. 87, *ita ŏmnis*. **scelesta:** see note at 22.

896. quid . . . quippiam: presumably the repetition is rhetorical: "nothing, not a thing".

898. piscatum: supine.

900. ludos: cf. 470. **retiam** = *rete*. Priscian, who quotes the line for the form *retiam*, gives *facit*, the MSS of Plautus *dat*; the meaning is the same either way.

903. ita: on the meaning, see note on 87.

ACT IV, SCENE ii. *Gripus has fished up a heavy traveller's trunk; he is carrying it in his net, from which trails a long rope. Its weight suggests to him a load of precious metal inside, and he goes into a day-dream about his future—freedom, riches, and power. Abruptly awaking from this, he decides to conceal the trunk for the present.*

METRE: see Appendix B.

908. quom . . . expedivit: on the indicative, cf. 245 and note.

909. templis is in apposition to *locis*; the word does not in its older sense imply an edifice, but a space (of earth or sea or air) appropriated to a god.

151

909. redducem = *reducem* (from *redux*): this scansion is also found at *Captivi* 923; and *reducere* is the older scansion of *reducere*.

911. uberi is ablative.

913. Scan *piscj(um)* and *uncj(am)*, the *i* becoming consonantal.

915-19. The sentence is never finished. Gripus intended to sing, "When I rose up early and went fishing, I hauled up this trunk in my net"; but in his garrulous self-approval he loses the gist, and has to begin afresh at 924, *nam ego*.

919. Take *qui* (conjunction = *ut* final) before *paupertatem eri*. **opera** is ablative singular.

920. This anapaestic line (if it is one—Lindsay scans it otherwise) is very full of short syllables, as though Gripus's self-conceit were bubbling over.

921. decēt has kept its original long *e*, but *suscitet* in the next line has not; this seems to be dictated merely by metrical convenience. Perhaps in view of the scansion *temperi*, we should here write the word *tempore*; this ablative and the adverb are originally identical.

925. repperi ut siem: "found how to be".

926. quidquid inest, grave quidem est: *as a piece of comic business, Gripus may drop the trunk on his toe, and display anguish.*

928. Legal freeing of a slave at Rome normally took place before a praetor. A similar un-Greek reference to this is found at *Pseudolus* 358. Scan *occasjo* as three syllables; cf. *piscjum* and *uncjam* in 914. But 928 is corrupt in the MSS, and our text is conjectural.

930. igitur demum: "in that case (but only in that case)", like *tum demum*.

932. "*Stratonicus*, the celebrated musician of the time of Alexander the Great, who travelled from place to place in Greece in order to exhibit his art" (Sonnenschein): a topical allusion by Diphilus, kept by Plautus.

934. To fit into the anapaestic metre, *oppidum* is usually scanned *oppidŭm*, on the theory that a following stressed syllable (*magn-*) will lighten a syllable after a light one, in *breves breviantes*; for there is no stress on the preceding light syllable *-pid-*. But neither does there seem to me to be any great stress on *magn-*, either by sense or metre; and I prefer to suppose a pronunciation with a single *p*, *ŏ'pidum*. Either way, anapaests compelled the Romans to strange expedients; see p. 25.

935. Take *qui* (= *ut* final) before *ibi*.

936. hic: I take this to mean "in my head", or rather, in

Roman terms, "in my breast"; but Sonnenschein says, " 'here', in this desolate place where I now am". *agito* governs *instruere*: "I am arranging to organise". **vidlum** = *vidulum*, which the MSS have; so also at lines 999, 1106, 1127, 1130.

937. pulmento: the Greeks and Romans divided food into bread or porridge on the one hand, and on the other anything that one ate with this; the latter was called *pulmentum* or *obsonium*: it could be meat or cheese, but most often fish.

Act IV, Scene iii. *Gripus was too late in his decision: he has been observed by Trachalio, who seizes the rope which trails from the net, and thereby prevents Gripus from going away with the trunk, which is still entangled in the net—it is assumed that he has no time to disentangle it, and no means of cutting the rope. Trachalio, after putting the case in a fictitious form, demands a share of the contents. After a long altercation the two agree to submit to arbitration by Daemones, whose connection with Gripus is not known to Trachalio. On the whole situation see pp. 39-40.*

Metre: see Appendix B.

938-9. Trachalio pretends to be helpfully coiling the rope for Gripus, and gives as his reason, "A good turn done to a good man is not wasted".

940. *habe*(o) *adul-*, four light syllables, corresponds to the two heavy which would be here permissible in the iambic metre.

941. postules: cf. note on 17.

942. retem: the word is usually neuter, and the MSS give *rete*, but metre and Priscian (cf. note on 900) guarantee *retem* here. **sqamoso pecu** is in mock-heroic style, perhaps a quotation or parody of a line in an old tragedy.

943. Before *piscis* understand *tam*, correlative with *quam*, "so much as".

944. Scan *e-nĭcăs*: the word is here stressed as would be the uncompounded *nécas*, and so gets the benefit of *breves breviantes*. In colloquial Latin *odio enicas*, or *enicas* alone, means "I'm tired of you", "You're a nuisance".

945. sis: cf. 465 and note on 249. **malo** is ablative of *malum*, used as a noun, governed by *cave*. **malum:** cf. 492 and note. **nam** goes with *quid*, making up *quidnam*.

946. at ... qui makes up *atqui*. The point of *post* is, "since you'll have to later, you may as well now". Gripus accepts this and listens. **quin:** as at 628.

947. eho (cf. note on 578) is usually prefixed to a question or a command, but not usually to a statement; hence editors suspect the text is faulty: if it is sound, *modo* goes with *eho*, "Come on now, ...".

948. eloqueren = *eloquere* (present indicative) + *ne*, equivalent to a command.

956. The object of **vidi** is understood as "a man", antecedent to *qui*: **furtum** is object of *faciebat*. **quoi** refers to *dominum*, **id** is subject of *fiebat*.

958. istuc ... furtum is subject of *factum est*.

960. *Gripus has been completely taken in by Trachalio's tale, and encourages him to proceed with blackmail, partly out of fellow-feeling (it is what he would do himself), and partly in the hope that his advice and complicity will earn him a commission.*

963. This is a mixture of two constructions: (1) "I know the trunk, who owns it" (i.e. "I know who owns the trunk"), indirect question; and (2) "I know the man who owns the trunk", relative clause.

964. quo pacto periit is indirect question, despite the indicative; for the meaning of *periit*, cf. 39 and note.

966. quanti is superfluous in translation; like *pluris*, it is genitive of value. Smith's Dictionary, *refert* A a, quoting this line, ascribes it by oversight to Terence.

967. Probably **tŭ ĭllum**, scanned with hiatus and lightening of *tu*, though this cannot be proved.

968. potis: sc. *esse*, is equivalent to *posse*.

969. The *-a* of *frustra*, normally long, is always short in this phrase.

971. itane vero?: "Really?"; so again at 1003.

973. manu adseruntur: "are legally claimed"; cf. note on 719-20.

974. pro: "as", "on the understanding that they are".

975. omnibŭs: light syllable for heavy at the change of speakers.

976. qui: adverb. **minus**, as often, virtually means "not".

977. esne: "*-ne* often = *nonne* in comedy, as in all forms of less strict Latin" (Shipp, on Terence's *Andria* 17). Cf. *Rudens* 865, 1184. **impudenter impudens** is an unsophisticated specimen of *figura etymologica*.

154

979. quippe is a causal particle: sometimes it is to be translated as a conjunction ("for", "seeing that"), sometimes, as here, reinforcing another causal connecting word, and so not to be translated.

980. emat: "would buy", subjunctive as in a remote future conditional apodosis.

983. in manu non est mea: "It doesn't depend on me", a common phrase.

986. quod: indefinite adjective.   **siquidem ... excepisti:** either "if you have fished up", or "if you have made an exception of . . . .". Trachalio ingeniously argues from the pun.

987. enumquam: "ever . . . ?"; like *ecquando*, an interrogative adverb; it is not common, and some dictionaries do not list it; it occurs again at 1117.   **venefice,** like *inpure* in line 990, is used merely as a term of abuse, without any special appropriateness. Diphilus may have written φάρμακε, which however has a technical meaning (see Liddell and Scott), which Plautus did not appreciate.

990. vitorem (listed in Smith as *vietor*): "one who makes articles of *vimina*, 'a basket-maker'" (Sonnenschein).   The *vidulus* had a basket framework and was covered (cf. 998) with leather.

991. qui: adverb.

992. ne feras depends on *oportet*.

993. scelus: vocative; for the concrete sense, cf. 506.

996. dare verba: cf. 325.

997. If Trachalio wants the natural history of the trunk-fish, Gripus is ready to oblige him.

1001. scelus: concrete, as at 993.

1003. Thales was one of the Seven Sages of Greece; Gripus uses it as an ironical retort to *stultus es*.   **salve** "is often so used in greeting a person *who appears in a new light*, cf. 358, 1173, 1175" (Sonnenschein).

1004. hodie: see note on 177.

1005. sanun = *sanusne*.

1006. elleborosus: hellebore was a drug used to calm lunatics. Trachalio is trying to scare Gripus, in vain.

1007. in cerebro, etc.: i.e. "punch your brain-box in"; *colaphus*, Greek for "a box on the ear", after becoming *colpus*, produced the Italian word *colpo* and the French *coup*.

1008. te, intended as the object of some verb of violence, is in the next line replaced by *quidquid umoris tibi est*.   **peniculus:** ("wee tail") meant either a brush, or, as here, a sponge; from the second diminutive *penicillus*, used in the sense of the brush-like growths of mould, comes the name of the modern drug penicillin.
novos: nominative singular.

1010. On the treatment of cuttle-fish, see 659 and note. *polypus* has a long *o* in Latin.

1011. Neither slave really intends to proceed to extremities.

1012, 1014. nisei ... frunisei ... sei: a bunch of old forms preserved in the MSS, for *nisi, frunisci, si.*

1013. hinc: "from where I am". **offlectam:** "turn about (to face the way I want)". The notion of *facing* is basic to compounds of *ob*: this one occurs only here, and some dictionaries do not list it.

1015. rūdentem: This is the only place in Plautus where the length of the *u* in *rudens* is certain; in later Latin it is short.

1016. ramenta: "scraping", "scrap", from *rado*; it is ablative. **hodie:** cf. note on 177.

1018. redeitur = *reditur*; old form: it is impersonal passive. **sequestro:** predicative dative of *sequestrum*, "as a deposit".

1019. quemne: cf. 111 and note; the antecedent of *quem* is the understood subject of *ponitur*, viz. *vidulus*. Hiatus at the change of speaker.

1022. nihilo: Gripus gives this answer carelessly; he has not understood Trachalio's line of argument, and seizes too eagerly on what looks like an admission of being in the wrong. Trachalio promptly takes advantage of his lapse.

1023. facdum = *fac + dum.*

1025. nisi quia: "except that"—though this is not logical: Gripus merely means "but". Hiatus at the change of speaker.

1028. indicassis: cf. 731, 811, *exoculassitis, invitassitis.*

1029. *tacere* and *mussitare* mean the same.

1030-2. *condicionem ferre* is "make an offer", *condicionem referre* is "make a counter-offer"; then Gripus picks up the verb *ferre* again in *te aufer*, "make a get-away". **audes:** 870, note.

1033. heis = *his.* **oportet:** sc. *me novisse.* Gripus answers vaguely, and then in the next line untruthfully: he already guesses what Trachalio's proposal will be, and he considers it to be to his advantage to have his master as the arbitrator.

1035. fieri: impersonal, "the business to be dealt with".

1037. salva res est: cf. note on 172.

1038. intra praesepis meas: "on my home ground", a colloquial expression, also used at *Casina* 57 and *Curculio* 223.

1039. hodie: cf. note on 177. **suo:** "his man", i.e. Gripus himself.

1040. ne iste: cf. note on 821. **tetulerit:** cf. 68 and note. **eo** is equivalent to a future. The MSS in fact give *ibo,* but the metre suggests that something is wrong: one could also emend to *tulerit*. *ibo*. The sentence is still part of the aside.

1041-4. *The hypocritical protestations in which Gripus wraps his acceptance were no doubt typical of litigants.*

1042. nunc places: "That's better."

1043. adpellis is from *adpellere*, "drive", "force to". The main clause is *notus*, sc. *est*, i.e. "I will regard him as known, and trust him".

ACT IV, SCENE iv. *As the two litigants approach the farm-house door, they are forestalled by the hasty entry of the girls and of Daemones himself: it transpires that his wife's jealousy has forced the girls to leave the house. The pair approach Daemones, and Trachalio, though hampered by continual interruptions from Gripus, puts his case: that the trunk belongs to Labrax, and contains a casket belonging to Palaestra, the contents of which might help her to find her parents.*

1047. paelices: cf. pp. 37-8. **adduxe** = *adduxisse*.

1048. potius quam ego: sc. to escape his wife's wrath.

1049. sistam: "set", i.e. "render", "make"; cf. 1303.

1051. ex praesidio praesides: "Guards off guard!" This "sounds almost like a military command" (Sonnenschein).

1052. quid fit?: cf. 1303; like *quid agitis? quid agis?* (311, 337), it is a friendly greeting rather than a serious enquiry for information.

1054. em: cf. 463 and note on 177. **optume:** sc. *factum est*, 1054-9. *In what tone and with what emotion does Trachalio speak? He had not known till line 1052 that Daemones was Gripus's master; and Gripus thought this gave him, Gripus, an advantage. On finding out the truth, does Trachalio speak, in this line and in line 1057, with bitter irony? If so, line 1058 shows his feelings undisguised. But unknown to Gripus Trachalio had made the acquaintance of Daemones, and found him (after the short initial confusion) sympathetic and helpful; so he may speak in lines 1054 and 1057 quite sincerely. (Marx, taking the latter view, assigns the angry line 1059 to Gripus; but whereas Trachalio might ask Daemones to punish Gripus, his slave, it would be no use for Gripus to ask him to punish Trachalio, whom he did not own.) The scene could be played either way.*

1056. accersitum: supine.

1061. rem facesso: "I am on the job", i.e. "I am doing the talking". As claimant, Trachalio has the right to speak first.

1062. hinc facessas: "you would clear off": Gripus plays on the two meanings of *facesso*. But what is the point of *sis pudicus*? Presumably *rem facesso* could be taken *sensu obscoeno*, and Gripus chooses to do so: he indulges in the same form of humour at lines 1074-5.

1063. For *ut* introducing an indignant question, cf. 1244, *egone ut . . . celem?* **alienon** = *alieno* + *ne:* "to someone else's man?".

1064. ut: "How . . . !" **nequitur,** passive with a passive infinitive, like *coeptum est*.

1065. illum, in the case of *quem*, is superseded in the next line by *eiius*: "That pimp . . . his trunk". Cf. 1240-1, *ille qui . . . cavet, . . . (ei) licet . . . uti.*

1066. eccillum: cf. 576.

1067. ne videas: not merely "not see it", but "go blind".

1068. habeo, non habeo: equivalent to *sive habeo, sive non habeo.* **quid tu me curas quid rerum geram?:** The "I-know-thee-who-thou-art" construction.

1069. Hiatus after *modo*: Trachalio pauses impressively to emphasise his point.

1071. retia: ablative; for the 1st declension form, cf. 900 and note. **qui:** adverb.

1072. verba dat: cf. 325 and note.

1073. quod is relative. "What a respectable man would say" answers *quid tu ais?* Then follows what he would say, spoken to Daemones.

1076. modo: "only". Daemones, who has laughed at Gripus's dirty joke, hastens to assure Trachalio that it will not affect the serious business.

1078. isti: adverb; so also at 1082, but not in 1083, 1085.

1081. crepundia: "a variety of miniature objects . . . sometimes given as birthday presents, and often made into a necklace" (Sonnenschein). Palaestra describes hers in 1156-71.

1083. isti: pronoun; so also in 1085.

1084. id is explained by *qui*; the latter is instrumental case of the relative pronoun: "what she can recognise her parents by".

1086. crepundiă . . . aureă: light syllables for heavy at the change of speaker.

1090. unum is stressed by its position: "The one thing I ask you is . . ."

1092. Either *nisi de opinione* or *certum* would be enough: both together make the sentence slightly illogical.

1093. aucupatur: the context suggests some such meaning as "hedge", "prevaricate"; but the metaphorical meaning of *aucupari* is "lie in wait for", "try to catch". Since Trachalio is not trying to incriminate Gripus in anything, the meaning is perhaps that by temporising he hopes to learn something which he may later use to support his argument. The similar metaphor *expiscari* is so used in Terence, *Phormio* 382.

1095. haec: nominative plural feminine. **ain?** = *aisne?*

1097. quidum = *qui* (adverb) + *dum.*

1100. Scan *omnja*, two syllables; cf. 1359, and Vergil, *Georgics IV*, 221. **a me:** "on my side"; *hinc* means the same.

1101. "No, he may be standing on your side, but he'll take his evidence from ours." The *atqui* marks the contrast between the previous sentence and the *second* clause of 1100, as though *aps te stat* were subordinate in syntax, as it is in sense.

1102. paucis: sc. *verbis*, cf. 120.

1105. surrupta is from *surrupio* = *surripio* or *subripio.*

1106. sint: indirect question.

1107. scelus: vocative; cf. 993.

1109. isti: adverb. **caudea:** The word is only found in use in *Rudens*; later Roman grammarians explain it as "made of rushes".

1110. qui = *ut.*

1111. quibu'cum: the antecedent of course is *signa*, not *parentes.* **periit:** cf. 39 and note.

1112. venefice: cf. 987 and note.

1113. quae ... non queant: the relative is used consecutively: "so that they cannot".

1114. eo: cf. 24 and note. **quam,** for *potius quam*: cf. 684.

1115. pro portione: "correspondingly".

1116. quidum: cf. 1097. **enim** is not separately translatable here; it merely reinforces the causal *quia*; cf. what is said about *quippe* in note on 979.

1117. enumquam: cf. 987 and note.

1123. dudum: Gripus refers to 960. **immo etiam nunc peto:** This is inconsistent with the offer at 1120-1. Though there was now no question of hush-money, Trachalio might hope for a substantial reward from the owner; and no slave, or no slave in comedy, would forgo a claim to money, even though insistence on it might slightly weaken the altruism of his pleading.

1124. petere: "probably a technical term" (Sonnenschein); "aim" and "aim at" will cover the sense in 1123 and here. **miluom** is subject; no object is expressed.

NOTES

1126. sine: verb. **parti** is old ablative.

1127. cedo: cf. 243 and note.

1128 ac, like *atque* at 22, almost has the meaning of *atqui,* "and yet". **ut mihi reddas** (*ut* = "on condition that") depends on *concredam tibi,* understood to be repeated after *ac*: **si istorum nil sit** ("if there's nothing in what he says") depends on *ut mihi reddas.*

1129-90. *To test Palaestra's claim to the casket, Daemones questions her about its contents. Not only does she answer correctly, but the contents prove her to be his long-lost daughter, to the disgust of Gripus and the delight of everybody else.*

1129. atque Ampelisca is, as the singular *audi* shows, added as an afterthought.

1131. uti: adverb, exclamatory, "The way that . . . !" **ilico:** see 62 and note.

1131-2. plane . . . planam. The basic meaning of *planus* is not "visible", but "level", "flat", and the translation "plain" should be used with caution. Here *plane* = "definitely", *planam* = "straightforward". There is a gap in the MSS before the last three letters of *planam,* so that that word and *ex ardua* are guesses at what Plautus wrote; if *ex ardua* is right, *ex* means "instead of".

1135. nullum ostenderis: not "show me nothing", though this would fit the sense well enough, but "don't show it me at all"; cf. 143 and note; here *nullum* is neuter, referring to *quidquid inerit* of the line before. *ostenderis* may be either perfect subjunctive or future perfect; it hardly matters to the general sense.

1136. vos tamen . . . habebitis: "and you shall have it . . . in spite of me". The contrast indicated by *tamen* is not with *frustra dixero,* but with the general sense of the preceding lines.

1138. Hiatus at the change of speakers.

1139. superstitiosa: the older meaning of the word is "uncanny", "having the second sight".

1140. insit: subjunctive of virtual indirect speech, "everything that according to her is in it". Since Gripus's assumption is that she will guess right, subjunctive of what Palaestra may say and indicative of the facts come to the same thing.

1141. hariolabitur: Daemones plays on the exact meaning and on its figurative meaning of "guess" (for which see 347).

1143. hoc habet: "He's had it!" This, or merely *habet,* was

160

the cry when a gladiator was struck down. **solutum est:** *vidulus* is masculine, but the neuter is vague, referring to the net, the cord round the trunk, and any other obstacles.

1144-8. istaec ... hic ... huc ... istinc: The changes in the demonstrative suggest that Palaestra steps forward and is allowed to handle the box, without of course opening it, then at a gesture from Daemones moves back again.

1145. vostrum cognoscendum: genitive plural, "of recognising you".

1146. A similar joke is made at *Curculio* 605-6, when Planesium sees her father's ring: *PL opsecro, parentes ne meos mihi prohibeas. CURC sub gemmane apstrusos habeo tuam matrem et patrem?*

1149. facie: see note on 314.

1150. peccassis: cf. 731 *exoculassitis.* **quod:** the nearest, but clumsiest, translation is "as to the fact that"; say "if" or "though".

1152. Though *ius bonum oras* was a normal phrase, Trachalio affects to understand *bonum* as masculine, "You are asking a good man for justice" (*oro* takes accusative both of the thing and the person); hence his retort.

1154. primo: not "the first", but "the beginning of".

1156. dicedum = *dice + dum.*

1157. litterarum depends on *quid.*

1158. altrinsecus refers to the toy's position as strung on the necklace; for Palaestra could hardly know where it lay in a box that had suffered shipwreck and salvage. However, Daemones is only half attending to her words, because he is trying unsuccessfully (the ancients had no spectacles) to read the lettering on the little sword.

1160. quid, subject; **nomen paternum,** complement.

1161-90. *The conflicting motives and emotions of the characters now reach their highest pitch, and make the passage highly effective as drama, despite the hackneyed incidents of recognition.*

1163. per me quidem: "so far as I'm concerned".

1166. The first *qui* is the adverb, introducing a wish, like *ut.*

1167. adeo: cf. note on 36. **scelestum:** cf. note on 50.

1168. priu' with *quam* = *priusquam.* **rete:** probably ablative.

1170. sucula: "a piglet". The word can also mean "a windlass", which Sonnenschein strangely prefers here. **diērecta** (Smith gives the quantities wrong) is of uncertain derivation; it is an adjective, but only used predicatively, meaning "to ruin", "to the devil".

1174. Eccam: cf. 309 and note.

1175. *This is the culminating point of the scene, indeed of the whole play. The reunion is to be played sincerely: if the audience are inclined to deride it as too sentimental and stale, the discordant reactions of Gripus and Trachalio offer a convenient outlet for their laughter.*

1176. "I congratulate you on your well-deserved good fortune"; *ex* means "according to". Trachalio is no doubt sincere in his congratulations, but he also hopes for a reward.

1177. capedum = *cape* + *dum.*

1178. Gripi scelera = *Gripum scelestum.* **male evenit:** the usual congratulations of course had *bene evenit* or some such phrase; cf. 1367.

1180. argumentis: not "arguments", but "proofs"; though Daemones does not really require any more proof.

1181. signa: cf. 1110; but here birthmarks, if any, would naturally be included.

1182. Hiatus at mid-line. **promiscam** may be either adjective or adverb; the meaning will be the same either way. It is an early form: the classical adjective is *promiscuus.*

1184-90. *Gripus's soliloquy is partly pathetic, but more ludicrous, and is to be played so: slaves in comedy are comic; we are neither expected nor allowed to sympathise deeply with their disappointments. Hence the absurd logic of 1186-7, and the even more absurd threat of temporary hanging in 1189-90: Gripus has a penchant for suicide; cf. 1288 and 1415.*

1184. sumne: cf. 865 and note on 977.

1185. qui non . . . apstrusi: causal; "for not putting it away". Classical Latin would prefer a subjunctive.

1187. evenerat: not merely "came out of the sea", but also "fell to my lot".

1188. argenti et auri: partitive genitive with *largiter*, as though the latter were a noun; cf. 1315, and a similar construction with *abunde* in Vergil *Aeneid VII*, 552, and elsewhere.

ACT IV, SCENES v AND vi. *Daemones expresses his satisfaction with his good fortune, and modestly hints that it is a reward for his piety; then he despatches Trachalio to fetch Plesidippus: the latter is to marry Palaestra; to the former is virtually promised freedom and marriage with Ampelisca.*

NOTES

METRE: Daemones's soliloquy, like the soliloquies at 593-614 and 892-905, is naturally in the quiet six-beat iambics. These give way to seven-beat trochaics for his lively banter with Trachalio.

1193. satin: cf. 187 and note.

1194. optingit optatum piis: Daemones runs together two different ideas, viz. (1) if the gods want a thing to happen, it will, however improbable; (2) if you are pious, your prayers will be answered in the end.

1196. is replaces, or is in apposition with, *ego* of the previous line, as the natural antecedent for *qui*.

1199. adeo: cf. 36 and note.

1201. Drop the *id* in translating.

1204. For English idiom take *paene* before *nimis*.

1208. sunt domi means little more than "we possess"; cf. the metaphorical use of the same expression at 1335. **porci sacres** (*sacres* 3rd declension, and with a long *a*) is an old religious phrase.

1212-26. licet: *The insistent repetition of the same word, "O.K.", is a simple form of humour or high spirits. If Diphilus wrote such a passage, Plautus in imitating it became so enthusiastic that he decided to use the same device over again in 1269-79 (their Roman allusions show these to be his work). Played at high speed, with plenty of laughing and back-slapping, the scenes still go down quite well—better than the* licet-*epilogue at 1227, which to a reader seems a more amusing, because subtler, joke.*

1216. omnian licet : *licet* is quoted as a sort of noun; understand *sunt* as verb to *omnia*: "Is everything 'O.K.'?", i.e. "Is that the only word you can say?"

1217. ut memineris depends on *volo*; **quod promisisti** on *memineris*.

1221. gratum "has passive sense" (Sonnenschein). **factis:** "by your actions".

1225. cum sua licentia: "with his own brand of *licet*". *licentia* is humorously used in some such sense, and *sua* is by position emphatic; it refers not to the grammatical subject, *Hercules*, but to *istum*; cf. note on *se* in 47.

1226. ita: cf. note on 87.

ACT IV, SCENE vii. *Gripus wants Daemones to appropriate the trunk and its valuable contents—and, of course, to pay him something*

163

NOTES

in consideration. Daemones firmly refuses, to Gripus's renewed disgust. This scene fills in the time while Trachalio fetches Plesidippus; perhaps in Diphilus's play, though not Plautus's, the time was also needed for the Palaestra actor to change into Plesidippus's costume; cf. p. 13.

METRE: six-beat iambics.

1229. si sapias, sapias: "a dark hint, made explicit in the next sentence" (Sonnenschein).

1230. alienum belongs inside the relative clause.

1231. quodne ego inveni . . . : cf. 1019, and note on 111.

1234. isto: ablative neuter; "for that reason", picked up by *quom.*

1236. Hiatus at the pause after *transennae.*

1238. quam: relative adjective, agreeing with *escam.*

1240. ille: for its attraction into the case of the relative, cf. 1065, *illum.*

1241. uti: verb, governs *partum bene;* it does occasionally govern an accusative.

1242. "I think that your catch is going to be caught." The Latin is ungrammatical; perhaps Plautus was having difficulty with translation. *praedatum irier* is the so-called future infinitive; but grammatically it means "there is a movement afoot (*irier* or *iri*) to plunder (supine, *praedatum*)", and so would require an accusative, *istam praedam* (there is no possibility of its being a passive form with active meaning, like the other parts of deponent verbs); in that case *videtur* would be impersonal, "it seems", which is the usual construction in English. But *videor*'s habit of taking a personal construction of *nominative* and infinitive has misled the writer. It also confused him at *Curculio* 260-1, *visus sum viderier procul sedere . . . Aesculapium,* where what he is trying to say is "It seemed to me that it seemed (i.e. I thought I had a dream) that Aesculapius sat far off".

1244. cum maiore dote: "a metaphor from the law of divorce" (Sonnenschein): if so, Plautus is mixing his metaphors; difficulty in translation may again be the reason.

The general meaning of these two lines, metaphor apart, is that the trunk will be reclaimed, and they fined for dishonesty in trying to keep it.

1245. minume is, as usual, a virtual negative. **noster Daemones** is a complacent way of referring to himself, like the frequently used *nos.*

NOTES

1246. sapientis: accusative plural, subject of *cavere*.

1247. malefici: genitive of *maleficium*.

1248. conlusim is a conjecture, for *cum lusi* of the MSS; it is an adverb, "in collusion". If the conjecture is correct, understand some such infinitive as *fieri*, depending on *nil moror*; for which phrase cf. 583 and note.

1249-53. *Daemones's sermon has been sincere and (within the limits of ancient morality) sound; part at least of the audience will have listened with approval. But in case there are also scoffers, Plautus (or Diphilus) anticipates their mockery by Gripus's, and so disarms it.*

1250. is is dative plural; **plaudier,** infinitive passive, is impersonal.

1251. poplo = *populo*, not uncommon in early Latin.

1253. nullus erat: not, I think, "nobody was", but "he (the person indicated by *quisque*) wasn't at all . . ."; cf. note on 143.

1254. molestu's = *molestus es*, where *es* is imperative.

1255. ne frustra sis: on the scansion, see note on 969.

1258. illuc est quod: "that's how it is that . . ." or "that's why it is that . . .".

1259. illic: pronoun.

1260. furti: genitive of the crime.

1261. censeret: subjunctive because the clause is part of a supposition: obviously an indicative would be unsuitable, because *ex hypothesi* there *was* no time that could be described factually as *dum censet*.

ACT IV, SCENE viii. *Trachalio returns with Plesidippus; both are in high spirits, which they vent in facetious word-play before going into the farm-house. The virtually untranslatable jokes on the word* censeo, *being Roman, not Greek, in their allusions, show that the scene is Plautus's work rather than Diphilus's.*

METRE: eight-beat trochaics.

1266. mi liberte: So Trachalio has got his freedom! **mi patrone** is, like *mi pater*, an absurd exaggeration: in fact Plesidippus is now Trachalio's *patronus*, the relationship of a former master to his freedman; Trachalio is his *cliens*.

1267. popularis means the same as *mea popularis* at 605 and 740.

1269. censen = *censes-ne*. The two indicatives *censes* and *despondebit* are put side by side by parataxis; cf. p. 43.

1271. quid matri eiius?: understand *faciam* or *dicam*. To this question Trachalio's *censeo* is no complete answer (perhaps he hesitates); and Plesidippus breaks in with *quid ergo censes?* This question, and the answer *quod rogas censeo*, are drawn from the formal language of the Roman senate, where *censere* means "vote".

1272. quanti censes : *quanti* is genitive of value. Plesidippus now plays on a different use of the word *censere*, viz. to estimate a citizen's wealth at the quinquennial census, in order to assign him to his appropriate class in the army and citizen-roll. Trachalio's reply is apparently a mere stop-gap. Either we must suppose his master's nimbler wit has defeated him, or his reply is again interrupted.

1273. Yet another turn is given to the word. *censio* meant a fine laid by the censor on defaulters; so Plesidippus protests in *adsum equidem* that he is no defaulter. Again Trachalio's answer appears to have no point except to keep the ball rolling.

1275. etiamne: cf. 467 and note. **eam** disappears in scansion, and there is hiatus after *censeo*.

1277. eius patrem is unexpectedly substituted for *eam*, reversing the order of the list: Plesidippus is not really interested in hugging his in-laws, but chooses to lead up gradually to the question *quid eampse illam?*; according to pattern, Trachalio would still be answering *censeo*. But Plesidippus is disappointed; for Trachalio changes his pattern. To the first two *non censeos* Plesidippus raises no objection, but the third so disgusts him that, with one more quibble, he breaks off the conversation.

1279. dilectum dimisit: "He has dismissed the review", i.e. "He has finished the census", i.e. "No more *censeo*".

If we regard Rudens *as a romantic comedy, it is time for the play to close: virtue has been rewarded, and the lovers are reunited. But the ancients found comic rogues quite as entertaining as the course of true love, and would be delighted to have a scene between Gripus and Labrax, a pair who have not yet met. Moreover, Gripus, whose rope gives the play its title, deserves to have his story too brought to a happy end, whether or not he knows of it when the plaudite is spoken. So we have another act to run.*

ACT V

ACT V, SCENES i AND ii. *Labrax, deprived of possession of Palaestra, returns towards the temple to claim his remaining piece of property, Ampelisca. From Gripus he accidentally learns that his trunk has been found, and after haggling, agrees to pay a talent if he is put in possession of it and its contents: to this bargain he solemnly swears.*

METRE: seven-beat iambics till 1337, then six-beat iambics: on the effect of the change, see note at 1338.

1281. qui vivat: subjunctive is required in all relative clauses depending on a negative or virtual negative. **alter** is to be taken with *mortalis*.

1282. recuperatores is a Roman technical term for a commission which dealt with complaints brought by aliens against citizens: Diphilus would have had a similar Greek term; for a similar adaptation cf. 373 and note. **damnavit:** Labrax means, of course, "got me condemned".

1284-5. "The thought is obscurely conceived" (Sonnenschein). Perhaps it was clearer in Diphilus.

1285. ita omnes: both for the meaning of *ita* and for the scansion of *omnes*, cf. 87 and note.

1286. visam: future indicative of *viso*.

1287. reliquiarum: partitive genitive, depending on *quod*.

1290. If the text is sound, the subject of *tundat* must be understood to be *vidulus*. But from other passages of Plautus, e.g. *Pseudolus* 1045, one would expect it to be "my heart". Most editors suppose something is missing, perhaps a whole line, containing the word *cor*.

1291-2. ego qui . . . ei: cf. 1065-6, *illum quem . . . eiius*.

1292. Hiatus in the pause after *vidulum*. **rete:** ablative, as at 913, 1168. **darei:** old form of *dari*; the accusative *quicquam* is its subject.

1294. cubitum depends on *longis*: "eighteen inches tall".

1295-6. The proposed wording of the advertisement, given in Latin in indirect speech, would in English be given in direct.

1296. feretis: the subject is vague, but plural; Gripus feels that all the world is against him; cf. Ampelisca's *voluistis* at 273, if that is the right reading. **istum:** i.e. the trunk, *vidulum*.

1299. Gripus half hears Labrax's aside, but mistakes it for a call from indoors.

1301. ita: again, for the meaning see note on 87. **rutilum** is loosely constructed where the comparative would be regular.

1302. věrum: in classical Latin, 4th declension, *veru*. It is generally supposed that this line is an alternative for the preceding two, "introduced into some acting edition" (Sonnenschein): *nam quidem* is not a Plautine phrase, though otherwise the line is quite passable.

1303. te ... cum inraso capite: "you and your long hair". *This is clearly a piece of rudeness, but what was its exact point? Had Labrax long hair? Or is it an ironic reference to his baldness in front (for which, see 317)? If he had long hair, what did it imply? Fashions change in this matter. To Horace at Odes II, xv, 11 intonsi Catones represent rugged old-fashioned virtue; to St Paul, on the other hand, at 1 Corinthians, xi, 14, long hair apparently advertised the male prostitute. Whatever the point of the insult was, at* quid fit? *Labrax swallows it, and tries again to enter into amicable conversation.*

1304. To Labrax's *quid fit?* and *ut vales?* Gripus returns facetious and defensive answers. **verum:** as in 1302.

1305. una littera: ablative. In the next line Gripus guesses the riddle.

1306. tetigisti acu: Though this phrase occurs only here, it has been generally assumed to be a proverb equivalent to "hit the right nail on the head". Marx explains *acu* not as an ordinary needle, but as the surgeon's probe; the implication of the answer then is not merely "That's right", but "That hurts". **digna:** "appropriate". **forma:** sc. *tua*.

1307. quid tibi est: "What's the matter?" **alli:** dative.

1310. ecquid, neuter used adverbially, merely serves as an interrogative particle. **in vidulo** belongs to the *quid* clause, but having been put early it is resumed by *ibi*.

1311. rěfert: the impersonal verb. **qui,** referring to *vidulus*, has its antecedent unexpressed and vaguely dependent on *refert*: "(about a trunk) which . . .". More freely, it may be translated "since it . . .". If *sine hoc* is the right reading (the MSS give *si non*, which does not scan), *sine* is verb, and *hoc* accusative. Labrax makes a feint of being uninterested (in keeping with the casual affability of his opening words), as a preliminary to the bargaining that lies ahead.

NOTES

1312. qui: cf. 98 and note. **signa:** as at 1110, 1181.

1313-end of play. To understand the financial dealings which follow, the student should refer to pp. 41-2.

1313. Hiatus after *octingenti*: a pause throws emphasis on to *aurei*; for not all *nummi* were *aurei*; see pp. 41-2.

1314. minăria: the MSS of Plautus have *mna*; the line is quoted by the grammarian Nonius, and his MSS give *denaria*. If *minaria* is right, it is a diminutive of *mina*, and is perhaps used in the sense of "(so many) minae *approximately*". **Phĭlĭppa:** this spelling and scansion appear to be necessary in various places in Plautus, where the word is an adjective describing coins, though only in one, *Trinummus* 959, is this spelling found; for the meaning, see p. 42.

1315. mercedis: for the construction cf. 1188 and note.

1318. commodum, adjective: "in full measure", the original meaning, from *modus*.

1319. These vessels are clearly all intended for drinking-parties: their nature and use appears to be as follows: The *sinus* (2nd declension) was a large wine-bowl; the *gaulus* a still larger bowl or urn for drinking-water; from these two, the servant would ladle out, with the *cyăthus*, wine and water, in the proportion decided by the *arbiter bibendi*, into a jug, *epichўsis*; from this jug he would pour the mixture into the goblets, *canthări*, for the guests.

1320. Hiatus after *quidem;* a pause throws emphasis on to *habuisti*, the point of which is underlined by Labrax in the next line.

1322. Understand *ei* as antecedent to *qui*.

1323. nummos trecentos: these *nummi* are not *aurei*; Labrax begins at six *minae*.

1325. minutos: perhaps in its original meaning as the participle of *minuo*, "chopped up".

1326. os calet, and the rest, is a way of saying "You are wasting your breath".

1327. nummum: genitive plural, = *nummorum* (but *nummum* is the usual form), depending on *mille*, which in Plautus is a noun like the plural *milia* in classical Latin.

1328. Labrax begins blusteringly, but being in a weak position for bargaining, he concludes lamely: the threat *hic non ero*, in so far as it *is* a threat, means "you won't have another chance".

1329. quo: relative adverb; the antecedent is to be understood as *id*: "A sum to which you need not add anything, if you don't want to"—a facetious mock-concession.

1331. vel . . . vel: cf. note on 582. Gripus could have

said *aut . . . aut*, since obviously there is an exclusive choice (Labrax could not say both "Yes" and "No"); but the use of *vel* ("Please yourself") gives a lordly air of indifference; so does the permissive subjunctive *aias . . . neges*, instead of the more definite imperative. Ampelisca uses the same expression in dealing with Sceparnio, at 427. Actually Gripus's indifference is feigned; he is just as interested as is Labrax. **quid istic :** literally "What is there there?" (*istic* is adverb); hence "What can I do about that?". But the English equivalent is a resigned "Oh, well!".

1332. accededum = *accede + dum*. **Venus haec** is subject of *adroget*; the clause is paratactic with *volo*. **adroget** is in its original meaning of "put a formal question to": Venus is, figuratively, to administer the oath (*sacramento rogare*, "bind by oath", was a normal idiom).

1335. praei verbis. In 1338-49 the oath is *not* dictated and repeated verbatim: it would be tedious if it were, and Plautus is not the man to bore his audience for the sake of consistency. *domi est*: in colloquial Latin merely "I possess", "I have available"; cf. 1208.

1336. Hiatus after *viduli*: Gripus is pausing emphatically after each phrase, *te mi argentum daturum, eodem die, tui viduli, ubi sis potitus.*

1338. The METRE changes to staid six-beat iambics, normally used for formal documents; cf. Beare, p. 217.

The division of the following lines between speakers is not certain: we have adopted the arrangement in Sonnenschein. At 1342 the insertion of *tum ego huic* mends unsatisfactory metre, and, with the changes of speaker shown, it implies some amusing stage-business; see note on the line.

1342. tum ego huic: As Labrax says these words, he unostentatiously indicates himself, intending thus to alter the whole meaning of the oath. Gripus observes and frustrates this trick.

1343. For *huic* as two syllables, cf. 39, 750.

1345, 1348. fraudassis, peccasso: old future perfects.

1345. dic introduces an indirect petition, so translate it as "pray".

1346. caput atque aetatem tuam is in apposition to *te*: "you, viz. your person and life".

1347. tecum hoc habeto: "Keep this for yourself." At this point Gripus detaches Labrax's hand from himself, that he may

NOTES

not himself participate in the curses called down—the opposite of the gesture which he insisted on at 1342.

1348. illaec depends on *advorsum*.

1348-9. Venus, veneror: for the pun and the meaning of *veneror*, cf. 305.

In including all his confrères in the curse, Labrax goes further than he was asked to. Now that he has failed in all his attempts to get the better of Gripus in bargaining and to trick him in the taking of the oath, he concedes defeat with this generous gesture—with the full intention of merely disregarding the bargain and breaking the oath. With this intention, there was no need for the bargaining and trickery, but they came natural to him, and they delighted the audience.

1350. Gripus's comment " is a general reflection on the character of *lenones*". (Sonnenschein).

1351. faxo exibit: for the syntax cf. 365, *scibis faxo*.

1352. eum refers to *senem*. Like *rogo*, *posco* can take two accusatives, of the person and of the thing.

1353. si maxume: "however much", "even if".

1354. hodie: cf. note on 177.

1355. meus arbitratust: "It's my decision", "It's for me to decide". **lingua quod iuret mea** is not an indirect question (which would require *quid*, not *quod*), though this would be the natural construction in English, but a relative clause, its antecedent understood as *id*: "anything that my tongue is to swear".

ACT V, SCENE iii. *Labrax gets back his trunk and its contents (except Palaestra's casket), but refuses to pay Gripus the promised reward. But, when Daemones intervenes on Gripus's behalf, he agrees under pressure to hand over to him Ampelisca as the equivalent of half a talent, and to pay the other half in cash: this money Daemones will treat as the price for freeing Gripus; he concludes the play by inviting the two to dine with him.*

METRE: eight-beat trochaics.

1357. Hiatus in the pause after *tu*.

1359. quidquid is used after *ut* with the same meaning as *quidque*; this usage is also found in Livy. **infuere:** plural according to sense, despite the grammatically singular *quidquid*. **omnia** is dissyllabic, as at 1100. **salva sistentur:** cf. 1049.

1361. tuo'ne = *tuus-ne*.

1362. *The other diminutive* cístŭla *would have fitted the rhythm more neatly than* cistella, *which slows it up; but Daemones is drawling his words as he watches to see how Labrax takes the news.* **modo** modifies *una*: "just one".

1363. quibu'cum implies that Palaestra and her toys were found together. This is somewhat misleading (it sounds as though she had been wearing them round her neck); yet it is in some sense true (their finding coincided), and Plautus would not worry over the inaccuracy.

1365. bene factum was a standard phrase of congratulation, as was also a *quom* clause followed by *gratulor* or some such word, cf. 1178. One cannot but admire Labrax's self-control. **ex sententia** had two meanings: 1. (as here) "to one's satisfaction"; 2. "to the best of one's knowledge and belief". An amusing anecdote depending on this double meaning is quoted in Lewis and Short, *sententia* IB2.

1366. The normal acknowledgement of congratulations was *credo*.

1367, 1369. immo: the old standard translation "nay rather" needs to be adapted to context: in 1367, since Labrax is protesting against the negative *non credo*, we must translate "Yes, really!"; but in 1369 "No really!"

1368. ne duis: This is the main clause, "don't you give me..." *For the form* duis, *cf.* 580, interduim, *and note. Labrax's air of generosity is doubly shameless: Palaestra was no longer his property, first because the court had deprived him of her* (1283), *and secondly because she had been proved free-born.*

1369. Hiatus after *vero*, at the change of speakers.

1370. quid had better be translated "What" than "Why", to fit Gripus's answer.

1372. quae haec factio est : "What's this carry-on?", "What are you up to?". For the verbal noun in *-io* used in indignant questions, cf. 502-3.

1374. ius iurandum: "the oath", i.e. oaths in general. **rei servandae:** dative of purpose.

1375, 1380. cedo: cf. 243.

1375. sis: cf. 465.

1376. istum: i.e. Labrax.

1377. dare: Plautus is casual about the rule of accusative and infinitive with verbs of "hoping and promising"; and even Caesar has *pollicentur dare*.

The *pontifex* had the duty of taking cognisance of perjury and expiating by sacrifice the curse that it might bring upon the people.

NOTES

1379. si redegissem: "If I restored"; the pluperfect subjunctive stands in the indirect speech for the future perfect *redegeris* ("if you restore") of the direct speech. **iuratus:** sc. *est.*

1380. quicum habeam iudicem: "somebody with whom I can have a judge", i.e. "somebody to act as your representative against me before a judge (or arbitrator)"; for a slave could not act for himself; cf. p. 40. The suggestion of legal procedure is facetious, not serious, as the next line shows; moreover, the implication that Gripus is a slave, is only a guess, and perhaps merely intended as an insult; it is only at 1384 that Labrax learns the fact for certain.

1381. On *ni* and *si*, see note on 714. Labrax claims (1) that Gripus has used false pretences; (2) that he, Labrax, is under age: both are impudent falsehoods. In any case, there was no legal contract; see p. 40.

1382. By the *Lex Plaetoria quinavicenaria* (cf. *Pseudolus* 303), in Roman law a binding contract could not be made by any one under the age of twenty-five. **habe cum hoc:** "Deal with *him*", i.e. with Daemones, answering *cedo quicum habeam iudicem.* But Gripus regards Daemones less as his representative (Labrax has to remind him of it at 1403) than as the arbitrator. In fact Daemones informally combines both functions; and it is to having him as arbitrator that Labrax really objects in *aliost opus*: he could object to the choice of arbitrator, but not to his opponent's choice of representative, though 1383 confuses this.

1383. "I shouldn't dare remove it from him, if I won my action against him." The text and the meaning are very doubtful, but this (Lindsay's text, but Marx's interpretation) makes some sort of sense, viz.: "If I win a law-suit against this man (about your talent), he will take his revenge by withholding the *vidulus* from me (and therefore I object to him as representative or arbitrator)." If this is the meaning, *condemnavero* means "get him condemned", as at 1282.

1384. servo meo: *This is Labrax's first intimation that Daemones is Gripus's master, or, for that matter, that Gripus is a slave. It shakes him.* "*From* 1384 *to* 1392 *the pimp does not get a word in; he is overwhelmed with demands and reproaches, by Gripus as well as by Daemones. Thus the words* servo meo *are the turning-point of the scene*" (*Marx*).

1386. fide lenonia: for the sentiment, cf. 346. **iam** belongs to *nactum* (*esse*) rather than to *ratu's.*

173

1387. huc: i.e. into Gripus's hand, illustrated by a suitable gesture.

1388. adeo: see note on 36; it is *not* linked to the following *ut*, which is final, not consecutive.

1391. tum te mihi, etc., completes the interrupted sentence that began at *quando*.

1392-3. nemp' pro meo iure oras: "I gather you admit my right to it?" This sentence could have two meanings, the first as above (more literally, "You plead *on the basis of* my right?"), which is what Labrax means. The other meaning, which Daemones chooses to take, is of course "You are pleading *for* my right?"—an absurd thing for an opponent to do.

1393. mirum quin + subjunctive is used to ridicule a question, by introducing in exaggerated form what is assumed to be implied in it. It is not a matter of answering "Yes" or "No" to it, merely of suggesting that it was a silly question to ask. "(Of course I'm not pleading for your right.) Do you think I'd be spending my pains (or running a legal risk), merely to prove *you* right?" Cf. *Trinummus* 966-7, *CH nempe ab ipso id accepisti Charmide? SY mirum quin ab avo eiius aut prcavo acciperem, qui sunt mortui.*" "Did you receive it from Charmides himself?" "(Of course I did!) Did you expect me to receive it from his dead ancestors?" Literally *mirum quin* means "it's a marvel that . . . not", and its use is ironical. **periclo:** If this means "pains", cf. 432; but it is often used of the risk of loss in litigation.

1394. salvos sum: for the implication of this phrase, cf. note on 172. *It must be assumed that the uncompromising tone of Daemones's reply disconcerts Labrax, and that his demeanor shows it. See further, p. 40.*

1395. Daemones resumes his conciliatory tone. **illud,** like *ille*, refers to Gripus, but is attracted (quite normally) into the gender of *mancupium*.

1396. hunc, like *istum* in the line before, refers to the *vidulus*, but the change of pronoun implies "and here it is".

1397. de talento: "about the talent". **feras:** sc. *id* (the talent).

1398. quod: relative. **heus tu** is, I think, addressed to Labrax. **dato** (imperative) . . . **si sapis:** "Better give it me!" Cf. 96 and note.

1399. tacen = *taces-ne*. **simulas . . . agere:** for the simple infinitive, cf. Plautus's casual attitude to verbs of promising,

174

NOTES

line 1377; classical Latin requires *simulas te agere*. **meam rem agere:** "to be looking after my interest". **tibi munis viam:** adversative asyndeton; insert "but" in English. *munis viam* (Koch, Lindsay), *munificus es* (Sonnenschein), *multum sapis* (Marx) are various conjectures to complete the MSS *mu* . . .

1400. istoc, the talent. **aliam praedam,** the *vidulus*.

1401. isto: adverb; i.e. "to what you have just said". The unnatural placing of the stress, *unúm*, throws a rhetorical emphasis on to that word; so already in 1007. **vel:** see note on 551.

1403. tibi is emphatic: "It's your interests he's pursuing." **hoc** = *huc.*

1406. Ampeliscam?: MSS and editors add this word to Daemones's speech; but though he knew the name at 1129, he seems at 1408 to be still unfamiliar with it, and the dialogue is livelier and more natural if in 1406 it is supplied by Labrax. **mille nummum:** cf. 1327 and note. The sum is 20 minae, two-thirds of the value that Daemones puts on her. **vin** = *vis-ne.*

1407. dividuom . . . faciam: "I will split." **bene facis,** "Thank you", is merely polite: Labrax does not yet see why the *condicio* is described as *luculenta.* **pro illa altera:** i.e. as the price of Ampelisca. If we suppose there is any truth in the assertions of Trachalio at lines 649, 736, 1104, that she too was free-born, Labrax would be glad to get rid of her.

1410 and **1413.** Hiatus at the mid-line pause.

1412. Gripus has not heard lines 1405-11.

1413. me: sc. *habere.*

1415. gratiam facias: "let him off". **nisi me suspendo occidi:** The sentence is an absurdity similar in spirit, though not in form, to 1189-90.

1417. condicio placet: Labrax's acceptance is facetiously couched in commercial terms.

1419. ni: "except that". **pollucti:** cf. 425; but here the participle is neuter, used as a noun.

1420. adeo: cf. 36 and note.

1422. comissatum: supine. The verb is another Greek-derived drinking-term; cf. note on 360. **ad annos sedecim:** "in sixteen years' time"; the number is chosen at random.

1423. ambó is thrown into relief by its unnatural metrical stress (cf. *unúm* at 1401), and by bridging the normal half-line gap. It emphatically includes Gripus, and thereby promises him freedom; for no slave would be invited to lie down at table with his master (cf. Luke XVII. 7-8). *In performance Gripus should be seen to understand this; hence our conjectural stage-directions.*

175

NOTES

plausum date. *An appeal for applause is the standard end of a Latin comedy. Greek comedies, presented at competitive festivals, ended with a prayer to "Victory", or a hint to the judges, that this play ought to win first prize: in Menander's* Dyscolus, *and therefore perhaps in other Greek New Comedy, a formal appeal for applause came just before this.*

Appendix A

Act I, scenes 3–4, present the modern producer with two problems. First there is the improbability that the girls should fail to observe either the temple, or the farm-house, or each other, all being within a few feet and in clear view; and this is made the more implausible by their loud protestations that nothing is to be seen. For the Romans it must simply be supposed that this was conventionally acceptable; as Beare says (pp. 171–2), "The actor does not see what the dramatist does not want him to see. . . . The efforts of the two girls to find each other are frustrated for so long by nothing but the fact that they take care not to look in the right direction". A modern producer can ease this part of the improbability by having on stage a small mountain (five or six feet high), round which the girls can play hide-and-seek: it can also have other uses, as a look-out for Sceparnio in 160–84, as a screen for Labrax's vomit at 511, as a seat for Trachalio and Ampelisca in conversation and for Gripus polishing his spit. But the farm-house and temple are still in full view.

The second problem is the sheer length of Palaestra's monody. The Romans had a great appetite for such solos, and in less moving circumstances than Palaestra's: both the rake Philolaches in *Mostellaria* and the virtuous Lysiteles in *Trinummus* spend even longer in lyrical soliloquy about their own morals. No doubt much depended then as now on the quality of the performance, and the passages were written to give a virtuoso his chance. A modern audience, and perhaps a modern reader, will find Palaestra's lament more than enough, and the producer will make cuts.

APPENDIX A

Yet obviously it cannot disappear entirely: Palaestra and Ampelisca are to be introduced, and are to move the audience to pity. Nor is Palaestra's lament (the harder and longer of the two) to be dwarfed by Ampelisca's; for though in comic business Ampelisca has a bigger role to play (331–441), in serious drama Palaestra is her leader (664–701, and of course 1130–83). In putting the scenes across much depends on enlisting a good singer and getting attractive music written; this involves understanding the metre, which is the subject of the next appendix.

Appendix B

THE LYRIC METRES OF I 3-5, III 3, AND IV 2-3

I. 3. The prevailing rhythms of Palaestra's lament are bacchiacs and cretics, but almost all the lyric metres are there except anapaests, which are left for Ampelisca.

185, 187 are a pair; each is a four-beat iambic, followed by Reiz's tag. 186, 188 are also a pair: each has the pattern ∪ ∪ − − | ∪ ∪ − − (called "ionic"), followed by a double-trochee tag. An English imitation of this rather complicated stanza is:—

> "Too little of human woe we see
> In the tales that deceive us!
> 'Tis our own hardship that only
> Showeth our error.
> Is it this the god has will'd for me?—
> In plight so grievous,
> In a lost world to be lonely,
> Wreckt, in terror?"

189–94 are bacchiacs, slow and despondent (an English imitation of 191–2 is given on p. 27); then, as Palaestra's indignation against the injustice of Heaven mounts, the rhythm becomes more animated: 195–6 are of the same pattern as 185 and 187. Again she droops into bacchiacs (197), and again, as scorn and indignation rouse her, she turns to a more animated metre, aeolic, in 198–9. 200–3 are a stanza-like pattern of cretics with trochaic tags. 204–5 are slow again, bacchiacs; then 206 is a short iambic couplet:—

> "Here are rocks and roaring sea,
> And not a soul to meet with me."

207–16 are a second set of cretics and trochee-tags (not quite the same pattern as the last); near the end the tags become more frequent; and then in 217–18 we hear aeolics again:—

> "Free was I born, with right to be free;
> Free birth prov'd no use to me:
> My slavery now no more could be,
> Were I born of a slave-girl."

219 is a seven-beat iambic; cf. note on the line.

I. 4.   220–8, anapaests; see pp. 24-6.

229–32, short trochaic and iambic lines.

233–53, cretics, punctuated by a trochaic tag at 237, and ending with Reiz's tag at 253.

254–6, iambic lines, of increasing length.

257–8, eight-beat trochaics.

The changes between metres mark new developments in the action; see notes at 233, 253, 257.

I. 5.   259–64 are slow, dignified bacchiacs, which break off when the Priestess notices the girls' unceremonious appearance.   265–77 are cretics, rather faster and more agitated.   In 278–82 bacchiacs are resumed, as the girls droop wearily, and the Priestess relents.   283–5 are conversational and lighter in rhythm, trochaic and iambic; then, as the party enters the temple with dignity, the scene ends with a slow quatrain, alternate lines bacchiac and syncopated-trochaic $(-|-|-\smile|-\smile|-\smile)$.   An English imitation of 282–9 is:—

> "But, girls, my resources are but poor and slender—
> Barely a livelihood for me:
> Serving Venus I get no fee.—
> Is it Venus' temple, pray, ma'am?—
> It is so; and I by fame am
> The temple-tender.
> So far, though, as means give me power of bestowing
> Kindness now, I shall be glad to.—
> Come in with me!—Thank you!   You're most kind in showing,
> Ma'am, respect to us.—I had to."

APPENDIX B

III. 3. 664–73 are cretics, expressing the girls' agitation (667 and 668 have trochaic tags); at 674, as agitation gives way to despondency, the cretics change to bacchiacs. Trachalio's matter-of-fact comment at 677 is spoken in iambics (but the text is conjectural), and his call to Palaestra at 678, with her reply, makes a short trochaic line: but as her words happen also to form a cretic, this leads neatly back into cretics, appropriate because the girls' agitation is renewed by his call, and he himself is flustered by their emotion. Finally he rounds off the singing with a trochaic tag, *nimis inepta's*; and the scene then proceeds more quietly in seven-beat iambics.

IV. 2. 906–11 and 914–18, bacchiacs, whose slow pace fits Gripus's laborious steps as he carries the heavy trunk; perhaps he puts it down for a rest at 912–13 and 919, when the metre changes to anapaests—the latter change marks his transition from gloomy reflexion on his hardships to a lively contemplation of his virtues.

924–6 are jaunty trochaics and iambics. In 927–37 his day-dream sweeps majestically through another passage of anapaests.

IV. 3. As Trachalio breaks in on Gripus, there is a sharp change from the anapaests to short iambics. When Gripus has been frustrated in an attempt to withdraw, and the pair almost come to blows, this rhythm is jerkily varied by trochaic and aeolic: 945–6 form a sort of quatrain:—

> "You be careful! Why the hell do *you*
> Hold me?—Listen here, you!—
> I won't.—Oh yes you will, in due
> Time.—Oh well, I'll hear you."

947–8 is another quatrain:—

> "Psst! A moment! You'll find it'll pay.
> Listen to what I'm waiting to say.—
> Well, will you tell me? What *is* it?—Look out!
> Make sure nobody's prowling about!"

APPENDIX B

949–51, cretics.

952–5, another aeolic quatrain:—

> "Only on the condition that you
>   Swear to keep this dark.—
> Yes, I will; I swear to be true,
>   What's-your-name!—Now hark!"

956–62, Trachalio plays his opening gambit in anapaests. Thereafter the scene proceeds in eight-beat trochaics.

Select Bibliography

I. EDITIONS OF *Rudens*

T. Macci Plauti Comoediae, W. M. Lindsay (Oxford, 1903).
T. Macci Plauti Rudens, for the use of schools, Edward A. Sonnenschein (Oxford, 1901).
T. Macci Plauti Rudens, Friedrich Marx [Amsterdam, 1959 (a reprint), in German].

II. BACKGROUND MATERIAL

W. Beare, *The Roman Stage* (London, 1965).
Margarethe Bieber, *The History of the Greek and Roman Theater* (Princeton, 1961).
G. E. Duckworth, *The Nature of Roman Comedy* (Princeton, 1952).

III. TRANSLATIONS

P. Nixon, in the Loeb Classical Library, *Plautus* (London, 1916-38), vol. 4 (scholarly; its "stage directions", not directed to staging, are helpful to understanding).
E. F. Watling, in the Penguin Classics (London, 1965).
H. C. Fay, in *Three Classical Comedies* (verse) (Leeds, 1967).
F. A. Wright, in *Three Plays of Plautus*, Broadway Translations, Routledge (verse) (London, 1925).

Vocabulary

[vb. 5 refers to the conjunction of verbs like *capere*]

A

a, ab, aps, prep. + abl., *from; by* (of agent); *on the side of,* n 1100.

ab-dūcere, vb. 3, *lead away, remove.*

ab-esse, vb., *be absent, be away.*

ab-īre, vb., *go away.*

ā-bītere, vb. 3, *go away.*

abitiō, abitiōnis, noun f., *departure.*

ab-iūdicāre, vb. 1, *judge ... away from, give judgment against ... for.*

ab-iūrāre, vb. 1, *deny on oath.*

ab-ripere, -ripuī, -reptum, vb. 5, *tear away, seize.*

ac-cēdere, vb. 3, *approach, come* or *go towards.*

accept-us, -a, -um, ptc. of *accipere;* as adj., *acceptable.*

accersere, accersīvī, accersītum, vb. 3, *summon, fetch.*

accidere, accidī, vb. 3, *fall; happen.*

accipere, accipere, accēpī, acceptum, vb. 5, *receive, accept, welcome.*

accola, noun m., *neighbour.*

ācer, ācris, ācre, adj., *sharp, keen.*

acerb-us, -a, -um, adj., *bitter.*

acētum, noun n., *sour wine,*

vinegar.

acus, acūs, noun f., *needle,* n 1306.

ad, prep. + acc., *to, towards, against; at, near; after the fashion of.*

ad-decēre, vb., *befit, be appropriate,* n 112.

ad-dere, -didī, -ditum, vb. 3, *add.*

ad-dīcere, vb. 3, *sentence.*

ad-dūcere, vb. 3, *bring.*

1 **ad-eō,** 1 from **adīre.**

2 **adeō,** adv., n 36.

ad-esse, vb., *be present, be here.*

adfect-us, -a, -um, 1 from *adficere,* 2, adj., *sick.*

ad-ferre, vb., *bring.*

adflīctare, vb. 1, and **ad-flīgere, -flīxī, -flīctum,** vb. 3, *knock down, knock about.*

ad-gerere, vb. 3, *carry ... to.*

ad-grediri 4, and **ad-gredī** 5, **-grēssus,** vb. depon., *approach, go* or *come towards.*

adhibēre, vb. 2, *use, display.*

ad-igere, -ēgī, -āctum, vb. 3, *drive ... to, compel.*

ad-imere, -ēmī, -emptum, vb. 3, *take away,* n 389.

ad-īre, vb., *approach, go* or *come to.*

ad-iuvāre, -iūvi or **-iui, -iūtum,** vb. 1, *help.*

adligāre, vb. 1, *bind.*

admodum, adv., *very, very*

much, exactly.

ad-mōlīrī, -mōlītus, vb. 4, *make an effort.*

adornāre, vb. 1, *prepare.*

ad-pōnere, vb. 3, *place, put . . . near by.*

adpōt-us, -a, -um, adj., *in liquor, having drink taken.*

adprīmē, adv., *in the first degree, highly.*

ad-rigere, -rēxī, -rēctum, vb. 3, *set up.*

ad-ripere, -ripuī, -reptum, vb. 5, *seize.*

adrogāre, vb. 1, n 1332.

ad-sentīre,-sēnsī,-sēnsum, and depon. **adsentīrī,** vb. 4, *agree.*

ad-serere, -seruī, -sertum, vb. 3, *claim, appropriate.*

adservāre, vb., *watch.*

ad-sidēre, -sēdī, -sessum, vb. 2, *sit near by.*

adsīdere, vb. 3, *sit down (beside* or *near by).*

adsistere, vb. 3, *stand by.*

adulēscēns, adulēscentis, noun c., *young man* or *woman.*

adulēscentula, noun f., *young woman*

ad-vehere, vb. 3, *bring, ship.*

ad-venīre, vb. 4, *arrive, come.*

advocāt-us, -a -um, 1 from *advocāre,* 2 as noun, *supporter,* n 890.

advolāre, vb. 1, *fly up, fly to.*

advorsārius, noun m., *opponent.*

advorsum, prep. + acc., *against.*

aedēs, aedis, noun f., singular, *temple, shrine;* plural, *house.*

aedīlis, aedīlis, noun m., *aedile,* n 373.

aegrimōnia, noun f., *vexa-*

tion, distress.

aegrōtāre, vb. 1, *be sick.*

aemul-us, -a, -um, adj., *rivalling, imitating;* as noun, *rival, imitator.*

aequ-os, -a, -om, adj., *equal, level, fair, right;* + abl. n 47.

aerumna, noun f., *misery, hardship, affliction.*

aerumnōs-us, -a, -um, adj., *afflicted.*

aetās aetātis, noun f., *life, age;* **aetatem agere,** *spend one's life.*

aetātula, noun f., *age.*

ager, agrī, noun m., *field, farm, countryside.*

agere, ēgī, actum, vb. 3, *do, deal with, plead, drive, spend (time);* imperative, **age,** *come on!*

agitāre, vb. 1, frequentative of *agere.*

agnus, agnī, noun m., *lamb.*

agricola, noun m., *farmer.*

Agrigentīn-us, -a, -um, adj., *of Agrigentum.*

aha, interj., *ooh!*

(āiere), vb. defective, *say, say yes.*

Alcumēna, noun f., *Alcmena.*

aleātor, aleātōris, noun m., *dice-thrower, gambler.*

alere, aluī, altum, vb. 3, *feed, rear.*

algēre, alsi, vb. 2, *be cold.*

algor, algōris, m., and **algū, algūs,** n., nouns, *shivering, cold.*

aliā, adv., *in different places.*

alicubī, adv., *somewhere.*

aliquī, aliqua, aliquod, adj., *some.*

aliquis, aliquid, pron., *somebody, something.*

aliquō, adv., *to some place, somewhere.*

VOCABULARY

alius, alia, aliud, pron. and adj., *other, some.*

alm-us, -a, -um, adj., *kindly.*

alter, altera, alterum, pron. and adj., *other, one (of two), second.*

altrīnsecus, adv., *on the other side.*

alt-us, -a, -um, adj., *high, deep;* **altum** n. as noun, *the deep.*

alvos, alvī, noun f., *belly, bowels.*

amāre, vb. 1, *love;* **amo te,** n 363; **amabo,** n 249.

amātio, amationis, noun f., *petting.*

ambō, ambae, ambo, adj., *both.*

ambulāre, vb. 1, *walk, march.*

ambūstulāt-us, -a, -um, adj., *scorched, toasted.*

amict-us, -a, -um, adj., *covered, cloaked.*

amīcus, amīcī, noun m. and **amic-us, -a, -um,** adj., *friend, friendly.*

ā-mittere, vb. 3, *send away, let go, lose.*

amor, amōris, noun m., *love, love affair.*

amplectī, amplexus, 3, and **amplexārī,** 1, verbs deponent, *embrace, hug.*

amplius, adv., *more, further.*

ampullārius, ampullarii, noun m., *flask-maker.*

an, interrogative particle, usually not to be translated, sometimes *or.*

anancaeō, adv., n 363.

ancilla and **ancillula,** nouns f., *servant-girl.*

ancipēs, gen. **ancipitis,** adj., *two-edged.*

anetīn-us, -a, -um, adj., *of ducks.*

angust-us, -a, -um, adj., *narrow, constricted.*

animus, animī, noun m., *mind, spirit;* locative, **animī,** *in heart;* **animum advorsāre** or **advortere,** *pay attention, keep one's mind on the job,* **animō male fit,** n 510.

anne = an.

annus, annī, noun m., *year.*

antīqu-os, -a, -om, adj., *old, ancient.*

antistita, noun f., *priestess-in-charge.*

anus, anūs, noun f., *old woman, old lady.*

aperīre, aperuī, apertum, vb. 4, *open.*

apīscī, aptus, vb. 3 deponent, *get, win.*

apparāre, vb. 1, *prepare, get, find.*

appellāre, vb. 1, *address.*

ap-pellere, -pulī, -pulsum, vb. 3, *drive . . . to, push.*

aps = a.

aps-cēdere, vb. 3, *go away.*

apsēns, gen. **apsentis,** adj., *absent.*

ap-solvere, vb. 3, *set free; get rid of (i.e. finish describing).*

apstinēre, vb. 2, trans. or intrans., *keep away, keep off.*

aps-trudere, -trusi, -trusum, vb. 3, *push away, shove,* n 1007.

apud, prep. + acc., *with, at home with, at.*

aqua, noun f., *water.*

āra, noun f., *altar.*

arbiter, arbitrī, noun m., *arbitrator.*

arbitrārī, vb. 1 depon., *decide, think.*

arbitrātus, arbitrātūs, noun m., *arbitration, decision.*

VOCABULARY

ardu-os, -a, -om, adj., *up-hill, difficult.*

ārēre, vb., *be dry.*

ārēscere, vb. 3, *dry out, become dry.*

argenteol-us, -a, -um, adj., *silver.*

argentum, argentī, noun n., *silver, money.*

argūmentum, argūmentī, noun n., *proof; subject-matter.*

ārid-us, -a, -um, adj., *dry.*

āritūdō, āritūdinis, noun f., *dryness.*

arrabō, arrabōnis, noun m., *earnest-money, first instalment.*

ars, artis, noun f., *skill.*

ascendere, ascendi, ascēnsum, vb. 3, *climb.*

ascēnsiō, ascēnsiōnis, noun f., *climb, ascent.*

aspicere, aspexī, aspectum, vb. 5, *look at, catch sight of.*

asportāre, vb. 1, *carry away, ship off.*

astāre, astitī, vb. 1, *stand by.*

astringere, astrīnxi, astrīctum, vb. 3, *bind, involve.*

astū, adv., *cunningly, cleverly.*

astūt-us, -a, -um, adj., *clever.*

at, conj., *but.*

āter, ātra, ātrum, adj., *black.*

Athēnae, Athēnārum, noun f., *Athens.*

atque, conj., *and; and yet,* n 22; *even,* n 121.

atquī, conj., *and yet, nevertheless.*

Attic-us, -a, -um, adj., *Attic, Athenian.*

attinēre, vb. 2, *pertain (to), concern* (with *ad*).

attingere, attigī, attāctum, vb. 3, *touch.*

attrectāre, vb. 1, *handle.*

aucupārī, vb. 1 depon., *trap birds;* n 1093.

audāx, gen. **audācis,** adj., *daring.*

audēre, ausus, vb. 2, semidepon., *wish,* n 870; *dare.*

audīre, vb. 4, *hear, listen.*

auferre, apstulī, ablātum, vb., *carry off, take away.*

au-fugere, vb. 5, *escape.*

augēre, auxī, auctum, vb. 2, *increase, bless.*

aula, noun f., *pot,* n 135.

aureol-us, -a, -um and **aure-us, -a, -um,** adj., *golden.*

auris auris, noun f., *ear.*

aurum, auri, noun n., *gold.*

auscultāre, vb. 1, *listen.*

auscultātiō, auscultātiōnis, noun f., *listening,* n 502.

auspicāre, vb. 1, *take the auspices* (+ dative), n 717.

aut, conj., *or, or else.*

autem, conj., *and, but.*

autumāre, vb. 1, *say, declare.*

auxilium, auxilī, noun n., *help.*

avāritia, noun f., *greed.*

avār-us, -a, -um, adj., *greedy,* adv., **avāriter.**

a-vehere, vb. 3, *carry away, ship abroad, export.*

avid-us, -a, -um, adj., *eager, desirous.*

avis, avis, noun f., *bird.*

ā-vortere, vb. 3, *turn away, turn aside.*

B

balanus, balanī, noun f., *acorn; a shell-fish.*

balinea, noun f., *bath.*

balineātor, balineātōris, noun m., *bath-attendant.*

ballaena, noun f., *sea-monster, whale.*

barathrum, barathrī, noun n., *pit.*

barba, noun f., *beard.*

barbar-us, -a, -um, adj., *barbarous, uncivilised.*

basilic-us, -a, -um, adj., n 431.

belliāt-us, -a, -um, adj., *beautified, prettified.*

bell-us, -a, -um, adj., *pretty.*

bēlua, noun f., *animal, beast.*

bene, adv., *well.*

beneficium, beneficī, noun n., *good deed.*

benīgn-us, -a, um, adj., *kind.*

bēstia, noun f., *beast, creature.*

bibere, bibī, vb. 3, *drink.*

blandīmentum, blandī-mentī, n., and **blanditia,** f. nouns, *coaxing, sales-talk.*

bolus, bolī, noun m., n 360.

bon-us, -a, -um, adj., *good,* n. pl., **bona,** as noun, *goods, property.*

bulla, noun f., *locket.*

C

cadere, cecidī, cāsum, vb. 3, *fall.*

(caeles) gen. **caelitis,** noun m., *dweller in heaven, sky-god.*

caelum, caelī, noun n., *heaven, sky.*

caerul-us, -a, -um, adj., *blue.*

calātor, calātōris, noun m., *servant, attendant.*

cale-facere, vb. 5 and **cale-factare,** vb. 1, *warm, heat.*

calēre, vb. 2, *be warm, be hot.*

campus, campī, noun m., *plain.*

candidāt-us, -a, -um, adj., *dressed in white.*

candid-us, -a, -um, adj., *white, brilliant.*

canis, canis, noun c., *dog.*

cantāre, vb. 1, *sing, cry aloud.*

cantharus, cantharī, noun m., n 1319.

capere, cēpī, captum, vb. 5, *take.*

capessere, capessīvī, cap-essītum, vb. 3 trans., *take;* **se capessere,** *betake oneself, go;* so also intransitive, 178.

capillus, capillī, noun m., *hair.*

capitālis, capitale, adj., *affecting one's life, deadly.*

captāre, vb. 1, *try to capture, hunt, fish for.*

caput, capitis, noun n., *head; life, person, self,* n 885.

carbō, carbōnis, noun m., *coal.*

carcer, carceris, noun m., *gaol.*

carēre, vb. 2, *be without, be free from, be deprived of.*

carnufex, carnuficis, noun m., *hangman, executioner.*

castra, castrōrum, noun n. pl., *camp, fortress.*

caude-us, -a, -um, adj., n 1109.

caussa, noun f., *matter, cause, reason;* abl. **caussā,** *for the sake of,* n 31.

cavēre, cāvī, cautum, vb. 2, *beware, take care, avoid,* n 833; **cave** + subjunctive, a common form of negative command.

-ce, demonstrative suffix

often attached to *hic, iste, ille* and their derivatives.

cēdere, cēssi, cēssum, vb. 3, *yield, withdraw.*

cedo, interjection, n 243.

cēlāre, vb. 1, *conceal, hide.*

celer, celeris, celere, adj., *swift, quick.*

cĕna, noun f., *supper, (evening) dinner.*

cēnāre, vb. 1, *dine.*

cēnāt-us, -a, -um, ptc. of **cenare,** *having dined.*

cēnsēre, cēnsuī, cēnsum, vb. 2, *estimate, think;* n 1271-2.

cēnsiō, cēnsiōnis, noun f., n 1273.

centiēns, adv., *a hundred times.*

centum, adj., indeclinable, *a hundred.*

cerebrum, cerebrī, noun n., *brain.*

Ceres, Cereris, noun f., *Ceres, goddess of corn.*

cerrīt-us, -a, -um, adj., *crazy, lunatic.*

cert-us, -a, -um, adj., *definite, certain, determined;* **certiōrem facere,** *inform;* adv., **certē, certō,** n 344.

cēssāre, vb. 1, *hesitate, hang back.*

cēter-us, -a, -um, adj., *remaining, the rest of.*

chlamydāt-us, -a, -um, adj., *wearing a chlamys or military cloak.*

cibus, cibī, noun m., *food.*

ciccus, ciccī, noun m., *the membrane surrounding a pomegranate seed.*

ciēre or **cīre, cīvī, cītum,** vb. 2 or 4, *call for.*

cinis, cineris, noun m., *ash.*

circumcursāre, vb. 1, *run round.*

circum-īre, vb., *go round.*

circum-spicere, -spexī, -spectum, vb. 5, *look around.*

circumvectāre, vb. 1, *carry round;* in passive, *sail round.*

circum-vincīre, -vinxī, -vinctum, vb. 4, *tie round.*

cīre, see **ciēre.**

cistella, cistellula, and **cistula,** nouns f., *casket, little box.*

cito, adv., *quickly;* comparative **citius.**

cīvis, cīvis, noun c., *citizen, fellow-countryman (-woman).*

cīvitās, cīvitātis, noun f., abstract *citizenship;* concrete *body of citizens, state.*

clam, adv., *secretly;* prep. + abl., *without the knowledge of.*

clāmor, clāmōris, noun m., *shout, yell.*

clanculum, adv. diminutive of *clam, secretly.*

clār-us, -a, -um, *bright, shining, famous.*

clāva, noun f., *club, cudgel.*

clāvātor, clāvātōris, noun m., *club-man.*

clāvos, clāvī, noun m., *nail.*

clienta, noun f., *dependant, retainer;* p. 35.

cluēre, vb. 2, *be renowned, bear the name.*

cognāt-us, -a, -um, adj., *kindred;* as noun, *kinsman (-woman).*

colaphus, colaphī, noun m., n 1007.

colere, coluī, cultum, vb. 3, *cultivate.*

colōr, colōris, noun m., *colour.*

collus, collī, noun m., n 888, *neck.*

columbar, columbāris, noun n., n 888.

columbus, columbī, noun m. *dove, pigeon.*

VOCABULARY

comb-ūrere, -ūssi, -ūstum, vb. 3, *burn.*

comes, comitis, noun c., *companion.*

cōmicus, cōmicī, noun m., *comedian.*

cōmis, cōme, adj., *friendly, kind.*

cōmitās, cōmitātis, noun f., *friendliness, kindness.*

commeāre, vb. 1, *go and come (frequently), visit.*

commercium, commercī, noun n., *business, dealings.*

com-minuere, -minuī, -minūtum, vb. 3, *smash.*

com-mīscēre, -mīscuī, -mīxtum, vb. 2, *bring into contact.*

com-miserēscere, -miseruī, -miseritum, vb. 3, *take pity on* (+ genitive).

com-mittere, vb. 3, *entrust.*

commodāre, vb. 1, *lend or supply (free).*

commodul-us, -a, -um, adj., n 468, *moderate.*

commod-us, -a, -um, adj., *convenient, suitable;* n 468.

commonēre, vb. 2, *warn, advise, remind.*

commūnīre, vb. 4, *build and fortify.*

commūnis, commūne, adj., *common, belonging to all, shared.*

compāct-us, -a, -um, from *compingere.*

comparāre, vb. 1, *get together; put together, compare.*

compellāre, vb. 1, *address.*

compendium, compendī, noun n., *saving, abbreviation.*

com-pingere, -pegī, -pāctum, vb. 3, *put together, pack.*

com-placēre, vb. 2, *please* (+ dat.).

complectī, complexus, vb. 3 depon., *embrace, hug.*

com-plicāre, -plicuī, -plicitum, vb. 1, *fold up, coil.*

complūscul-ī, -ae, -a, adj. *several.*

comportāre, vb. 1, *carry (together).*

compotīre, vb. 4, *put in possession of* (+ acc. + abl.).

com-prehendere, vb. 3, *catch, arrest.*

com-primere, -pressī, -pressum, vb. 3, *squash.*

concha, noun f., *shell, shellfish, anything shaped like a shell.*

Conchīta, noun m., *Shellican*, n 310.

con-cēdere, vb. 3, *withdraw.*

con-cidere, -cidī, -cāsum, vb. 3, *collapse.*

concinnāre, vb. 1, *fix, put right.*

con-clūdere, -clūsī, -clūsum, vb. 3, *shut up, pack.*

con-crēdere, vb. 3, *entrust.*

con-dere, -didī, -ditum, vb. 3, *put away; found.*

condiciō, condiciōnis, noun f., *bargain, terms.*

condīmentum, condīmentī, noun n., *seasoning.*

condōnāre, vb. 1, *give, present* (+ acc. of thing and dat. of recipient, or + acc. of recipient and abl. of thing).

condormīscere, vb. 3, *fall asleep.*

con-dūcere, vb. 3, *bring together; hire.*

cō-nectere, -nexuī, -nexum, vb. 3, *join, link.*

con-ferre, vb., *bring together, contribute.*

con-ficere, -fēcī, -fectum, vb. 5, *perform, complete.*

confīdēns, gen. confidentis, adj., *self-confident.*

confīdentia, noun f., *self-confidence.*

con-flare, vb. 1, *blow up (of fire)*.

con-fodere, vb. 5, *dig*.

con-fringere, -frēgi, -frāctum, vb. 3, *smash, wreck*.

con-fugere, vb. 5, *flee, take refuge*.

con-gerere, vb. 3, *collect*.

con-icere, -iēci, -iectum, vb. 5, *throw, put together*.

coniectūra, noun f., *guess, interpretation*, n 612.

conlūsim, adv., n 1248.

con-ruere, -ruī, vb. 3 intrans., *collapse;* transit. n 542.

cōn-scendere, -scendi, -scēnsum, vb. 3, *climb, go aboard*.

cōnsci-us, -a, -um, adj., *in the know*.

cōn-senēscere, -senuī, vb. 3, *decay, crumble*.

cōn-sequī, vb., *overtake, keep up with*.

cōnserva, noun f., *fellow-servant*.

cōnsilium, consilī, noun n., *counsel, good sense, plan*.

cōnsociāre, vb. 1, *ally, go into partnership*, n 551.

cōnsōlārī, vb. 1 depon., *console, offer sympathy to*.

cōnspicārī, vb. 1 depon., *catch sight of*.

cōn-sulere, -suluī, -sultum, vb. 3, *plan, consult, take thought*.

cōnsult-us, -a, -um, participle from *consulere;* as adj., *wise*.

con-tendere, -tendī, vb. 3, *compete*.

con-terere, -trīvī, -trītum, vb. 3, *wear out*.

con-ticīscere, -ticuī, vb. 3, *stop talking*.

con-tinēre, -tinuī, -tentum, vb. 2, *restrain, hold back, hold*.

continuŏ, adv., *immediately*.

contrā, adv., *on the other hand, opposite;* prep. + acc., *against, to meet*.

con-trahere, vb. 3, *draw together;* contracta fronte, *scowling*.

contrōvorsia, noun f., *dispute*.

convenīre, vb. 4, intrans., *come together;* transit. *meet, befit*.

convīva, noun m., *guest, fellow-guest*.

con-vorrere, -vorrī, -vorsum, vb. 3, *sweep together, sweep up*.

con-vortere, -vortī, -vorsum, vb. 3, *turn*.

cōpia, noun f., *supply, resources, ability*.

coquere, coxī, coctum, vb. 3, *cook*.

corium, corii, noun n., *hide*.

corpus, corporis, noun n., *body*.

corusc-us, -a, -um, adj., *flickering, agitated*, n 525-6.

cottīdiē, adv., *daily*.

crāpula, noun f., *sick headache (brought on by drinking)*.

crass-us, -a, -um, adj., *thick, fat*.

crēber, crēbra, crēbrum, adj., *thick, frequent;* adv., crēbrō, *thickly, at close intervals:* comparative crēbrius.

crēdere, crēdidī, crēditum, vb. 3, *trust, believe* (+ dative).

crepitāre, vb. 1, *make a noise, clatter*.

crepundia, crepundiōrum, noun n. pl., n 1081.

crībrum, crībrī, noun n., *sieve*.

crīsp-us, -a, -um, adj., *curly-headed*.

cruciātus, cruciātūs, noun

m., *torment.*

crumīna, noun f., *purse.*

crūs, crūris, noun n., *leg.*

crux, crucis, noun f., *cross, gallows.*

cubāre, cubuī, cubitum, vb. 1, *lie down, go to bed.*

cubitum, cubitī, noun n., *cubit, ell, foot and a half.*

culter, cultrī, noun m., *knife.*

cult-us, -a, -um, from *colere.*

cultus, cultūs, noun m., *livelihood.*

cum, prep. + abl., *with.*

cupere, cupīvī, cupītum, vb. 5, *desire.*

cūra, noun f., *care, anxiety.*

cūrāre, vb. 1, *care for, attend to, take care of* (usually transit., but n 182).

curculiunculus, curculiunculī, noun m., *wee weevil.*

currere, cucurrī, cursum, vb. 3, *run.*

curriculum, curriculī, noun n., *run.*

custodēla and **custōdia,** nouns f., *protection, guard-duty.*

cyathus, cyathī, noun m., n 1319.

Cyrēnēnsis, adj., *Cyrenaean.*

D

dare, dedī, datum, vb. 1, *give; make,* n 900; **verba dare,** n 325.

dē, prep. + abl., *down from, from; about.*

dēbēre, vb. 2, *owe.*

decēre, vb. 2, *be fitting.*

de-cipere, -cēpī, -ceptum, vb. 5, *cheat.*

decōr-us, -a, -um, adj.,

befitting, worthy, n 255; *handsome.*

dēfendere, defendi, defēnsum, vb. 3, *ward off,* n 774; *defend.*

dēfēnsāre, vb. 1, *defend.*

dē-ferre, vb., *bring, offer.*

dē-fierī, vb., *fail, run out.*

dēfrūdāre, vb. 1, *defraud.*

dēierāre, vb. 1, *swear.*

dēlicia, noun f., *delight, pleasure, fun.*

de-linquere, -līquī, -lictum, vb. 3, *fail to do, do wrong.*

dē-litēscere, -lituī, vb. 3, *hide.*

dēlūdificāre, vb. 1, *fool.*

dē-mittere, vb. 3, *let down.*

dēmorārī, vb. 1 depon., *delay, keep waiting.*

dēmum, particle to emphasise and make precise a preceding pronoun or adverb, n 930.

dēns, dentis, noun m., *tooth.*

dēnuō, adv., *over again.*

deorsum, adv., *downwards, down.*

dē-ripere, -ripuī, -reptum, vb. 5, *tear away.*

dē-serere, -seruī, -sertum, vb. 3, *abandon.*

dēsidia, noun f., *slackness, laziness.*

dē-silīre, -siluī, or **-suluī, -sultum,** vb. 4, *jump down.*

dē-sinere, vb. 3, *cease.*

dē-sistere, -stitī, -stitum, vb. 3, *cease.*

dē-spondēre, -spondī, -spōnsum, vb. 2, *betroth, promise in marriage.*

dēstināre, vb., *fasten; determine;* n 45.

dē-stituere, -stituī, -stitūtum, vb. 3, *station, leave in position.*

dē-tegere, vb. 3, *uncover, unroof.*

dē-tinēre, -tinuī, -tentum, vb. 2, *detain.*

dēturbāre, vb. 1, *knock down.*

deus, deī, noun m., *god.*

dē-venīre, vb. 4, *come down, come.*

dēvītāre, vb. 1, *avoid.*

dēvorāre, vb. 1, *devour.*

dextera, noun f., *right hand.*

dextrōvorsum, adv. *to the right.*

dī, nom. pl. of *deus.*

dīcere, dīxi, dictum, vb. 3, *say, tell, speak, call.*

dictum, 1. from *dīcere;* 2. as noun n., *word, saying.*

didicī, from *dīscere.*

dīerect-us, -a, -um, adj., n 1170.

diēs, diēī, noun m. or f., *day.*

dif-ferre, vb. transitive, *separate;* intrans., *differ.*

dif-fīdere, -fīsus, vb. 3 semi-depon., *distrust* (+ dat.).

digitulus, digitulī, and digitus, digiti, nouns m., *finger.*

dign-us, -a, -um, adj., *worthy* (+ abl.).

dīlectus, dīlectūs, noun m., *levy, enrolment,* n 1279.

dīligentia, noun f., *care.*

dī-luere, -luī, -lutum, vb. 3, *wash away; clear up.*

dīmidi-us, -a, -um, adj., *half;* neuter dimidium as noun.

dī-mittere, vb. 3, *send away, dismiss.*

dīs, dat. or abl. pl. of *deus.*

dīscere, didicī, vb. 3, *learn.*

disparāre, vb. 1, *set at intervals.*

disputāre, vb. 1, *argue.*

dītiae, see dīvitiae.

diū, adv., *for a long time;* comparat. diūtius, *longer.*

diūtin-us, -a, -um, *long-lasting;* adv. diūtinē, *for a long time.*

dīves, genitive divitis, adj., *rich.*

dī-videre, -vīsī, -vīsum, vb. 3, *divide.*

dīvidu-os, -a, -om, adj., *halved.*

dīvīn-us, -a, -um, adj., *divine, of,* or *for the gods.*

dīvitiae, dīvitiārum (dītiae, ditiārum), noun f. pl., *wealth, riches.*

dīvors-us, -a, -um, adj., *far apart, in different directions.*

dīv-os, -a, -om, adj., *divine;* as noun m. or f., *god, goddess.*

doct-us, -a, -um, participle of *docere;* as adj. *clever.*

dolus, dolī, noun m., *trick.*

domus, domūs, noun f., *house, home;* locative domi, *at home;* n 1208, 1335.

dōnābilis, dōnābile, adj., *qualified for a presentation.*

dōnec, conj., *until.*

dōnum, dōni, noun n., *gift, present.*

dormīre, vb. 4, *sleep.*

dōs, dōtis, noun f., *dowry, endowment.*

dūcere, dūxi, dūctum, vb. 3, *lead, bring.*

dūctitāre, vb. 1, *lead about, deal in.*

dūdum, adv., *lately, just now.*

duis, n 580, 1368.

dum, adv., *so long,* n 779; enclitic, *well, just, just a moment,* n 32, 720; conj., *while; so long as.*

du-o, -ae, -o, adj., *two.*

VOCABULARY

E

ē, ex, prep. + abl., *out of, from, of.*

eādem, adv., *by the (same) way.*

ēcastor, interjection, *by Castor!*

ecce, interjection, *behold! see here! there you are!* (+ acc.).

eccill-um, -am, -ud = *ecce* + *illum*, etc.

ecc-um, -am, etc., n 309.

echīnus, echīnī, noun m., *hedgehog;* anything like it, e.g. *sea-urchin.*

ecquis, ecquid, pron., interrog., *anyone? anything?*

ēdentāre, vb. I, *de-tooth, knock out the teeth from.*

edo, esse, ēdi, es(s)um, vb. irreg., *eat.*

ēdormīscere, vb. 3, *sleep off.*

ēducāre, vb. I, *breed, rear.*

ē-dūcere, vb. 3, I. *lead out, remove;* 2. same as *educare.*

effigia, noun f., *image, picture.*

egēre, vb. 2, *be in want* (+ gen. or abl.).

ego, mē, meī, mihĭ, (mī), mē, (mēd), pron., *I, me.*

ē-gredī, -grēssus, vb. 5 depon., *go (or come) out, leave.*

ehem, interjection, n 177.

ĕheu, interjection, *alas!*

eho, interjection, n 578, 947

ē-icere, -iēcī, -iectum, vb. 5, *fling out, cast ashore.*

ei(i)usmodī = *eius modī*, *of that sort.*

ē-lavāre, vb. I, *wash out;* n 537.

ē-līdere, -līsi, -līsum, vb. 3, *knock out.*

ellebor ŏs-us, -a, -um, adj., *needing hellebore,* n 1006.

ē-loquī, vb. 3 depon., *speak out, speak up.*

ē-luere, -luī, vb. 3, *wash out;* n 537.

em, interjection, n 463.

emere, ēmī, emptum, vb. 3, *buy.*

ē-mittere, vb. 3, *send out, release;* **manū ēmittere,** *free from slavery.*

ēnāre, vb. I, *swim out.*

ē-nicāre, -nicuī (or **necāvī**), **-nectum** (or **-necātum**), vb. I, *murder (slowly);* n 944.

enim, I. asseverative particle, *definitely* (922, 989, 1116); 2. conjunction *for.*

ēnsiculus, ēnsiculī, noun m., *little sword.*

ēnumquam, adv., interrog., *ever?*

eō, vb., see *īre.*

eō, pron. ablative of *is; for that reason;* especially with comparatives, *that much . . . , the . . .*

eō, adv., *thither, to that place, there,* n 61, *to it.*

epichysis, epichysis, noun f., n 1319.

equidem, emphatic form of *quidem,* used for *ego quidem.*

equos, equī, noun m. *horse.*

era, noun f., *mistress, owner* (of a slave).

ērādīcāre, vb. I, *uproot, root out.*

ergā, prep. + acc., *in relation to, towards.*

ergō, adv. or conj., *therefore.*

erīlis, erīle, adj., *belonging to the master (or mistress).*

ē-ripere, -ripuī, -reptum, vb. 5, *tear away, seize.*

errāre, vb. I, *stray, lose one's*

195

way.

errātiŏ, errātiŏnis, noun f., and **error errōris,** noun m., *straying, being lost.*

erus, erī, noun m., *master* (of a slave).

esca, noun f., *food, bait.*

esse, fuī (present *sum*), vb., *be.*

ēsse, ēdi, ēs(s)um (present *edo*), vb., *eat.*

et, adv. or conj., *even, also; both; and.*

etiam, adv., *still; even.*

etiamdum, adv., *still; after negative, ever yet.*

eugae and **eugepae,** interjections, *hurrah!*

Eurīpidēs, Eurīpidī, noun m., *Euripides.*

ē-vādere, -vāsī, -vāsum, vb. 3, *escape, get out.*

ē-venīre, vb. 4, *come out; result.*

ēventus, ēventūs, noun m., *outcome, result.*

ēvocāre, vb. 1, *call out.*

ex, see **ē.**

exaequāre, vb. 1, *equal, compensate for, counterbalance.*

exagōga, noun f., *export,* n 631.

exanimālis, exanimāle, adj., *deadly, paralysing.*

exanimāt-us, -a, -um, adj., *fainting, paralysed.*

exārēscere, vb. 3, *dry out.*

ex-cidere, -cidī, -cāsum, vb. 3, *fall out.*

ex-cipere, -cēpī, -ceptum, vb. 5, *take out, catch, fish up.*

excitāre, vb. 1, *rouse, call out.*

excruciāre, vb. 1, *torment.*

exemplum, exemplī, noun n., *pattern, example,* n 370.

exercēre, vb. 2, *train.*

exercitus, exercitūs, noun

m., *training.*

exhibēre, vb. 2, *provide.*

exicāre, vb. 1, n 122.

ex-imere, -ēmī, -emptum, vb. 3, *take out.*

exīre, vb., *go* (or *come*) *out.*

exitium, exitī, noun n., *destruction.*

exoculāre, vb. 1, *knock out the eyes from.*

exoptāre, vb. 1, *pray for, desire.*

exōrāre, vb. 1, *move by pleading, persuade, succeed* (in a request).

exorīrī, vb. 4 or 5, *rise up.*

expedīre, vb. 4, *disentangle; explain.*

expendere, vb. 3, *weigh out, counterbalance.*

ex-perīrī, -pertus, vb. 4, *experience.*

expetere and **expetessere,** vb. 3, *seek, desire, ask for.*

exsul, exsulis, noun c., *exile.*

exsulāre, vb 1, *be in exile.*

ex-quīrere, -quīsīvī, -quīsītum, vb. 3, *seek out, enquire, investigate.*

ex-scrībere, -scrīpsī, -scrīptum, vb. 3, *write out.*

exsequī, vb. 3 depon., *follow, apply to.*

exsolvere, vb. 3, *untie.*

exspectāre, vb. 1, *await, wait for.*

ex-sūrgere, -surrēxī, -surrēctum, vb. 3, *rise up.*

extāris, extāre, adj., *for cooking exta* (offal).

extemplō, adv., *promptly.*

ex-tergēre, -tērsī, -tērsum, vb. 2, *wipe, rub clean.*

extrahere, vb. 3, *pull out, pull up.*

ex-unguere, -ūnxī, -ūnctum, vb. 3, n 580.

VOCABULARY

ex-ūrere, -ūssi, -ūstum, vb. 3, *burn out.*

ex-urgēre, -ūrsī, vb. 2, *force out, squeeze out.*

F

faber, fabrī, noun m., *workman, smith.*

fābula, noun f., *talk, story; play.*

fābulāri, vb. 1 depon., *talk, speak.*

facere, fēcī, factum, vb. 5, *make; do; cause; estimate* (+ gen. of value); **certiōrem facere,** *inform.*

facessere, facessīvī, facessītum, vb. 3 transit., *perform, deal with;* intrans., *go away.*

faciēs, faciēī, noun f., *appearance.*

facile, adj. neuter of *facile;* adv., *easily.*

facilis, facile, adj., *easy.*

facinus, facinoris, noun n., *deed, action* (usually wicked, but n 162).

factiō, factiōnis, noun f., *action,* n 1372.

factum, from *facere;* ptc. neuter as noun, *action.*

fallere, fefellī, falsum, vb. 3, *elude, keep in the dark.*

fals-us, -a, -um, 1. from *fallere;* 2. as adj., *false.*

fāma, noun f., *fame, reputation.*

famēlic-us, -a, -um, adj., *starveling.*

famēs, famis, noun f., *hunger, starvation.*

familiāris, familiāre, adj., *belonging to the household, familiar.*

fānum, fānī, noun n., *shrine, temple.*

fastīdiōs-us, -a, -um, adj., *fastidious, fussy.*

fatērī, fassus, vb. 2 depon., *admit, confess.*

faucēs, faucium, noun f. pl., *throat.*

fēlēs, fēlis, noun f., *cat,* n 748.

fēmina, noun f., *woman.*

fēnstra (fenestra), noun f., *window, sky-light.*

ferōx, adj., *valiant, fierce.*

ferrāmentum, ferrāmentī, noun n., *iron tool,* i.e., *spade.*

ferrāri-us, -a, -um, adj., *of iron, of iron-work;* **fabrī ferrariī,** *blacksmiths.*

ferre, tulī, lātum, vb., *bear, fetch, bring, get.*

fīcus, fīcī, noun f., *fig.*

fidēs, fideī noun f., *faith, loyalty, honesty; promise; protection.*

fidicini-us -a, -um, adj., *for flute-playing.*

fīd-us, -a, -um, *faithful, discrete, reliable.*

fierī, factus, vb. passive of *facere.*

fīlia and **fīliola** nouns f., *daughter.*

flagrantia, noun f., *blaze, flagrancy,* n 733.

flēre, flēvī, flētum, vb. 2, *weep.*

floccus, floccī, noun m., *tuft of wool;* **floccī facere,** *care two pins for.*

flūctuāre, vb. 1, *heave, swell, surge.*

flūctuōs-us, -a, -um, *heaving, surging.*

flūctus, flūctūs, noun m., *wave, billow.*

fodere, fōdī, fōssum, vb. 5, *dig.*

follis, follis, noun m., *leather bag.*

forās, adv., *out, away,* n 171.

fore, forem, future infin. and imperf., subjunc. of *esse.*

foris, foris, noun f. (usually in plural), *door.*

fōrma, noun f., *shape, appearance.*

fortasse, adv., *perhaps.*

fortis, forte, adj., *brave, energetic.*

fortūna, noun f., *fortune, luck.*

fortūnāt-us, -a, -um, adj., *fortunate, lucky.*

forum, forī, noun n., *market place.*

frangere, frēgī, frāctum, vb. 3, *break, wreck.*

fraudāre, vb. 1, *defraud, swindle.*

fraudulent-us, -a, -um, adj., *swindling.*

fraus, fraudis, noun f., *deceit, wickedness.*

frīgefactāre, vb. 1, *cool.*

frīgid-us, -a, -um, adj., *cold.*

frōns, frontis, noun f., *forehead.*

frūnīscī, frūnītus, vb. 3, *get, win.*

frūstrā, adv., *in vain;* **frūstrā esse,** *be mistaken.*

fugere, fūgī, vb. 5, *flee, run away.*

fundāmentum, fundāmentī, noun n., *bottom.*

fūr, fūris, noun m., *thief.*

fūrārī, vb. 1 depon., *steal, commit burglary.*

furcifer, furciferī, noun m., *a (bad) slave, fastened as a punishment to a plank across his shoulders; gallows-bird, whip-stock.*

fūstis, fūstis, noun m., *cudgel.*

G

galea, noun f., *helmet.*

gaulus, gaulī, noun m., n 1319.

gēns, gentis, noun f., *tribe, nation.*

genus, generis, noun n., *race; kind, type.*

genū, genūs, noun n., *knee.*

gerere, gessī, gestum, vb. 3, *carry; do.*

germān-us, -a, -um, adj., *true-born.*

gestāre, vb. 1, *wear.*

gladius, gladiī, noun m., *sword.*

glāns, glandis, noun f., *acorn.*

glōria, noun f., *glory, boast, pride.*

gnār-us, -a, -um, adj., *aware of, acquainted with* (+ gen.).

gnāta, noun f., *daughter.*

gradus, gradūs, noun m., *step.*

Graecia, noun f., *Greece.*

Graec-us, -a, -um, adj., *Greek.*

grassārī, vb. 1 depon., *roam.*

grātia, noun f., *favour; gratitude;* **grātiam habēre, grātiās agere,** *be grateful, thank;* abl. **grātiā** as prep., like **caussā,** *for the sake of.*

grātulārī, vb. 1 depon., *congratulate* (+ dat.).

grāt-us, -a, -um, adj., active, *grateful;* passive, *welcome, acceptable.*

gravări, vb. 1 depon., *begrudge.*

gravăt-us, -a, -um, partic. of *gravari*, as adj., *grudging.*

gubernător, gubernătŏris, noun m., *pilot, steersman.*

gutta, noun f., *drop.*

gymnastic-us, -a, -um, adj., *athletic.*

H

habēre, vb. 2, *have, hold, regard as;* **sē habēre,** *be.*

habitāre, vb. 1, *dwell, live.*

hāc, pron. or adj. from *hic;* adv., *this way.*

haec, pron. or adj. from *hic;* n 282, 294.

haerēre, haesi, haesum, vb. 2, *stick, be caught.*

hāmātilis, hāmātile, adj., *by hooks, hook-.*

Hāmiŏta, Hāmiŏtae, noun m., *Hookamite,* n 310.

hāmus, hāmi, noun m., *hook.*

hancine = **hanc** + **ne.**

hariola, noun f., *fortuneteller.*

hariolāri, vb. 1 depon., *tell fortunes, guess.*

harundō, harundinis, noun f., *reed, cane, fishing-rod.*

hāsce = **hās** + **ce.**

hau, haud, haut, adv., *not.*

heia, interjection, n 339.

hem, interjection, n 177.

herclē, interjection, *by Hercules* (often not worth translating).

heri, adv., *yesterday.*

heu, interjection, *alas! oh dear!*

heus, interjection, *hi! hoy!*

hey!

hībern-us, -a, -um, adj. *wintry, stormy.*

hic, haec, hoc, pron. or adj., *this* (*hic* and *hoc* nominative are usually heavy syllables, as standing for *hicc, hocc,* though their vowels are short).

hĭc, adv., *here.*

hilaritūdō, hilaritūdinis, noun f., *merriment.*

hilar-us, -a, -um, adj., *merry.*

hinc, adv., *from here; on this side,* n 1100.

hirundinīn-us, -a, -um, adj., *of swallows, swallow-.*

hirundō, hirundinis, noun f., *swallow.*

hisce = **hīs** + **ce;** n 294.

hŏc, pron. or adj. from *hic.*

hŏc, adv. = **hūc.**

hodiē, adv., *to-day;* n 177.

homō, hominis, noun c., *human being.*

homunculus, homunculī, noun m., *diminutive of homo.*

honest-us, -a, -um, adj., *honourable* (*with outward marks of respect*).

honōr, honōris, noun m., *honour, respect, consideration,* n 196.

hŏria, noun f., *fishing-boat.*

hŏrsum, adv., *in this direction.*

hospes, hospitis, noun c., *host; guest.*

hospitium, noun n., *hospitality.*

hostia, noun f., *sacrifice.*

hostiāt-us, -a, -um, adj., *provided with a sacrifice.*

hostis, hostis, noun c., *stranger,* n 434; *enemy.*

hūc, adv., *hither, to this place, here,* n 61.

huī, interjection (a whistle of surprise).

VOCABULARY

I

ibĭ, adv., *there*.

ibĭdem, adv., *in the same place*.

idcircō, adv., *for that reason* (referring either back, as 28, or forward, as 700).

igitur, adv. or conjunction, *therefore, in that case*.

ignāv-us, -a, -um, adj., *idle, cowardly*.

ignis, ignis, noun m., *fire*.

ignōscere, ignōvi, ignōtum, vb. 3, *pardon* (+ dat.).

ignōt-us, -a, -um, adj., *unknown*.

īlicō, adv., n 62.

illāc, 1. pron. or adj. from *illic;* 2. adv., *that way*.

ille, illa, illud, and **illic, illaec, illuc,** or **illoc,** pron. or adj., *that; he she it* (on the vowel-length of *illic, illuc, illoc,* cf. *hic, hoc*).

illīc, adv., *there*.

imitārī, vb. 1 depon., *imitate*.

im-mergere, -mērsī, -mērsum, vb. 3, *plunge in* (usually transit., but at 397 intrans.).

immō, adv. or conj., n 671.

impedīre, vb. 4, *hamper, get (somebody or something) into difficulties*.

imperāre, vb. 1, *give orders*.

imperātor, imperātōris, noun m., *commander, ruler*.

impetrāre, vb. 1, *get (for the asking); get leave*.

im-pingere, -pēgī, -pāctum, vb. 3, *punch in, drive in*.

implōrāre, vb. 1, *plead for*.

im-pōnere, vb. 3, *put in, load*.

im-prans-us, -a, -um, adj., *without any lunch*.

in, prep. + acc., *into, on to, to; for;* + abl., *in, on*.

incān-us, -a, -um, adj., *hoary, white*.

in-cēdere, vb. 3, *approach, advance, go, come* (with slow dignity).

incēnāt-us, -a, -um, adj., *supperless*.

incert-us, -a, -um, adj., *uncertain, unknown*.

in-cipere, -cēpī, -ceptum, vb. 5, *begin*.

inclēmēns, adj., *rough, rude*.

in-colere, vb. 3, *inhabit*.

incrēdibilis, incrēdibile, adj., *unbelievable*.

increpāre, vb. 1, *roar (at)*.

incursāre, vb. 1, *run at, attack*.

inde, adv., *from there, from it*.

indecōr-us, -a, -um, adj., *unfitting, improper*.

in-dere, -didī, -ditum, vb. 3, *put on, bestow on* (+ acc. + dat.).

indicāre, vb. 1, *inform against, denounce*.

indicium, indicī, noun n., *information;* **indicium facere**, *lay information*.

indigēre, vb. 2, *be in want, be in need* (+ gen. or abl.).

indign-us, -a, -um, adj., *unworthy, outrageous*.

ind-ipīscī, -eptus, vb. 3 depon., *get*.

indolēs, indolis, noun f., *character*.

in-dūcere, vb. 3, *bring in;* **in animum suom indūcere**, *persuade oneself*.

induere, induī, indūtum, vb. 3, *put on, dress in* (+ two accusatives).

inept-us, -a, -um, adj., *silly*.

200

in-esse, vb. *be in* (+ dat.).

infēlīcāre, vb. 1, *curse, damn.*

infēlīx, adj., *wretched, accursed.*

infīd-us, -a, -um, adj., *untrustworthy, unsafe.*

(infierī), vb., *begin.*

infortūnium, infortūnī, noun n., *misfortune,* n 118.

ingenu-os, -a, -om, adj., *free-born.*

ingrātieis (ingrātiīs), adv. or prep., *in despite, without leave.*

ingredīrī 4, or ingredī 5, ingressus, vb., *enter; advance, go.*

inhūmān-us, -a, -um, adj., *inhuman, uncivilised;* n 767.

inīqu-os, -a, -om, adj., *unfair.*

iniūria, noun f., *wrong, violence.*

iniūri-us, -a, -um, adj., *in the wrong.*

inlūstris, inlūstre, adj., *bright; famous.*

inmodest-us, -a, -um, adj., *indecent, outrageous.*

inmortāl-is, -e, adj., *immortal.*

innocēns and innoxi-us, -a, -um, adj., *innocent, harmless.*

in-nuere, -nuī, -nūtum, vb. 3, *nod at* (+ dat.).

inopia, noun f., *want, deprivation.*

inops, gen. inopis, adj., *poor, needy.*

inpiāre, vb. 1, *disgrace.*

inpietās, inpietātis, noun f., *wickedness.*

in-piger, -pigra, -pigrum, adj., *active, energetic.*

inpi-us, -a, -um, adj., *impious, wicked.*

inpiare, vb. 1, *bring guilt upon.*

inportūnitās, inportūnitā-tis, noun f., *harshness, oppression.*

inprāns-us, -a, -um, adj., *dinnerless.*

in-probus, adj., *bad, worthless.*

inprōvīs-us, -a, -um, adj., *unforeseen;* ex inprovīso, *unexpectedly.*

inpudēns and inpudīc-us, -a, -um, adj., *shameless, indecent.*

inpūrāt-us, -a, -um and inpūr-us, -a, -um, adj., *dirty, filthy.*

inquam (no infinitive), vb., *I say.*

inrās-us, -a, -um, adj., *unshaven, uncut.*

īnscēnsio, īnscēnsiōnis, noun f., *going aboard, boarding,* n 502.

īnscīt-us, -a, -um, adj., *unknown, uncanny.*

īn-sectārī, -sectātus, vb. 1 depon., *chase.*

īnsidiae, īnsidiārum, noun f. pl., *trap.*

īnsignīt-us, -a, -um, adj., *notable.*

īn-silīre, siluī, -sultum, vb. 4, *jump into* or *on to.*

īnspectāre, vb. 1, *look at, watch.*

īnspērāt-us, -a, um, adj., *unhoped for, unexpected.*

īnstipulārī, vb. 1 depon., *bargain, make conditions.*

īn-stituere, -stituī, -stitū-tum, vb. 3, *set up, arrange.*

in-struere, -struxi, -structum, vb. 3, *set up.*

īnsula, noun f., *island.*

īnsuls-us, -a, -um, adj., *unsalted, insipid, stupid.*

in-tegere, -tēxī, -tēctum,

vb. 3, *cover*, *thatch*.

intel-legere, -lēxī, -lēc-tum, vb. 3, *understand*, *know*.

inter, prep. + acc., *between, among*.

interdiūs, adv., *by day*.

inter-dare, vb. 1, *put between*.

interibi and **interim**, adv., *meanwhile*.

inter-primere, -pressī, -pressum, vb. 3, *interrupt by pressing, throttle*.

intervallum, intervallī, noun n., *interval*.

inter-vortere, vb. 3, *swindle* (+ acc. of person and abl. of thing).

intrō, adv., *inside*.

intuērī, vb. 2 depon., *look upon*.

intum-us, -a, -um, adj., *inmost*.

intus, adv., *inside*.

in-venīre, vb. 4, *come upon, find*.

inverēcund-us, -a, -um, adj., *shameless, immoral*.

investīgare, vb. 1, *track down*.

invītāre, vb. 1, *invite*.

invīt-us, -a, -um, adj., *unwilling*; used adverbially, *against the will of* . . .

ipse, eapse, or **ipsa, ipsum**, pron. or adj., *(him)self, (her)self, (it)self; the very*.

īrāt-us, -a, -um, adj., *angry*.

is, ea, id, pron. and adj., *he, she, it; that, the*.

is = eis, dative and abl. pl. of *is, ea, id*.

iste, ista, istum, and **istic, istaec, istuc**, or **istoc**, pron. or adj., *he, she, it; that (of yours)*; for the vowel and syllable length of *istic, istoc*, cf. *hic, hoc*.

istīc and **istī**, adv., *there (by you)*.

istīcin = istīc + ne.

istine, adv., *from where you are*.

istīusmodi, *of that sort*.

ita, adv., *so, thus*; often as a causal connection, n 87.

itaque = ita + que, n 589; usually as a conjunction, *so, therefore*.

item, adv., *in the same way, likewise*.

iterāre, vb. 1, *repeat*.

iterum, adv., *again*.

itidem, adv., *in the same way*.

I Consonant

iacere, iēcī, iactum, vb. 5, *throw*.

iactāre, vb. 1, *throw about, toss*.

iam, adv., *now, already, soon*.

ioculus, ioculī, noun m., *little joke*.

Iovis, see Iuppiter.

iubēre, iussī, iussum, vb. 2, *tell, order, invite*.

iūdex, iūdicis, noun c., *judge, arbitrator*.

iuncus, iunci, noun m., *rush*.

Iuppiter, Iovis, noun m., *Jupiter, Jove*.

iurāre, vb. 1, *swear*; perfect ptc. with active sense, *after swearing, on oath*.

iūs, iūris, noun n., *right, justice*.

iūs iūrandum, iūris iūrandī, noun n., *oath*.

L

labāscere, vb. 3, *totter, falter*.

labōr, labōris, noun m., *labour, hardship*.

laetari, vb. 1 depon., *be glad.*
lapis, lapidis, noun m., *stone.*
Lār, Laris, noun m., *Family God.*
largiter, adv., *generously, in generous quantity,* n 1188.
lāserpīcium, lāserpīcī, noun n., n 630.
latebrae, latebrārum, noun f. pl., *hiding-place, lair.*
laudāre, vb. 1, *praise.*
laut-us, -a, -um, perfect participle of *lavare;* as adj., n 301.
lavāre, lāvī, lautum\ or lavātum, vb. 1, *wash.*
lēgerupa, noun m., *law-breaker,* n 652.
lēgerupiō, lēgerupiōnis, noun f., *law-breaking,* n 652.
lēnis, lēne, adj., *mild.*
lēnō, lēnōnis, noun m., *pimp, slave-dealer,* p. 35.
lēnōni-us, -a, -um, adj., *a pimp's.*
lepid-us, -a, -um, adj., *nice.*
lepōs, lepōris, noun n., *charm.*
levāre, vb. 1, *lighten, relieve.*
lēx, lēgis, noun f., *law.*
līber, lībera, līberum, adj., *free.*
līberālis, līberāle, adj., *befitting a free-born person, gentlemanly, ladylike.*
līberāre, vb. 1, *free.*
lībertās, lībertātis, noun f., *freedom.*
licentia, noun f., *leave, "all-rightness",* n 1225.
licēre, vb. 2, *be permissible, be all right* (translate by *may*).
ligne-us, -a, -um, adj., *wooden.*
lignum, noun n., *wood.*
lippitūdo, lippitūdinis, noun f., *sore eyes.*

līs, lītis, noun f., *law-suit, award.*
lītigāre, vb. 1, *go to law, dispute.*
littera, noun f., *letter.*
litterāt-us, -a, -um, adj., *lettered, bearing letters.*
lītus, lītoris, noun n., *shore.*
locāre, vb. 1, *place, hire out.*
locuplēs, gen. locuplētis, adj., *rich.*
locus, noun m. (plural usually loca, n.), *place.*
long-us, -a, -um, adj., *long;* adv., longē, *at a distance, far off.*
longulē, adv., diminutive of *longe.*
lopas, lopadis, noun f. (*some kind of shell-fish*).
loquī, locūtus, vb. 3 depon., *speak, talk.*
lōrārius, noun m., *strap-man, i.e. slave-constable.*
lubēns, adj., *willing, glad* (used adverbially).
lubēre, vb. 2, *be acceptable, be agreeable* (translate by *like to, be glad to*).
lucrum, noun n., *gain, profit.*
lūculent-us, -a, -um, adj., *brilliant, striking.*
lūdus, noun m., *game, laughing-stock,* n 470, 593; *school.*
lutum, noun n., *mud.*

M

macellum, noun, *food-market.*
machaera, noun f., *a (Greek) sword.*
mactāre, vb. 1, n 96.
maest-us, -a, -um, adj., *sad, gloomy;* adv. maestiter.

magis, comparative adv., *more.*

magistrātus, magistrātūs, noun m., *magistrate.*

magnidic-us, -a, -um, adj., *boastful, salesman's.*

magȳdaris, magȳdaris, noun f., n 630.

māiŏr, māius, comparative adj., *bigger, greater.*

māla, noun f., *jaw.*

male, adv., *badly,* n 221, 337.

maledīcere, or separately **male dīcere,** vb., *abuse, revile;* ptc., **maledictum,** as noun n., *bad language.*

malitia, noun f., *wickedness.*

mal-us, -a, -um, adj., *bad;* neuter, **malum** as noun, *misfortune.*

mancupium, mancupī, noun n., *chattle, possession; ownership,* p. 36.

mandāre, vb. 1, *entrust; give instructions.*

mandūcus, noun m., n 535.

māne, adv., *in the morning.*

manēre, mānsī, mānsum, vb. 2, *remain, wait.*

manicula, noun f., *little hand.*

mantāre, vb. 1, *wait.*

mare, maris, noun n., *sea.*

marīn-us, -a, -um, and **maritum-us, -a, -um,** adj., *of the sea, sea-.*

marsuppium, marsuppī, noun n., *pouch.*

mās, maris, noun m., *male.*

mastīgia, noun m., *branded slave.*

māter, mātris, noun f., *mother;* as a term of respect, *ma'am.*

māvelle (mālo, mālle, māluī), vb., *wish rather, prefer.*

maxum-us, -a, -um, superlative adj., *greatest, very great;* *biggest, very big.*

mēd., pron. abl. of *ego.*

medicus, medicī, noun m., *physician.*

mehercule, interjection, *by Hercules.*

meliŏr, melius, comparative adj., *better.*

membrum, membrī, noun n., *limb.*

meminisse, vb. perfect, *remember.*

memorāre, vb. 1, *tell of, relate, report.*

mendācium, mendācī, noun n., *falsehood.*

mendāx, adj., *lying, false.*

mendīcitās, mendīcitātis, noun f., *beggary.*

mendīcus, mendīcī, noun m., *beggar.*

mēns, mentis, noun f., *mind, thought.*

mentiō, mentiōnis, noun f., *mention.*

mercārī, vb. 1 depon., *buy.*

mercātūra, noun f., *trade.*

mercēs, mercēdis, noun f., *payment.*

meretrīcula and **meretrīx, meretrīcis,** nouns f., *whore.*

mergae, noun f., *pitchfork.*

meritō, adv., *deservedly.*

mer-us, -a, -um, adj., *unmixed, pure.*

(merx), gen. **mercis,** *goods for sale.*

messis, noun f., *harvest.*

metus, metūs, noun m., *fear, dread.*

me-us, -a, -um, adj., *my.*

mī, 1. for *mihi,* dative of *ego;* 2. masc. sing. voc. of *meus.*

mille, noun n. indeclinable, n 1327, *thousand.*

mīluos, mīluī, noun m., *kite.*

mina, noun f., *mina.*

mināciae, noun f. pl., *threats.*

minarium, noun n., n 1314.

minim-us, -a, -um, superl. adj., *smallest, least;* adv., **minime,** as virtual negative, *not in the least.*

minitārī, vb. 1 depon., *threaten.*

minŏr, minus, comparative adj., *smaller;* adv., **minus,** *less;* in an "if" clause, *not.*

minuere, minuī, minūtum, vb., *break up, chop up.*

mirārī, vb. 1 depon., *marvel, wonder.*

mīr-us, -a, -um, adj., *wonderful, strange.*

misell-us, -a, -um and **miser, misera, miserum,** adj., *wretched, miserable.*

miserārī, vb. 1 depon., *express pity for.*

miserēre, vb. 2 impersonal, *move to take pity* (+ acc. of person, gen. of thing), translate by *pity,* personal.

miseria, noun f., *wretchedness.*

misericors, gen. **misericordis,** adj., *merciful.*

mittere, mīsī, missum, vb. 3, *send.*

modŏ, 1. noun, abl. sing. of *modus;* 2. adv., *just, only, just now.*

modus, modī, noun m., *method, way;* n 147.

moenia, moenium, noun n. pl., *city-walls, fortifications.*

molest-us, -a, -um, adj., *tiresome.*

monēre, vb. 2, *warn, advise.*

mōnstrāre, vb. 1, *show, point out.*

monumentum, noun n., *memorial.*

mora, noun f., *delay;* **morae esse,** *cause delay.*

morārī, vb. 1 depon., *linger, wait, wait for, have time for,* n 583.

morīrī or **morī, mortuus,** vb. 4 or 5 depon., *die.*

mors mortis, noun f., *death.*

mortāl-is, -e, adj., *mortal;* masc. used as noun.

mōs, mōris, noun m., *manner, habit, custom;* pl. *character.*

movēre, mōvī, mōtum, vb. 2, *move, stir.*

mox, adv., *soon, subsequently.*

muliebr-is, -e, adj., *womanly, woman's, girl's.*

mulier, mulieris, and **muliercula,** nouns f., *woman, girl.*

murtētum, noun n., n 732.

muls-us, -a, -um, adj., n 364.

multa, noun f., *fine, penalty.*

multāre, vb. 1, *fine, punish.*

mult-us, -a, -um, adj., *much;* pl. *many.*

murmurillum, noun n., *muttering.*

mūsculus, mūsculī, noun m., *mussel.*

mussitāre, vb. 1, *keep one's mouth shut.*

mūtāre, vb. 1, *change, exchange.*

mūt-us, -a, -um, adj., *dumb.*

N

nam, adv., emphasising a question, attached to the interrogative word or put before it, n 678; conjunction, *for.*

nancīscī, nanctus or **nactus,** vb. 3 depon., *get.*

nārrāre, vb. 1, *tell, relate, speak of.*

născī, nātus, vb. depon., *be born.*

nātāl-is, -e, adj., *of birth, birth.*

natāre, vb. 1, *swim.*

nātiō, nātiōnis, noun f., *tribe.*

nāvis, nāvis, noun f., *ship.*

nē, adv. and conjunction, *not, lest,* etc., **nē ... quidem,** *not even.*

nē, adv., *for sure, certainly,* n 821.

nec and **neque,** adv. and conjunction, *neither, nor, and ... not.*

necessāri-us, -a, -um, adj., *necessary.*

necessitās, necessitātis, noun f., *necessity.*

necessum, noun n. indecl., *necessity.*

negāre, vb. 1, *deny, say no.*

negōtium, noun n., *business, trouble.*

nēmō, pron., *nobody.*

nempe, adv., n 268.

Neptūnus, Neptūnī, noun m., *Neptune.*

nēquam, adj. indecl., *wicked, worthless;* superl., **nēquissumus;** adv., **nēquiter,** *badly.*

neque, see **nec.**

nēquīquam, adv., *in vain.*

nequīre, vb. (like *īre*), *be unable.*

nervos, nervī, noun m., n 872.

nescioquis (nescio quis), pron., *somebody or other.*

nescīre, vb. 4, *not know.*

nesci-us, -a, -um, *unknowing; unknown.*

neu, 1 = **nē-ve,** *or not, and not;* 2 = **nī-ve,** *or if ... not.*

neuter, neutra, neutrum, adj. and pron., *neither.*

nī = **nisi.**

nīdāmentum, noun n., *material for a nest.*

nīdus, nīdī, noun m., *nest.*

nihil or **nīl,** noun n., *nothing;* as adv., *not at all;* genit., **nihilī,** *of no value;* abl. **nihilō** with comparatives, *none the ...*

nimis, noun indecl., *a lot, too much;* as adv., *very, too much.*

nimi-us, -a, -um, adj., *extreme, excessive;* n. **nimium,** as adv. = *nimis;* abl. **nimiō,** with comparatives.

nisi, conjunction, *unless, if not, except;* **nisi sī,** n 581.

nītī nīxus, vb. 3 depon., *lean on* + abl.

nīve = **nī** + **ve,** *or if ... not, or unless.*

nīxus, see **niti.**

nōbil-is, -e, adj., *famous, well known.*

nocēre, vb. 2, *do harm, hurt* + dat.

noctū, adv., *by night.*

nōlle, nōluī, vb., *be unwilling, not wish, wish not.*

nōmen, nōminis, noun n., *name.*

nōmināre, vb. 1, *call by name.*

nōn, adv., *not.*

nōs, nostrī or **nostrum, nōbīs,** pron., *we, us;* often used for singular, *I,* with an air of self-consequence.

nōscere, nōvī, nōtum, *get to know, learn;* perfect, *know.*

nōsmet = **nos** + **-met,** *we, us,* emphatic.

noster, nostra, nostrum, adj., *our;* n 1245.

novos, nova, novom, adj., *new.*

nox noctis, noun f., *night.*

nūbere, nūpsi, nūptum, vb., *marry* + dative.

null-us, -a, -um, adj., *no, none;* colloquially in adverbial sense, *not,* n 143.

nunc, adv., *now, as things are.*

num, interrog. adv. introducing a question, NOT necessarily expecting a negative answer.

nummus, nummī, noun m., *coin;* pp. 41-2.

nunciam, adv., *now* (= **nunc iam,** but three syllables).

nūntius, nūntiī, noun m., *messenger.*

nusquam, adv., *nowhere.*

O

ob, prep., *to meet; because of;* **ob viam (obviam),** *to meet* + dat.

obdormīscere, vb. 3, *fall asleep.*

ob-icere, -iēcī, -iectum, vb. 5, *throw to.*

oblectāre, vb. 1, *delight, console.*

ob-torquēre, -torsī, -tortum, vb. 2, *twist.*

occāsiō, occāsiōnis, noun f., *opportunity.*

occeptāre, vb. 1, *begin.*

oc-cidere, -cidī, -cāsum, vb. 3, *fall, set.*

oc-cīdere, -cīdī, -cīsum, vb. 3, *kill.*

oc-cipere, -cēpī, -ceptum, vb. 5, *begin.*

occupāre, vb. 1, *seize; get in first* + infin., n 248.

ocellus, ocellī, noun m., *eye, sweet eye.*

ōcior, compar. adj., *quicker;* adv. **ōcius,** practically used as positive.

octingent-ī, -ae, -a, adj., *eight hundred.*

oculus, oculī, noun m., *eye.*

odiōs-us, -a, -um, adj., *tiresome.*

ōdisse, vb. perfect, *hate.*

odium, noun n., *dislike; object of dislike, abomination.*

of-fendere, -fendī, -fēnsum, vb. 3, *bump into,* n 788.

offerre, optulī, oblātum, vb., *put in the way of, bring to.*

offerrūmenta, noun f., n 753.

officium, noun n., *duty.*

of-flectere, -flexī, -flexum, vb. 3, n 1013.

ōminārī, vb. 1 depon., *give an omen,* n 337.

ō-mittere, vb. 3, *let go.*

omnis, omne, adj., *all.*

opera, noun f., *doing, activity;* **operam dare,** *take an interest;* **operae pretium,** *worth while.*

opīnāre, or depon., **opīnārī,** vb. 1, *suppose, think.*

opīniō, opīniōnis, noun f., *opinion.*

oportēre, vb. 2 impersonal, *behove* (translate by *must* or *ought*).

op-perīrī, -pertus, vb. 4 depon., *wait, await.*

oppidō, adv., *entirely, definitely, very, quite.*

oppidum, noun n., *town.*

op-plēre, -plēvī, -plētum, vb. 2, *fill.*

opportūn-us, -a, -um, adj., *convenient.*

op-primere, -pressī, -pressum, vb. 3, *pounce on;* n 387.

(ops) opis, noun f., *help;* pl. *resources, wealth.*

opsecrāre, vb. 1, *beg, beseech.*

opsequēns, adj., *obliging.*

VOCABULARY

opservāre, vb. 1, *watch.*
op-sidēre, sēdī, -sessum, vb. 2, *sit by.*
opsidiō, opsidiōnis, noun f., *sitting opposite, blockade.*
optāre, vb. 1, *desire, choose, pray for.*
optestārī, vb. 1 depon., *call to witness, call upon.*
op-tingere, -tigī, vb. 3, *befall* (+ dat.).
op-torquēre, -torsi, -tortum, vb. 2, *twist.*
optum-us, -a, -um, superl. adj., *best, very good.*
opulentia, noun f., *wealth.*
opulent-us, -a, -um, adj., *wealthy.*
opus, operis, noun n., *work;* opus est, *there is need of* (+ acc. or abl. and dat.).
ōrāre, vb. 1, *plead, beseech.*
ōrātiō, ōrātiōnis, noun f., *speech.*
orb-us, -a, -um, adj., *deprived, destitute* (+ gen. or abl.).
ōrdō, ōrdinis, noun m., *rank, order;* ordine, *in order.*
orīrī, vb. 4 and 5, *rise, arise.*
ornāre, vb. 1, *equip, supply.*
ōrnātus, ōrnātūs, noun m., *equipment.*
ōs, ōris, noun n., *face; mouth.*
ōsculārī, vb. 1 depon., *kiss.*
ostendere, ostendī, ostensum, vb. 3, *show.*
ōstium, noun n., *door.*
ostrea, noun f., *oyster.*
ōtium, noun n., *spare time, leisure.*

P

pābulārī, vb. 1 depon., *forage.*
pābulum, pābulī, noun n., *fodder, food.*
pactum, noun n., *method, way* (only in abl.).

paelex, paelicis, noun f., *concubine.*
paene, adv., *nearly, almost.*
paenitēre, vb. 2 impers., *cause regret* (translate by *be sorry, regret*).
pāgus, pāgī, noun m., *country district, parish.*
palaestric-us, -a, -um, adj., *of wrestling.*
Palaemō, Palaemōnis, noun m., *a sea-god.*
palam, adv., *openly.*
pallium, noun n., *cloak.*
palpātor, palpātōris, noun m., *confidence-man.*
pālus, pālī, noun m., *stake.*
palūs, palūdis, noun f., *marsh, bog.*
papae, interjection, *crikey! gosh!*
pār, gen. paris, adj., *equal; right,* n 675; adv., pariter, *similarly.*
parāre, vb. 1, *get, prepare;* ptc., parātus, as adj., *ready,* n 506; adv., parātē, *readily, zealously.*
parcere, pepercī, parsum, vb. 3, *spare* (+ dat.).
parc-us, -a, -um, adj., *sparing.*
parēns, parentis, noun c., *parent.*
parere, peperī, partum, vb. 5, *bear, produce;* ptc., partus, n 506.
parricīdium, noun n., *parricide* (murder of a father or near relative).
pars, partis, noun f., *part share; quarter, direction.*
parum, adv., *little;* virtually a negative.
parvol-us, -a, -um, and parv-os, -a, -om, adj., *little, small;* gen. parvī, *at a low value.*

pasceolus, pasceolī, noun m., *pouch, leather money-bag.*

pater, patris, noun m., *father; sir,* n 103.

patern-us, -a, -um, adj., *father's.*

patī, passus, vb. 5 depon., *suffer, experience.*

patria, noun f., *fatherland, own country.*

patrōnus, patrōnī, noun m., *patron, protector,* p. 35.

pauc-ī, -ae, -a, adj., *few;* abl. pl., **paucis,** *briefly,* n 120.

paullisper, adv., *a little while.*

pauper, gen., **pauperis,** adj., *poor, needy.*

paupertās, paupertātis, noun f., *poverty.*

pausa, noun f., *stop.*

pauxillātim, adv., *little by little.*

pauxillul-us, -a, -um, adj., *very small;* neuter **pauxillulum** as adv., *very slightly.*

pavǒr, pavōris, noun m., *terror, panic.*

pāx pācis, noun f., *peace; permission,* n 698.

peccāre, vb. 1, *go wrong.*

pectere pexī pexum, vb. 3, *comb;* n 661.

pectus pectoris, noun n., *breast.*

pecū, noun n., *cattle.*

pecūliōs-us, -a, -um, adj., *wealthy, thrifty* (applied to a slave).

peiiūrium, noun n., *perjury, dishonesty.*

pendēre, pependī, vb. 2, *hang* (intrans.).

pendere, pependī, pēnsum, vb. 3, *hang, suspend; weigh;* **parvī pendere,** *set little value on.*

pēniculus, pēniculī, noun m., n 1008.

per, prep. + acc., *through, by;* **per mē quidem,** *as far as I'm concerned.*

perbene, adv., *splendid(ly).*

perbītere, vb. 3, *perish.*

percontārī, vb. 1 depon., *enquire.*

per-coquere, vb. 3, *cook thoroughly.*

perdere, perdidī, perditum, vb. 3, *lose; ruin.*

per-ferre, vb., *carry; endure.*

pergere, perrēxī, perrēctum, vb. 3, *proceed, go on.*

perhibēre, vb. 2, *report.*

perīclum, noun n., *attempt; risk;* n 144, 432, 1393.

per-īre, vb., *perish; be lost.*

periūrus (or **peiiūrus**), abj., *foresworn, false.*

perlubēre, vb. 2 impersonal, *be most acceptable* (translate by *should very much like*).

per-lūcēre, -lūxī, vb. 2, *shine through, let light in.*

per-nōscere, vb. 3, *get to know thoroughly.*

per-petī, -pessus, vb. 5 depon., *suffer, endure.*

perpetu-os, -a, -om, adj., *continuous; lasting;* **perpetuam noctem,** *all night long.*

perquam, adv., *very, exceedingly.*

perrēptāre, vb. 1, *crawl through.*

per-sequī, vb. 3 depon., *pursue;* with infin., *attempt,* n 667.

per-suādēre, vb. 2, *persuade* (+ dat.).

per-tegere, vb. 3, *cover, thatch.*

per-timēscere, -timuī, vb. 3, *be terrified.*

per-venīre, vb. 4, *arrive, reach* (+ ad).

pervestigāre, vb. 1, *track down.*

pes, pedis, noun m., *foot.*

pessum, adv., *to destruction.*

pessum-us, -a, -um, superl. adj., *worst, very bad, villainous, disastrous.*

petere, petīvī, petītum, vb. 3, *seek, aim at, want to get.*

Philippus, Philippī, noun m., *"Philip", two-drachma piece,* pp. 41-2, n 1314.

philosophus, philosophī, noun m., *philosopher, professor.*

pietās, pietātis, noun f., *goodness.*

piger, pigra, pigrum, adj., *lazy.*

pigēre, vb. 2 impersonal, *cause dislike* (translate by *refuse, object to, dislike*).

pignus, pignoris, noun n. *pledge, deposit.*

piscārī, vb. 1 depon., *fish.*

piscātor, piscātōris, noun m., *fisherman.*

piscatus, piscatūs, noun m., *fishing, a catch.*

piscis, piscis, noun m., *fish.*

pisculent-us, -a, -um, adj., *fishy, full of fish.*

pi-us, -a, -um, adj., *good, virtuous.*

plācāre, vb. 1, *pacify.*

placēre, vb. 2, *please, be acceptable* (+ dat.).

placid-us, -a, -um, and placidul-us, -a, -um, adj., *quiet, gentle.*

plagūsia, noun f., *a shell-fish, scallop.*

plān-us, -a, -um, adj., *level, flat; straightforward;* adv., plānē, *definitely;* n 1131.

plaudere, plausī, plausum, vb. 3, *clap.*

plausus, plausūs, noun m., *applause.*

plēn-us, -a, -um, adj., *full.*

plōrāre, vb., *lament, whine.*

pluere, vb. 3, *rain.*

plūrum-us, -a, -um, superl. adj., *most, very much;* pl., *very many.*

plūs, plūris, noun n., *more;* pl. plūres, plūra, adj.

pōculum, noun n., *drinking cup;* in pl. *drinks.*

pol, interjection, *by Pollux.*

pollentia, noun f., *power.*

pollicitārī, vb. 1 depon., *promise.*

pollūct-us, -a, -um, ptc., n 424, 1419.

pōlypūs, pōlypodis, noun m., *polypus, cuttle-fish, octopus.*

pondō, adv., *in weight.*

pōnere, posīvī (classical posuī), positum, vb. 3, *place, put; serve up; deposit.*

pontifex, pontificis, noun m., *high priest,* n 1377.

poplus, poplī, noun m. = populus, *people.*

populāris, populāre, adj., *of the people; of one's own people;* as noun, *fellow-country-man/woman.*

porculus, porculī, noun m., *piglet.*

porrō, adj., *further; further off; moreover.*

portiō, portiōnis, noun f., *share, proportion;* pro portiōne, *correspondingly.*

portus, portūs, noun m., *harbour.*

pōscere, popōscī, vb. 3, *demand, ask for.*

posse, potuī, vb., *be able.*

post, adv. and prep. + acc., *after, behind.*

posteā, adv., *afterwards.*

posterior, posterius, adj., *rear;* adv., posterius, *afterwards.*

posthāc, adv., *after this.*

postĭbĭ, postĭd, adv., *afterwards*.

postquam, and separately, **post quam**, conj., *after, when*.

postulāre, vb. l, *demand, expect*.

pōtāre, vb. I, *drink*.

potesse = **posse**.

potestās, potestātis, noun f., *power, possession*.

potin = **potis-ne**.

pōtiō, pōtiōnis, noun f., *drink, dose*.

potior, potius, compar. adj., *preferable;* adv., **potius**, *preferably;* superl. adv., **potissumum**, *best of all*.

potīrī, vb. 4 depon., *get, meet with* (+ acc. or gen. or abl.).

potis, indecl. adj., *possible*.

prae, prep. + abl., *before; compared with; by reason of, for*.

praecipēs, gen. **praecipitis**, adj., *headlong;* neut. as adv.

praecipu-os, -a, -om, adj., *especial, outstanding*.

praeda, noun f., *loot, catch*.

praedārī, vb. I depon., *plunder*.

praedicāre, vb. I, *declare*.

praedō, praedōnis, noun m., *brigand, pirate*.

praefestīnāre, vb. I, *be in a hurry*.

praefiscinē, adv., n 461.

praehibēre (classical **praebēre**), vb. 2, *offer, show*.

prae-īre, vb., *go before;* **verbīs, praeīre**, *dictate*.

prae-loquī, vb. 3 depon., *speak first*.

praemium, noun n., *reward*.

prae-pōnere, vb. 3, *prefer*.

praesēns, adj., *present*.

praesēpēs, praesēpis, noun f., *stall, manger*.

praesertim, adv., *especially*.

praeses, praesidis, noun m., *guard, protector*.

praesidium, noun n., *guard, protection*.

praestō, adv., *at hand, present*.

praeter, adv. and prep. + acc., *beyond, beside; besides*.

praetereā, praeterhāc, adv., *besides, in addition*.

praeter-īre, *go past, pass*.

praetor, praetōris, noun m., *praetor*, n 928.

prae-torquēre, -torsī, -tortum, vb. 2, *twist, wring*.

prae-vortere, or depon., **praevortī**, vb. 3, *give prior attention to*.

prandēre, prānsus, vb. 2 semi-depon., *lunch*.

prandium, noun n., *lunch*.

precārī, vb. I depon., *pray*.

prehendere, prehendī, prehēnsum, vb. 3, *grasp, catch*.

pretium, noun n., *price, value, payment;* **operae pretium**, *worth while*.

(prex) precis, noun f., *prayer, request*.

prīdem, adv., *in the past, some time ago*.

prīmāri-us, -a, -um, adj., *of the first rank*.

prīm-us, -a, -um, adj., *first; beginning of*, n 1154; neuter, **prīmum**, as adv., *first, firstly;* **quam prīmum**, *as soon as possible*.

prius, adv., *previously, before*.

priusquam, or separately, **prius quam**, conj., *before*.

prō, prep. + abl., *for; on behalf of; in recognition of; corresponding to;* n 1392.

prō, interjection, *oh!*

probrum, noun n., *scandal, disgrace.*

prob-us, -a, -um, adj., *good, honest.*

prō-cēdere, vb. 3, *go forward; pass.*

prōcreāre, vb. 1, *beget.*

prō-dere, -didī, -ditum, vb. 3, *bring out;* n 589.

prōd-esse, vb., *be useful.*

prōd-īre, vb., *go or come forward, come out.*

prōditor, prōditōris, noun m., *betrayer;* n 50.

prō-dūcere, vb. 3, *breed, rear.*

profectō, adv., *for certain, definitely.*

prō-ferre, vb., *bring forward, bring out.*

proficīscī, profectus, vb. 3 depon., *set out.*

prōgnāt-us, -a, -um, adj., *born, begotten.*

prohibēre, vb. 2, *prevent, stop.*

prōmīscam, adv., *in common,* n 1182.

prōmīsc-us, -a, -um, adj., *in common,* n 1182.

prō-mittere, vb. 3, *let out, allow to grow; promise.*

prope, adv. and prep. + acc., *near by, nearly; near;* compar. adj., **propior;** adv., **propius.**

prō-pellere, -pulī, -pulsum, vb. 3, *knock forward.*

propemodum, adv., *almost, pretty well.*

properāre, vb. 1, *hurry.*

propinqu-os, -a, -om, adj., *near; related.*

prōportāre, vb. 1, n 733.

propter, adv. and prep. + acc., *near; because of;* **propter viam,** n 150.

prōrēta, noun m., *look-out man (in the ship's bows).*

prō-ripere, -ripuī, -reptum, vb. 5, *pull out.*

prō-sequī, vb. 3 depon., *escort, follow in a friendly manner.*

proterv-os, -a, -um, adj., *violent, reckless.*

prō-vehere, vb. 3, *ship off,* n 863.

prō-venīre, vb. 4, *make progress;* n 837.

proxum-us, -a, -um, superl. adj., *nearest, very near; next; last.*

pudēre, vb. 2 impers., *cause shame* (translate by *be ashamed*).

pudīc-us, -a, -um, *decent, moral.*

pudor, pudōris, noun m., *shame, decency, morality.*

puella, noun f., *girl.*

pugilātōri-us, -a, -um, adj., *for punching.*

pugnāre, vb. 1, *fight.*

pugne-us, -a, -um, adj., *of fists, fist-.*

pugnus, pugnī, noun m., *fist.*

pulcher, pulchra, pulchrum, adj., *beautiful;* adv., **pulchre,** *splendidly.*

pulmentum, noun n., n 937.

pulmōne-us, -a, -um, adj., *of the lungs, lung-.*

pulsāre, vb. 1, *bang, knock at.*

pulvisculus, pulvisculī, noun m., *scrap of dust.*

pūnice-us, -a, -um, adj., *crimson.*

puplic-us, -a, -um, adj., *public.*

pūr-us, -a, -um, adj., *clean.*

puteus, puteī, noun m., *well.*

pūtid-us, -a, -um, adj., *rotten, mouldy.*

VOCABULARY

Q

quā, pron. from *qui* or *quis.*

quā, adv., relat. or interrog., *by which way, where.*

quadri(n)gent-ī, -ae, -a, adj., *four hundred.*

quaerere, quaesīvī, quaesītum, vb. 3, *seek, ask, enquire.*

quaeritāre, vb. 1, *ask, enquire.*

(quaesere); quaesō = **quaerō,** *I ask.*

quaestus, quaestūs, noun m., *profit, profession.*

quālis, quāle, adj., relative and interrog., *of what sort, of the sort that.*

quam, pronoun and adj. from *qui.*

quam, adv. relative or interrog., *as, as much as,* n 943; with superlatives *as . . . as possible; how;* conjunction, *than, rather than,* n 684.

quamvīs, adv. and conjunction, *as much as you like, however much;* n 372; *though.*

quandō, adv. relative and interrog., *when;* conjunction, *when, since.*

quant-us, -a, -um, adj. relat. and interrog., *as great as; how great.*

quāpropter, adv. and conjunction, *for which reason, wherefore; why.*

quasi, adv. and conjunction, *as if, as it were,* n 99.

-que, conjunction, *and; both.*

queo, quire, vb. like **eo,** *be able.*

quī, relative pronoun and adj., *who, which, what;* interrog. adj., *what, what sort of;* indefinite, *any, any sort of,* n 26, 98, 385.

quī, adv. relative, interrog. and indefinite, and conjunction, *as, how, why; in any way; in order that;* n 11.

quia, conjunction, *because; that,* n. 1025.

quid, pronoun and adj., neuter of *quis;* used as interrog. adv., *why.*

quīdam, quaedam, quoddam, adj., and **quīdam, quaedam, quiddam,** pronoun, *a certain one, some, somebody.*

quidem, particle; it emphasises the preceding word, and is usually not to be translated; **ne . . . quidem,** *not even.*

quiēs, quiētis, noun f., *rest, sleep.*

quiēscere, quiēvi, quiētum, vb. 3, *rest.*

quīn, adv. and conjunction, *why not,* n 122, 628; *nay more,* n 671; introducing subordinate clause with subjunctive, *but that, from;* **mīrum quīn,** n 1393.

quīn = quī-ne, n 767, 861.

quīnam, quaenam, quodnam, adj. interrog., *what? which?,* n 678.

quisnam, quaenam, quodnam, pron. interrog., *who? what?,* n 678.

quīngent-ī, -ae, -a, adj., *five hundred.*

quīnque, adj. indecl., *five.*

quippe, conjunction or particle, causal; alone *for;* before another conjunction or relative, not to be translated, but shows that the clause has causal force.

quīque, quaeque, quodque, adj., *each.*

quīque = quī-que.

(quīre), quīvi, vb., *be able, can.*

quis, quid, pronoun, interrog., *who, what;* indefinite, *anyone, anything.*

quispiam, quippiam, pronoun indefinite, *someone, something; anyone, anything.*

quisquam, quidquam, pronoun, *anyone, anything.*

quisque, quidque, pronoun, *each.*

quisquis, quidquid, pronoun, *whoever, whatever.*

quīvīs, quaevīs, quidvīs, quodvīs, pronoun and adj., *any, anyone you like.*

quō, pronoun and adj., from *quī* or *quis.*

quō, adv., relative and interrog., *whither, where to, to the point where,* n 287.

quod, pronoun and adj. from *qui.*

quod, conjunction, *because; that; as to the fact that,* n 1150.

quoi, pronoun or adj., dative sing. of *qui* or *quis.*

quoianam = quoia-nam.

quoi(i)us, pronoun or adj., genitive sing. of *qui* or *quis.*

quoi(i)-us, -a, -um, adj. relative or interrog., *whose.*

quoiusmodī = quoius modī, *of what sort, what sort of, what a.*

quom, adv. and conjunction, *when, since.*

quōmodō, or separately, **quō modō,** adv., *how.*

quōn = quō-ne, n 111.

quondam, adv., *once, formerly.*

quoniam, conjunction, *since, when,* n 67.

quoque, adv., *also, too.*

quot, adj. relative or interrog., indecl., *as many as, how many.*

qūr, adv., *why.*

R

rāmenta, noun f., *scraping, scrap.*

rapere, rapuī, raptum, vb. 5, *seize, snatch, hustle away.*

rār-us, -a, -um, adj., *rare.*

ratus, from *rērī.*

recalv-os, -a, -om, adj., *bald in front, going bald.*

re-cēdere, vb. 3, *retreat, go back.*

re-cipere, -cēpī, -ceptum, vb. 5, *take back, get back, receive.*

re-clūdere, -clūsī, -clūsum, vb. 3, *open.*

rēct-us, -a, -um, adj., *straight, upright, right;* adv., **recte,** n 747.

recuperātor, recuperātōris, noun m., n 1282.

red-dere, -didī, -ditum, vb. 3, *give back; pay.*

re(d)dux, genit., **re(d)ducis,** adj., *returning, safe home.*

red-igere, -ēgī, -āctum, vb. 3, *drive back; reduce.*

red-īre, vb., *go back, come back.*

re-ferre, vb., *bring back, pay back.*

rē-ferre, vb. impersonal, *matter, be important;* **pluris tuā refert,** *it matters more to you.*

regiō, regiōnis, noun f., *region, district.*

rēgnum, noun n., *kingdom.*

re-linquere, -līquī, -lictum, vb. 3, *leave, abandon.*

reliquiae, noun f. pl., *remains, leavings.*

re-mittere, vb., *send back; slack off.*

remorārī, vb. 1 depon., *delay, keep waiting.*

re-pellere, -pulī, -pulsum, *drive back, knock back.*

reperīre, repperī, repertum, vb. 4, *find.*

re-plēre, -plēvi, -plētum, vb. 2, *fill.*

VOCABULARY

re-pŏscere, vb. 3, *demand back, claim.*

repudiāre, vb. 1, *repudiate.*

rērī, ratus, vb. 2 depon., *think, suppose.*

rēs, rēī, noun f., *thing;* abstract, *matter, affair, business;* concrete *property;* in rem, *to the point;* rē, n 683; ācta rēs est, n 683; rēs dīvīna, n 130.

re-spicere, -spexī, -spectum, vb. 5, *look back, look back at.*

re-spondēre, -spondī, -spōnsum, vb. 2, *answer.*

respōnsor, respōnsōris, noun m., *answerer, someone to reply.*

restis, restis, noun f., *cord, rope.*

rēte, rētis, n., and rētis, rētis, m., and rētia, f., nouns, *net.*

retentāre, vb. 1, *hold back.*

re-tinēre, -tinuī, -tentum, vb. 2, *hold on to.*

re-trahere, vb. 3, *drag back.*

re-venīre, vb. 4, *come back.*

rēx, rēgis, noun m., *king.*

rōbīgō, rōbīginis, noun f., *rust.*

rogāre and rogitāre, vb. 1, *ask, ask for.*

rubicund-us, -a, -um, adj., *ruddy, red-faced.*

rŭdēns, rūdentis, noun m. or f., *rope.*

rumpere, rūpī, ruptum, vb. 3, *burst.*

rūsum, adv., *back again.*

rutil-us, -a, -um, adj., *red.*

S

saccipērium, noun n., *bag, kit-bag (made of sack-cloth).*

sacer, sacra, sacrum, adj., *sacred; cursed,* n 158.

sācer, adj., *sacred, for sacrifice,* n 1208.

sacerdōs, sacerdōtis, noun c., *priest, priestess.*

sacrileg-us, -a, -um, adj., *sacrilegious; irreligious.*

sacruficāre, vb. 1, *sacrifice.*

saepe, adv., *often.*

saevīre, vb. 4, *be savage, rage, act cruelly.*

saev-os, -a, -om, adj., *savage, furious, cruel.*

sal, salis, noun m., *salt.*

sals-us, -a, -um, adj., *salty, brine-soaked; witty,* n. 301.

saltem, adv., *at least.*

salūs, salūtis, noun f., *salvation, escape, happy ending; greeting.*

salūtāre, vb. 1, *greet.*

salvēre, vb. 2, *be healthy;* salvē, salvētō, salvēte, and salvēre iubeō, *used as a greeting.*

salv-os, -a, -om, adj., *safe, healthy;* salvos sīs, *as a greeting;* salvos sum, salva rēs est, n 172.

sānct-us, -a, -um, adj., *holy, religious.*

sān-us, -a, -um, adj., *healthy, sane;* adv. sāne, *certainly,* n 386.

sapere, sapīvī or sapiī, vb. 5, *have sense, be wise.*

sapiēns, adj., *wise, clever.*

sat and satis, noun indecl. and adv., *enough; quite, pretty well.*

satin = satis-ne; *in questions,* n 187.

saturitās, saturitātis, noun f., *satiety, fullness, exhaustion.*

sauciāre, vb. 1, *wound, cut to pieces.*

VOCABULARY

sāvium, noun n., *kiss, mouth for kissing.*

saxātilis, saxātile, adj., *rock-.*

saxum, noun n., *rock, cliff.*

scālae, noun f. pl., *ladder.*

scapha, noun f., *boat.*

scelest-us, -a, -um, adj., *criminal;* colloquial use, n 22.

scelus, sceleris, noun n., *crime, wickedness;* as a term of abuse, *crook, rascal;* n 1178.

scīlicet, adv., *of course;* with accusative and infinitive, 395.

scīn = scīs-ne.

scīre, scīvī, scītum, vb. 4, *know.*

scirpus, scirpī, noun m., *bulrush.*

scīt-us, -a, -um and scītul-us, -a, -um, adj., *nice, pretty.*

sē, suī, sibī, sē, reflexive pronoun, *him/herself, him, her.*

sē-clūdere, -clūsī, -clū-sum, vb. 3, *separate.*

secūricula, noun f., *toy axe.*

sectārī, vb. 1 depon., *follow.*

secundum, prep. + acc., *along, after, according to.*

secus, adv., *differently.*

sed, conjunction, *but; and what's more,* n 799.

sēdecim, adj., indecl., *sixteen.*

sedēre, sēdī, sessum, vb. 2, *sit.*

sēdulō, adv., *with all one's heart.*

sēmen, sēminis, noun n., *seed;* **sceleris sēmen,** *thoroughbred crook.*

sēmita, noun f., *path.*

semper, adv., *always.*

senex, senis, noun m., *old man, old gentleman;* in vocative, *sir.*

sententia, noun f., *opinion; feeling,* n 587, 1365.

sentīre, sēnsī, sēnsum, vb. 4, *feel; think, form an opinion.*

sēpia, noun f., *squid, cuttlefish.*

septingent-ī, -ae, -a, adj., *seven hundred.*

sequester, sequestrī, noun m., *trustee, in whose hands was placed a disputed article.*

sequestrum, noun n., *deposit;* **sequestrō pōnere,** *place (a disputed article) in trust.*

sequī, secūtus, vb. 3 depon., *follow.*

sēriō, adv., *seriously.*

servāre, vb. 1, *keep safe, guard.*

servīre, vb., *be a servant.*

servitūs, servitūtis, noun f., *slavery.*

servos, servī, noun m., *slave, servant.*

sēscent-ī, -ae, -a, adj., *six hundred.*

seu, conjunction (= **sīve**), *whether; or if.*

sī, conjunction, *if;* n 714.

sīc, adv., *thus, so, in that way;* **sīc ut,** or as one word **sīcut,** *just as, as.*

siccitās, siccitātis, noun f., *dryness, freedom from moisture.*

Sĭcilia, noun f., *Sicily.*

sīcīlicula, noun f., *toy sickle.*

Siciliēnsis, Siciliēnse, adj., *Sicilian.*

sīcine = sīc-ne.

Sicul-us, -a, -um, adj., *Sicilian.*

sīcut(ī) = sīc ut.

siem, subjunctive of **esse.**

signāre, vb. 1, *mark, write up.*

signum, noun n., *sign, mark; proof; statue; constellation.*

VOCABULARY

Sīlānus, Sīlānī, noun m., n 317.

simul, adv., *at the same time, together.*

simulāre, vb. 1, *pretend.*

sīn, conjunction, *but if.*

sincēr-us, -a, -um, adj., *unspoilt.*

sine, imperative of *sinere.*

sine, prep. + abl., *without.*

sinere, sīvī, situm, *let, let be.*

sīnus, sīnī, noun m., *bowl,* n. 1319.

siquidem = sī quidem; it usually implies that the condition is true, and is almost causal, *seeing that.*

sirpe, sirpis, noun n., *rush, bulrush.*

sīs, subjunctive of *esse.*

sīs, interjection (= **sī vīs**), *please;* n 249.

sistere, stitī, statum, vb. 3, *present, produce;* n 1049.

sitis, sitis, noun f., *thirst.*

sīve, seu, conjunction, *whether; or if.*

socia, f., and **socius socii,** m. nouns, *ally, partner.*

solēre, solitus, vb. 2, semidepon., *be accustomed.*

sollicitāre, vb. 1, *trouble, distress.*

sōl-us, -a, -um, adj., *alone, only.*

solvere, solvī, solūtum, vb. 3, *untie, loosen; pay; settle.*

somniāre, vb. 1, *dream.*

somnium, noun n., *dream.*

somnus, somnī, noun m., *sleep, slumber.*

sonāre, sonuī, sonitum, vb. 1, *sound, roar, be heard.*

sopor, sopōris, noun m., *sleep.*

sōrsus, adv., *separately* (in Smith, *seorsus*).

sōspes, genit., **sōspitis,** adj., *safe and sound.*

speciēs, speciēī, noun f., *appearance.*

spectāre, vb. 1, *watch, look at.*

spērāre, vb. 1, *hope.*

spernere, sprēvī, sprētum, vb. 3, *despise, reject.*

spēs, spēī, noun f., *hope.*

splendēre, vb. 2, *shine.*

squāma, noun f., *scale.*

squāmōs-us, -a, -um, adj., *scaly, fishy.*

statuere, statuī, statūtum, vb. 3, *set up;* ptc., **statūtus,** as adj., *well set up, of considerable stature.*

stēlla, noun f., *star.*

strēnu-os, -a, -om, adj., *energetic.*

striāt-us, -a, -um, adj., *striated, fluted.*

stult-us, -a, -um, adj., *stupid.*

suādēre, suāsī, suāsum, vb. 2, *give advice,* + dat.

subaquil-us, -a, -um, adj., *rather dark(skinned).*

sub-fringere, -frēgī, -frāctum, vb. 3, *break.*

sub-igere, -ēgī, -āctum, vb. 3, *force.*

subitāri-us, -a, -um, adj., *for a sudden crisis;* res subitāria, *emergency.*

sub-legere, -lēgī, -lēctum, vb. 3, *steal,* + dat., n 748.

sub-venīre, vb. 4, and **subventāre,** vb. 1, *come to help,* + dat.

subvolturi-us, -a, -um, adj., *rather vulturish,* n 422.

suc-cingere, -cīnxī, -cīnctum, vb. 3, *gird up, tuck up one's skirts.*

VOCABULARY

sucula, noun f., n 1170.

sūdāre, vb. 1, *sweat.*

sūd-us, -a, -um, adj., *bright, dry (of weather).*

suf-fundere, -fūdī, -fūsum, vb. 3, *pour in,* n 588.

sultis = si voltis = *if you please.*

summ-us, -a, -um, adj., *supreme, highest, top.*

sūmptus, sūmptūs, noun m., *expenditure.*

supercilium, noun n., *eyebrow.*

superstitiōs-us, -a, -um, adj., *magical,* n 1139.

sup-petere, vb. 3, *suffice, be available.*

suppetiae, noun f. pl., *help, rescue.*

supplicāre, vb. 1, *beg,* with dat. or *a* + abl.

sur-rigere (or **surgere**), **-rexi, -rectum,** vb. 3, *rise, get up.*

sur-rupere, -rupuī, -ruptum, vb. 5, *steal, kidnap.*

sus, suis, noun c., *pig.*

suscitāre, vb. 1, *wake.*

sus-pendere, -pendī, -pēnsum, vb. 3, *hang up.*

suspicārī, vb. 1 depon., *suspect.*

susurrus, susurrī, noun m., *whisper.*

su-os, -a, -om, adj., *his, her, its, their,* normally referring to subject, or to "speaker" of indirect speech, n 47.

T

tabula, noun f., *flat piece of wood; writing-tablet, note-book.*

tacēre, vb. 2, *be silent.*

tacit-us, -a, -um, adj., *silent.*

talentum, noun n., *talent,* p. 41.

tālus, tālī, noun m., *ankle.*

tam, adv., *so, so much.*

tamen, adv. or conj., *nevertheless, in spite of all.*

tandem, adv., *at last;* in impatient questions, n 468.

tangere, tetigī, tāctum, vb. 3, *touch; come to.*

tantā, adv., n 521.

tantillum, adv., *so little, ever so little.*

tantisper, adv., *for so long, meanwhile.*

tant-us, -a, -um, adj., *so great, so big, so much.*

tēctum, noun n., *roof.*

tēd = tē.

tegere, tēxī, tēctum, vb. 3, *cover, thatch.*

tēgillum, noun n., *mat,* n 576.

tēgula, noun f., *tile.*

temperāre, vb. 1, *control, moderate,* + dat.

temperī, adv., *in good time,* n 921.

tempestās, tempestātis, noun f., *weather, bad weather, storm.*

templum, noun n., *precincts,* n 909.

tempus, temporis, noun n., *time.*

tēn = tē-ne.

tenēre, vb. 2, *hold; catch hold.*

tergum, tergī, noun n., *back.*

terra, noun f., *land, earth.*

testārī, vb. 1 depon., *call to witness, appeal to.*

testimōnium, noun n., *evidence.*

testis, testis, noun c., *witness.*

tetigī, from *tangere.*

tetulī = tulī, from *ferre.*

Thēbae, Thēbārum, noun f. pl., *Thebes.*

218

VOCABULARY

thermipŏlium, noun n., *hot-drink counter.*
timēre, vb. 2, *fear.*
timid-us, -a, -um, adj., *frightened.*
tinnīmentum, noun n., *ringing.*
tolerāre, vb. 1, *make the best of.*
torquēre, torsī, tortum, vb. 2, *twist.*
totidem, adj. indecl., *as many, the same number.*
tŏt-us, -a, -um, adj., *whole.*
tractāre, vb. 1, *handle.*
trā-dere, -didī, -ditum, vb. 3, *hand over.*
trahere, traxī, tractum, vb. 3, *drag, draw.*
trāma, noun f., *cloth.*
trānsenna, noun f., *snare.*
trēcent-ī, -ae, -a, adj., *three hundred.*
tremōr, tremōris, noun m., *shivering.*
trēs, tria, adj., *three.*
trīcae, trīcārum, noun f. pl., *trash.*
trifurcifer, noun m., *three-times-furcifer;* see **furcifer.**
trigīnta, adj. indecl., *thirty.*
trīm-us, -a, -um, adj., *three-year-old.*
triŏbolum, noun n., *three-obol bit,* pp. 41-2.
trīticum, noun n., *wheat.*
tū, tē, tuī, tibĭ, tē, pronoun, singular, *you.*
tum, adv., *then; in that case; moreover,* n 644.
tumultuāre, vb. 1, *raise a riot.*
tumultus, tumultūs, noun m., *riot.*
tunc = **tum.**
tundere, tutudī, tūnsum or **tūsum,** vb. 3, *bang.*

tunica and **tunīcula,** noun f., *tunic, shirt.*
turbid-us, -a, -um and **turbulent-us, -a,- um,** adj., *confused, stormy.*
tutārī, vb. 1 depon., *protect.*
tūtē = **tū,** emphatic.

U

ūber, ūbera, ūberum, adj., *fertile.*
ubĭ, adv. relative or interrog., and conj., *where; when.*
ubinam, see **ubi** and **nam.**
ulcīscī, ultus, vb. 3 depon., *avenge.*
ull-us, -a, -um, adj., *any.*
ulme-us, -a, -um, adj., *of elm-wood,* n 636.
ultrō, adv., *without provocation, unnecessarily.*
ultum-us, -a, -um, adj., *furthest; last.*
ūmor, ūmōris, noun m., *moisture..*
umquam, adv., *ever.*
ūncia, noun f., *ounce.*
unda, noun f., *wave.*
unde, adv., *where from, whence.*
ūn-us, -a, -um, adj., *one; only;* emphasising superlative, n 70.
urbān-us, -a, um, adj., *city-.*
urbs, urbis, noun f., *city.*
urna, noun f., *pot.*
urtīca, noun f., *nettle.*
ūsquam, adv., *anywhere.*
ūsque, adv., *all the way, right.*
ūsquequāque, adv., *everywhere.*

219

ūsus, ūsūs, noun m., *experience;* **ūsus est,** *there is need of* + abl.

ut, adv., *how;* interrog., n 12; exclamatory, n 154, 421; relative, *as; to judge by the way that,* n 138; = *utinam,* n 82; conj. *in order that; so that; that.*

uter, utra, utrum, adj., *which (of two).*

utervīs, utravīs, utrumvīs, adj., *whichever (of two) you like.*

utĭ = ut.

ūtī, ūsus, vb. 3 depon., *use,* normally with abl., but n 602, 1241.

utinam, adv., before subjunctive expressing wish, *would that.*

utpote, adv., before a relative clause, indicating that it has causal force.

utrum, neuter of *uter,* used as adv., introducing double question.

ūvid-us, -a, -um, adj., *wet.*

uxor, uxōris, noun f., *wife.*

V

vadum, noun n., *shallow water.*

vae, interjection, n 374.

valēre, vb. 2, *be strong;* imperative, *farewell, good-bye.*

valid-us, -a, -um, adj., *strong.*

vāniloquentia, noun f., *chattering, talkativeness.*

vāpulāre, vb. 1, *get a thrashing.*

vās, vāsis, noun n., *receptacle* (*cooking-pots,* 135; *a trunk,* 986).

vāsculum, noun n. (diminu-

tive of *vas*), *cooking-utensil.*

vehemēns, adj., *vigorous, impetuous.*

vehere, vēxī, vectum, vb. 3, *carry.*

vel, adv., n 551.

vēlitātiō, vēlitātiōnis, noun f., n 525.

velle, voluī, vb., *wish, be willing.*

velut = **vel ut,** adv. and conj., *as (if you like), as for example, as.*

vēnālis, vēnāle, adj., *for sale,* n 584.

vēn-dere, -didi, -ditum, vb. 3, *offer for sale, sell.*

venēfic-us, -a, -um, adj., *poisoning,* n 987.

venēnāt-us, -a, -um, adj., *poisoned, bewitched.*

venerārī, vb. 1 depon., *pray to.*

veneri-us, -a, -um, adj., *of Venus.*

venia, noun f., *leave, pardon.*

venīre, vēnī, ventum, vb. 4, *come;* **in mentem venit,** n 685.

venter, ventris, noun m., *belly; greed.*

ventriōs-us, -a, -um, adj., *pot-bellied.*

ventus, ventī, noun m., *wind.*

Venus, Veneris, noun f., *Venus.*

venust-us, -a, -um, adj., *favoured by Venus, attractive, pretty.*

verbum, noun n., *word.*

verērī, vb. 2 depon., *fear.*

vērō, adv., *really, indeed;* conj., *but, and.*

verum, verī, and **verū, verūs,** noun n., *spit.*

vērum, 1. see **vērus;** 2. conj., *but.*

vēr-us, -a, -um, adj., *true,*

220

truthful; neuter as noun, *truth.*

vesper, gen. **vesperī** or **vesperis,** abl. **vespere** or **vesperī,** noun m., *evening; evening meal.*

vestīgāre, vb. 1, *track down.*

vestimentum, n., and **vestis, vestis,** f. nouns, *clothing, dress.*

vestīre, vb. 4, *clothe.*

via, noun f., *road.*

vicem, abl. **vice** (no nominative), noun f., *turn, alternation;* with gen., *instead.*

vīcīnia, noun f., *neighbourhood.*

vīcīn-us, -a, -um, adj., *neighbouring;* as noun, *neighbour.*

vīctitāre, vb. 1, *live.*

viden = **vidēs-ne.**

vidēre, vīdī, vīsum, vb. 2, *see;* **mē vidē,** n 680; passive, *seem;* n 1242.

vīdlus, vīdlī, or **vīdulus, vīdulī,** noun m., *trunk,* n 990.

viduitās, viduitātis, noun f., *deprivation.*

vīdulus, see **vīdlus.**

vigilāre, vb. 1, *stay awake.*

vīgintī, adj. indecl., *twenty.*

villa, noun f., *farm-house.*

vincere, vīcī, victum, vb. 3, *defeat, overcome.*

vinclum, noun n., *chain;* pl. *chains, captivity.*

vindicāre, vb. 1, *vindicate, assert one's rights.*

vīnum, noun n., *wine.*

violāre, vb. 1, *violate, do violence to.*

violentia, noun f., *violence.*

vir, virī, noun m., *man* (as opposed to *female* or *child*).

virga, noun f., *stick.*

virgidēmia, noun f., n 636.

virginālis, virgināle, adj., *of girls, girl-.*

virgō, virginis, noun f., *maiden, girl.*

virīlis, virīle, adj., *man's, male.*

virtūs, virtūtis, noun f., *virtue.*

vīs, acc., **vim,** abl., **vī;** noun f., *force;* pl. **vīres,** *strength.*

vīsere, vb. 3, *go to see.*

vīta, noun f., *life.*

vitium, noun n., *fault, vice.*

vītor, vītōris, noun m., n 990.

vīvere, vīxi, vīctum, vb. 3, *live;* n 127.

vīv-os, -a, -om, adj., *alive, living.*

vix, adv., *hardly, scarcely, barely.*

vocāre, vb. 1, *call.*

Volcānus, Volcānī, noun m., *Vulcan, god of fire.*

volup, adv., **volup est,** *it's a pleasure, I'm delighted.*

voluptāri-us, -a, -um, adj., *of pleasure, pleasure-loving.*

voluptās, voluptātis, noun f., *pleasure;* concrete, *darling, sweet-heart.*

vomere, vomuī, vomitum, vb. 3, *vomit, spew.*

vomitus, vomitūs, noun m., *vomit.*

vorāre, vb. 1, *devour.*

vortere, vortī, vorsum, vb. 3, *turn.*

vōs, vostrī or **vostrum, vōbis,** pronoun pl., *you.*

voster, vostra, vostrum, adj., *your.*

votare, votuī, votitum, vb. 1, *forbid, order not to.*

vōtum, noun n., *vow.*

vōx, vōcis, noun f., *voice.*

Printed in the USA/Agawam, MA
January 20, 2011

556213.044